KATE MULVANY OAM is an award-winning playwright, screenwriter and actor. Her epic adaptation of the Ruth Park trilogy, *The Harp in the South*, played to great acclaim for the Sydney Theatre Company in 2018, and she followed this with her adaptation of Schiller's *Mary Stuart* for the company in 2019 and Ruth Park's *Playing Beatie Bow* in 2021. *The Harp in the South* was also produced by the Perth International Arts Festival in 2022. Her play *Jasper Jones*, an adaptation of Craig Silvey's novel, has enjoyed great success at Belvoir Street Theatre, MTC, QTC and State Theatre Company of South Australia, after its Barking Gecko premiere in 2015. In 2015 Mulvany's play *Masquerade*, a reimagining of the much-loved children's book by Kit Williams, was produced by Griffin Theatre Company and performed at the 2015 Sydney Festival, the State Theatre Company of South Australia and Melbourne Festival. Her autobiographical play *The Seed* (Belvoir Street Theatre) won the Sydney Theatre Award for Best Independent Production. With Mulvany performing in the play, it toured nationally, and is currently being developed into a work for screen. Mulvany's *Medea*, co-written with Anne-Louise Sarks, was produced by Belvoir Street Theatre in 2012, won several awards including an AWGIE Award and five Sydney Theatre Awards, and has gone on to be produced in Poland, Basel, Auckland and at the Gate Theatre in London, to rave reviews. Other plays and musicals include the multi-award winning *The Mares* for the Tasmanian Theatre Company, *The Rasputin Affair* for Ensemble Theatre, *The Danger Age*, *Blood and Bone*, *The Web*, the musical *Somewhere* (with music by Tim Minchin), and *Storytime*, which won Mulvany the 2004 Philip Parsons Award. As a screenwriter, she has developed and written on several television projects, including the Emmy-award-winning Netflix series *Beat Bugs*, and the critically acclaimed *Upright*. She is also an award-winning stage and screen actor, with credits with many international theatre companies, television series and films.

The HARP in the SOUTH TRILOGY: The PLAY

Adapted by **KATE MULVANY**
From the novels by **RUTH PARK**

CURRENCY PRESS
The performing arts publisher

CURRENCY PLAYS

First published in 2018
by Currency Press Pty Ltd,
PO Box 2287, Strawberry Hills, NSW, 2012, Australia
enquiries@currency.com.au
www.currency.com.au

This revised edition first published 2023.

Copyright: *The Harp in the South Trilogy: The Play* © Kate Mulvany and Kemalde Pty Ltd, 2018, 2023.

COPYING FOR EDUCATIONAL PURPOSES

The Australian *Copyright Act 1968* (Act) allows a maximum of one chapter or 10% of this book, whichever is the greater, to be copied by any educational institution for its educational purposes provided that that educational institution (or the body that administers it) has given a remuneration notice to Copyright Agency (CA) under the Act.

For details of the CA licence for educational institutions contact CA, 12/66 Goulburn Street, Sydney, NSW, 2000; tel: within Australia 1800 066 844 toll free; outside Australia 61 2 9394 7600; fax: 61 2 9394 7601; email: memberservices@copyright.com.au

COPYING FOR OTHER PURPOSES

Except as permitted under the Act, for example a fair dealing for the purposes of study, research, criticism or review, no part of this book may be reproduced, stored in a retrieval system, or transmitted in any form or by any means without prior written permission. All enquiries should be made to the publisher at the address above.

Any performance or public reading of *The Harp in the South* is forbidden unless a licence has been received from the author or the author's agent. The purchase of this book in no way gives the purchaser the right to perform the play in public, whether by means of a staged production or a reading. All applications for public performance should be addressed to Cameron's Management, Locked Bag 848, Surry Hills NSW 2010, Australia; ph: 61 2 9319 7199; email: info@cameronsmanagement.com.au

Typeset by Currency Press.
Cover design by Lisa White for Currency Press.
Cover photograph from the Ted Hood collection, State Library of New South Wales.

A catalogue record for this book is available from the National Library of Australia

Contents

Introduction
  Michelle Arrow — v

THE HARP IN THE SOUTH

  Act One: Missus — 1
  Act Two: The Harp in the South — 40
  Act Three: The Harp in the South — 94
  Act Four: Poor Man's Orange — 144

The cast of Sydney Theatre Company's The Harp in the South, Part One and Part Two, *2018. (Photo: Daniel Boud)*

Introduction

The Harp in the South Trilogy is a sweeping Sydney story. It traces the story of Margaret and Hughie, a young couple in love, who move from rural NSW to the heart of the city to make a life together. Their marriage is enriched by the joy of family, but they are burdened by poverty, the endless grind of survival, and the tragedy of loss. Adapted from Ruth Park's enduringly popular novels *Missus*, *The Harp in the South*, and *Poor Man's Orange*, Kate Mulvany's lyrical play celebrates the humble, beautiful lives of Sydney's poor. The play is a love letter to the women who keep the Darcy family together: Eny Kilker, her daughter Margaret Darcy, and her daughters Roie and Dolour. These resilient women, determined to live their modest dreams in the face of often crushing bleakness and tragedy, come vividly to life in Mulvany's adaptation. Mulvany's love of the rich Irish-Australian vernacular, and her attention to moments of poetry of everyday life, make this story sing. She has transformed three novels into a six-hour play, with 90 roles played by eighteen actors: an epic theatrical experience for audience and performers alike.

The Harp in the South was Ruth Park's first novel. Born in Auckland in 1917, she moved to Sydney at the height of World War II, in 1942, and married fellow writer D'Arcy Niland later that year. Ruth and D'Arcy shared a dream to support themselves through writing, and wrote industriously, living week to week on their modest freelance incomes. Freelance writers lived in 'total insecurity', and perhaps that gnawing anxiety gave Ruth some insight into the mindset of the very poor in her story.[1] In 1943, Ruth and D'Arcy rented rooms in Surry Hills because, as she wrote in her memoir, 'like all working class suburbs, [it] was cheap, and I was cheaper still, hunting around to save threepence here and a shilling there.'[2] She described it as a 'queer, disreputable little village, half hidden under the hem of a prosperous city.'[3] They lived

---

1 Ruth Park, *Fishing in the Styx*, (Ringwood: Viking Penguin, 1993), 137.
2 Park, *Fishing in the Styx*, 43.
3 Park, *Fishing in the Styx*, 9.

next door to a Chinese grocery store, surely the inspiration for Lick Jimmy's little shop next to the Darcy's house in *Harp*. Life in Surry Hills was lived 'on the streets, rowdily and often outrageously'.[4] Ruth found living in such close proximity to her neighbours, with no bath, no gas, and an 'army of ferocious rats' difficult, and they escaped as soon as they could.[5]

At the time Ruth and D'Arcy settled in Surry Hills, it had long been a densely populated, neglected enclave of urban poverty: a slum. Much of the suburb's residential development, dating to the late Victorian era, suffered from poor planning and lack of amenities: sewerage and drainage was substandard, and it had become the home of criminal gangs and organised crime. World War II, and the influx of American troops on R&R gave a huge boost to the Surry Hills sex and sly grog trades, making criminal figures such as Kate Leigh wealthy, and infamous. By the late 1940s, areas of Surry Hills were being targeted for slum clearance. Historian Christopher Keating described post-war Surry Hills as 'notorious by reason of narrow streets, substandard housing and a general air of decay.'[6] Planned high-rise housing development looked set to sweep the slums of Surry Hills off the map, along with the poor families who called them home.

The Harp in the South might never have been written but for a competition run by *The Sydney Morning Herald* for an Australian novel in 1946. World War II had heightened Australia's patriotic fervour and the *Herald* contest can be seen as part of Australia's post-war reconstruction, an attempt to 'stimulate the development of Australian literature'.[7] Park recalled that the generous first prize of £2000 seemed like a 'colossal sum to us … certainly enough to put a deposit on a home' and while she originally encouraged her husband to enter the competition, eventually she decided to give it a go herself, even though she felt she didn't know enough about anything to manage

---

4 Park, *Fishing in the Styx*, 9.
5 'Author Lived in Surry Hills tenement', *Sydney Morning Herald*, 28 December 1946, 7.
6 Christopher Keating, *Surry Hills: The City's Backyard*, (Sydney: Hale and Iremonger, 1991), 94.
7 Shawn O'Leary, '1st prize novel is a social document', *Sydney Morning Herald*, 28 December 1946, 8.

80,000 words about it.⁸ She wrote at the kitchen table every night after her children went to bed, turning her less-than fond memories of her time in Surry Hills into the story of the Darcys, an Irish-Australian family living at 12½ Plymouth St, and their friends and neighbours. Their migrant Irish heritage offered Park, a migrant herself, a way to comment on Australian identity, and the Surry Hills of her novel is a melting pot of Irish, Anglo-Australian, Italian, Chinese and Indigenous voices.

All those nights at the kitchen table paid off: her vivid, warm novel won the *Herald* competition. Yet from the moment the paper published the book's synopsis, *The Harp in the South* generated huge controversy. Readers wrote in droves to condemn it. 'Disgusted' of Burwood declared that it 'was no better than an open sewer. Spreading death and disease all around.' 'Another critic' called it 'sordid reading [...] must our literary talent dig into cesspits to produce mental food for the people?' In a city still reeling from wartime privation and in the throes of a severe housing shortage, *The Harp In The South*'s frank acknowledgement of urban poverty was deeply unpopular. Another reader labelled it:

> an outrage against decency. To think that in a young clean country (clean as compared with the older countries) such unadulterated filth should be given first prize, and put out to the world as representing Australian life, makes my blood boil.⁹

This reader's objections were particularly telling. Part of the way Australian culture remained 'clean' was a heavy-handed regime of literary censorship which banned many works (especially those which acknowledged sex, contraception or abortion) from entering the country.¹⁰ This made a home-grown novel that addressed these issues even more shocking. Jon Cleary's novel *You Can't See Around Corners*, which was the runner up in the contest, was also about urban crime, but

---

8 Park, *Fishing in the Styx,* 146
9 'The Harp in the South—reader's opinions', *The Sydney Morning Herald*, 11 January 1947, 2.
10 Nicole Moore, *The Censor's Library*, (St Lucia: University of Queensland Press, 2012).

it generated no equivalent protest from *Herald* readers. Park concluded that she had committed two sins: she was a woman and she was not an Australian. A 'foreigner' had dared to depict Sydney's underclass, and Sydney residents objected strenuously: not to the fact that there were slums, and that people lived there, but to Park's decision to tell their stories.[11] The novel exposed a rich seam of anxiety about class, gender and national identity in post-war Australia.

Yet reader outrage proved to be wonderful publicity. The novel was serialised in the *Herald* from January 1947, and was published, reluctantly, by leading Australian publisher Angus and Robertson in 1948. Editor Beatrice Davis told Ruth that her novel was 'not the kind of book Angus and Robertson cares to publish but we have a gentleman's agreement with the *Herald*.'[12] Reviewers pointed out the novel's blend of sentimentality and social realism: *The Bulletin* praised Park's 'courage' in confronting abortion in the novel, but suggested that apart from some more extreme experiences, the novel was the story of a 'girl's love and marriage, essentially the same as a thousand romances that are published in women's magazines'.[13] This was faint praise indeed from the magazine that had long promoted a masculine national identity as the basis for Australian culture. *The Bulletin* also claimed the novel lacked 'the dynamic force of plot and characterisation necessary to hold the reader's interest.'[14] Yet it has remained in print— and inspired readers' devotion—for decades. Ruth Park definitely had the last laugh.

Mulvany's adaptation reminds us why these novels have endured for so long. While *The Harp in the South* was criticised for its episodic plot and lack of a central focus, adapting the three novels into a single play allows Park's larger themes and patterns to emerge. Margaret, the fresh-faced, naïve young woman of Act One, has, by Act Two, become 'Mamma'—her name, and many of her hopes and dreams, irretrievably lost. Yet she remains at the heart of the story, stoic and devoted to her clan, even while her life is worn away by daily domestic drudgery. In Act Two, Roie is the innocent young woman who learns painful

---

11 Park, *Fishing in the Styx*, 158.
12 Park, *Fishing in the Styx*, 151.
13 'The Harp in the South', *The Bulletin*, 3 March 1948, 2.
14 'The Harp in the South', *The Bulletin*, 3 March 1948, 2.

lessons about men, intimacy and love. In Act Three, as the story turns dark, it is Dolour's turn to learn the same lessons.

Park seemed to suggest that marriage and family were women's destiny and purpose: this made sense in post-war Australia, where women were encouraged to once again turn their full attention to home and family. Yet in Mulvany's hands, that sense of romantic fatalism is subtly challenged by the foregrounding of female characters who make their own, very different destinies: Delie Stock, the madam and sly grog entrepreneur, and the kindly nuns Sister Theophilus and Sister Beatrix, who share a secret love story in the play.

Yet even if marriage and family have their disappointments, the Darcys still have each other, unlike the lonely Patrick Diamond or sad Miss Sheily. The Darcy family might live in each other's pockets and get under each other's feet, but they are each other's great strength and support, too. The play is a hymn to the ways that love, in its many forms, sustains and supports us. From the devotion of a mother who still buys Christmas presents for her missing son, to the passionate romance of Roie and Charlie, and Lick Jimmy's kindness to the irrepressible Dolour, Mulvany reminds us that while these characters may be poor, they are also, in Margaret's words, 'lucky'.

When *The Harp in the South* was published in 1949, Surry Hills was a slum, a place Sydneysiders would rather not discuss. Today, Surry Hills is the embodiment of cosmopolitan, inner city Sydney, and like much of the city, it has been gentrified, priced well out of reach of today's poor. Unlike her left-wing contemporaries Mona Brand or Dorothy Hewett, who were writing novels and plays in the 1940s and 1950s that depicted the working class through the lens of socialist realism, Park was not political in her depiction of the residents of Surry Hills. Her characters are often far from noble in their willingness to wallow in self-pity, or in the case of Hughie, his alcoholism.[15] There is a fatalism in her characters' inability to escape Surry Hills, even as the walls close in on them in Act Three, as the suburb begins to be swallowed up by slum clearance and redevelopment.

For all the controversy the novel caused, *The Harp in the South*

---

15 F.C. Molloy, 'Hearts of Gold and a Happy Ending': The Appeal of *The Harp in the South, Australian Literary Studies*, 14 (3), 1990, 317.

arguably made Ruth Park's name. She quickly published the sequel, *Poor Man's Orange*, in 1949, and found even bigger fame as a children's author. She wrote *The Muddle-headed Wombat* in 1962, and then a series of books based on the character throughout the 1960s and '70s, and a number of novels for children, including *Callie's Castle* (1975) and *Playing Beattie Bow* (1981, and adapted for the stage by Mulvany in 2021). She returned to Margaret and Hughie Darcy with *Missus* in 1985. *The Harp in the South* and *Poor Man's Orange* were both adapted into popular television miniseries in 1987: the series introduced a new generation to Park's characters. Mulvany's trilogy will see the Darcy family endure in the Australian cultural imagination even longer.

Michelle Arrow
December 2022

Michelle Arrow is Professor of Modern History at Macquarie University and author of three books, including *Upstaged: Australian Women Dramatists in the Limelight at Last* (2002) and *The Seventies: the personal, the political and the making of Modern Australia (2019).*

The Harp in the South Trilogy: The Play was first produced by Sydney Theatre Company at the Roslyn Packer Theatre, Sydney, on 16 August 2018, with the following cast:

THADY DARCY	Joel Bishop
FAIRGROUND ANNOUNCER / KIDGER / DOCTOR EVANS / GUS MACINTOSH	Luke Carroll
FATHER DRISCOLL / PATRICK DIAMOND / BRETT'S DAD / HOTDOG SELLER	Tony Cogin
MARTIN DARCY / ADULT HUGH DARCY	Jack Finsterer
NOEL CAPPER / PUBLICAN / BARFLY / TOMMY MENDEL / SAILOR / BILL BRIGGS / BUMPER REILLY / FRANKY	Benedict Hardie
BERTIE / MAUREEN / THIRSTY WOMAN / LOLLY MOLLY / LYNETTE / BERNICE / NURSE WATKINS / SUSE / MINNIE	Emma Harvie
ELSPETH / ADULT MARGARET DARCY	Anita Hegh
FAIRGROUND NUN / BETSY / CLOTHES SELLER / SISTER THEOPHILUS / PHYLLIS / MRS SICILIANO / LYNDALL / FLORRIE	Lucia Mastrantone
ENY KILKER / MRS WILEY	Heather Mitchell
ALF / FLO / MISS SHEILY / MRS X / SISTER BEATRIX / MRS KILROY / SHIRLEY	Tara Morice
YOUNG HUGH DARCY / BARFLY / POLICE OFFICER / LOLLY'S MAN / STEVIE / SAILOR / DOCTOR / BRETT / TUG	Ben O'Toole
YOUNG MARGARET / ROIE DARCY	Rose Riley
HERB LENNON / JOHNNY SHEILY / HARRY DRUMMY / SAILOR / ERNEST BLAINEY / REPORTER / DOCTOR	Rahel Romahn
THADY DARCY	Jack Ruwald

JER / SOLDIER / BOOKSELLER /
POLICE OFFICER / PHOTOGRAPHER /
CHARLIE ROTHE — Guy Simon
JOHN KILKER / BARFLY / FATHER COOLEY /
MR KILROY / JOSEPH MENDEL /
MR GUNNARSON / EYE DOCTOR — Bruce Spence
FRANCES DARCY / ENID / DELIE STOCK /
DENISE / BRETT'S MUM — Helen Thomson
JOSIE / DOLOUR DARCY — Contessa Treffone
LICK JIMMY / SAILOR / DOCTOR / REPORTER /
CAVES ATTENDANT / USHER — George Zhao

All cast: BRASS BAND MEMBERS, FAIRGOERS, CAROLLERS, SCHOOLKIDS, PUBCRAWLERS, SURRY HILLS CITIZENS, STREET URCHINS, PADDY'S STALLHOLDERS, FIRE BRIGADE MEMBERS, POLICE OFFICERS, BARFLIES, CROWD MEMBERS, DUTCH SAILORS, REPORTERS, PHOTOGRAPHERS, QUIZ SHOW AUDIENCE, CONGREGATION, TRAIN PASSENGERS, LUNA PARK REVELLERS

Director, Kip Williams
Set Designer, David Fleischer
Costume Designer, Renée Mulder
Lighting Designer, Nick Schlieper
Composer, THE SWEATS
Sound Designer, Nate Edmondson
Musical Director, Luke Byrne
Assistant Director, Jessica Arthur
Fight and Movement Director, Nigel Poulton
Voice and Text Coach, Charmian Gradwell
Production Manager, Dominic Hamra
Deputy Production Manager, Lauren Makin
Stage Manager, Minka Stevens
Deputy Stage Manager, Todd Eichorn
Assistant Stage Managers, Katie Hankin and Jennifer Parsonage

Kate Mulvany would like to thank the following for their ongoing support of this adaptation:

The family of Ruth Park, Tim Curnow, Kip Williams, Andrew Upton, Jonathan Church, Polly Rowe, Anthony Blair, Hamish Michael and all the artists who gave their time to read and develop the work.

CHARACTERS

ACT ONE: MISSUS (1920)

    THADY DARCY, 8
    FRANCES DARCY, late 40s
    MARTIN DARCY, 50s
    HUGH DARCY, 22
    JER DARCY, 18
    MARGARET KILKER, 19
    JOSIE KILKER, 17
    ENY KILKER, 45
    JOHN KILKER, 55
    HERB LENNON, 19
    NOEL CAPPER, 19
    TOWNSFOLK
    FAIRGROUND ANNOUNCER
    BERTIE
    LITTLE GIRL
    FAIRGROUND NUN
    ALF, 22
    FATHER DRISCOLL, 50s
    MAUREEN
    ENID
    ELSPETH

ACT TWO & THREE: THE HARP IN THE SOUTH (1948–1950)

THADY DARCY, 8
DOLOUR DARCY, 13-15
ROIE DARCY, 18-20
MARGARET DARCY (MISSUS), 47-49
HUGH DARCY, 50-52
ENY KILKER, 73-75
CHARLIE ROTHE, 19-21, Aboriginal
LICK JIMMY, 40s, Chinese
PATRICK DIAMOND, early 60s
MISS SHEILY, early 40s
JOHNNY SHEILY, early 20s
DELIE STOCK, late 40s
KIDGER
PHYLLIS, teens
FLO, 50s
MOLLY, 20s
MOLLY'S MAN
PUBLICAN
ABORIGINAL SOLDIER
THIRSTY WOMAN
BARFLIES 1, 2 and 3
BOOKSELLER
CLOTHES SELLER
TOMMY MENDEL, 20
JOSEPH MENDEL, 40s
TEASING CHILDREN
SCHOOLCHILDREN
SISTER THEOPHILUS
SISTER BEATRIX

FATHER COOLEY
HARRY DRUMMY
MR GUNNARSON
POLICE OFFICERS 1 and 2
FIREMEN
CROWD MEMBERS 1, 2 and 3
MRS SICILIANO
MAN
MRS X
LYNETTE
DUTCH SAILORS 1, 2 and 3
STEVIE
BILL BRIGGS
LYNDALL
BERNICE
DENISE
ERNEST BLAINEY
USHER

ACT FOUR: POOR MAN'S ORANGE (1950-1953)

THADY DARCY, 8
DOLOUR DARCY, 15-18
ROIE DARCY, 20-21
MARGARET DARCY (MISSUS), 49-51
HUGH DARCY, 52-55
CHARLIE ROTHE, 21-24, Aboriginal
LICK JIMMY, 30s, Chinese
PATRICK DIAMOND, 60s
SUSE KILROY, 16
FATHER COOLEY
SISTER THEOPHILUS
SISTER BEATRIX
PHOTOGRAPHER
REPORTERS 1, 2 and 3
FLO
PHYLLIS KIDGER
LEERING BARFLY
POLICE OFFICERS 1, 2, 3 and 4
DOCTOR
TRAINEE DOCTORS 1, 2 and 3
MRS WILEY
FLORRIE
SCHOOLCHILDREN
HARRY DRUMMY
EYE DOCTOR
NURSE WATKINS
MR KILROY
MRS KILROY
BUMPER REILLY

GUS MCINTOSH, 50s
BRETT, 28
ELSE
BRETT'S DAD
HOTDOG SELLER
FRANKY
TUG
SHIRLEY
MINNIE
CAVES ATTENDANT

SUGGESTED DOUBLINGS

FRANCES DARCY / ENID / DELIE STOCK / DENISE / ELSE

THADY DARCY

MARTIN DARCY / ADULT HUGHIE

YOUNG HUGH DARCY / LOLLY MOLLY'S MAN / STEVIE / BRETT / POLICE OFFICER 2 / REPORTER 1 / CAVES ATTENDANT

FATHER DRISCOLL / MR DIAMOND / BRETT'S DAD / HOTDOG SELLER

ENY KILKER / MRS WILEY

JER / SOLDIER / BOOKSELLER / POLICE OFFICER 1 / CHARLIE ROTHE

YOUNG MARGARET KILKER / ROIE DARCY

JOSIE / DOLOUR DARCY

ELSPETH / ADULT MARGARET DARCY

JOHN KILKER / FATHER COOLEY / MR KILROY / JOSEPH MENDEL / MR GUNNARSON / EYE DOCTOR

BERTIE / MAUREEN / THIRSTY WOMAN / LOLLY MOLLY / LYNETTE / BERNICE / NURSE WATKINS / SUSE / MINNIE

NOEL CAPPER / PUBLICAN / TOMMY MENDEL / BILL BRIGGS / BUMPER REILLY / LEERING BARFLY / FRANKY

HERB LENNON / JOHNNY SHEILY / HARRY DRUMMY / ERNEST BLAINEY / REPORTER 3 / TUG

LICK JIMMY / USHER

ALF / FLO / MISS SHEILY / MRS X / SISTER BEATRIX / MRS KILROY / SHIRLEY

FAIRGROUND NUN / BETSY / CLOTHES SELLER / SISTER THEOPHILUS / PHYLLIS / MRS SICILIANO / FLORRIE

FAIRGROUND ANNOUNCER / KIDGER / PHOTOGRAPHER / REPORTER 2 / DOCTOR EVANS / GUS MACINTOSH

All actors play:

BRASS BAND MEMBERS, FAIRGOERS, CAROLLERS, SCHOOLKIDS, PUBCRAWLERS, SURRY HILLS CITIZENS, STREET URCHINS, PADDY'S MARKET STALLHOLDERS, FIRE BRIGADE MEMBERS, POLICE OFFICERS, BARFLIES, CROWD MEMBERS, DUTCH SAILORS, REPORTERS, PHOTOGRAPHERS, QUIZ SHOW AUDIENCE, CONGREGATION, TRAIN PASSENGERS, LUNA PARK REVELLERS

SETTINGS

Act One: Missus
 Trafalgar, rural NSW, Plymouth Street, Surry Hills, Sydney

Act Two: The Harp in the South
 Surry Hills and its surrounds

Act Three: The Harp in the South
 Surry Hills and its surrounds

Act Four: Poor Man's Orange
 Surry Hills and its surrounds

The play was written with the intention of a highly movable set, shifting fluidly from one locale to another, one home to another, one room to another.

This play was written on Gadigal land, on Eora Country. The adapter pays her respects to all First Nations people of this land. Always was, always will be Aboriginal land.

The adapter asks for all-inclusive casting and crewing.

Kirk Page, Helen Thomson and George Zhao in Sydney Theatre Company's The Harp in the South, Part One and Part Two, *2018. (Photo: Daniel Boud)*

ACT ONE: MISSUS

SCENE ONE

The outskirts of Trafalgar, New South Wales, 1920. A dam on the far edges of a rural property.

A small boy of eight, THADY DARCY, *wanders. He doesn't belong there. He is of another time and place. He wears navy trousers and red braces and clutches a bag of marbles. He watches as ...*

A woman, FRANCES DARCY *(late 40s), appears—an odd figure on the barren landscape.*

THADY: Frances Darcy.

> FRANCES *is dressed in a slip and an extravagant coat with deep pockets. She has a red embroidered shawl swathed around her neck. She sings as she travels.*

FRANCES: [*singing*] 'Tis the last rose of summer,
    Left blooming alone;
    All her lovely companions
    Are faded and gone …

THADY: Often she was fantastically merry, though falling suddenly from laughter into tears.

FRANCES: [*singing*] No flower of her kindred,
    No rosebud is nigh,
    To reflect back her blushes,
    Or give sigh for sigh.

> *A man appears in the distance—Frances's husband,* MARTIN DARCY *(50s). He watches his wife solemnly. He does not see* THADY.

THADY: Martin Darcy had brought Frances to Trafalgar at the start of the century when everything was hopeful. Long before today—1920.
    Long before her throat started to swell and her brain started to boil.

But now ... he did not know what to do with a madwoman.

FRANCES *drinks from a bottle of laudanum, wincing as it burns her throat.*

FRANCES: [*singing*] I'll not leave thee, thou lone one!
　　To pine on the stem;
　　Since the lovely are sleeping,
　　Go, sleep thou with them.

Although her song has ended ... another plays in the distance. A lone harp.

THADY: Perhaps she was haunted by the harp. Calling from a faraway land.

They all hear it. Like the call of a ghost.

FRANCES *removes her shawl to reveal a horrifically flayed neck. As she sings on, she gathers stones and places them in her pockets. Her husband watches on. As does* THADY ...

The harp plays on.

FRANCES: [*singing*] Thus kindly I scatter,
　　Thy leaves o'er the bed,
　　Where thy mates of the garden
　　Lie scentless and dead.
　　When true hearts lie withered,
　　And fond ones are flown,
　　Oh! who would inhabit
　　This bleak world alone?

She steps into the water and disappears. The harp echoes ...

MARTIN *wanders away.*

THADY *walks down to the dam. He looks into the water then out to us.*

THADY: We are all haunted by the harp.

The harp echoes ...

Blackout.

SCENE TWO

Two young men now stand over the dam. They are HUGH *and* JER DARCY.

HUGH: Ma …

> HUGH *is a small, muscular 22-year-old. 'He often found a lump in his throat for no reason. He began to look at things, stars, girls' hair, the way a paddock of cabbages was not green, but blue …'*
>
> JER *is his younger brother (18), but they don't look alike. Whereas* HUGH's *skin is pale and freckled,* JER's *is much darker. His feet are twisted awkwardly and he leans on a pair of crutches. 'Born a dark elvish thing with its feet back to front.'*

JER: Now what?

> HUGH *shrugs.*

We can't leave her in there.

> *The boys stare down at the water.*

She's been missing two weeks. We pull her out, she might fall apart.

> *Silence.*

I thought she could swim … We can't leave her in there.

> MARTIN *approaches. He stands between the two boys. Looks into the dam.*

It's Ma.

MARTIN: I know who it is.

JER: Reckon she fell in.

MARTIN: She didn't fall in.

> *Beat.*

Mad bitch. Madder than that goitre growing out of her bloody neck. Mad with shame. For you.

> *He glares at* JER.

She's gone. Now I want you gone too.

JER: But, Da—

MARTIN: Just because your ma opened her legs to any man that paid her mind, don't mean I have to atone for her sins.

JER: [*turning to his brother*] Hughie …?
MARTIN: Get him off my property, Hugh. She's gone. Now he can go too. Twisted black bastard.

> HUGH *snaps. He fights his father to the ground. It is a long, protracted grapple, as* JER *watches on.* HUGH *makes guttural grunts with each punch, beating his father brutally.*

JER: *Hugh, enough!*

> *But* HUGH *doesn't hear. Just keeps punching until his father lays still. The two boys stare down at* MARTIN *in silence.*

Is he dead?
HUGH: No.
JER: Why do you do that, Hughie?
HUGH: Cos he's a mean bastard, Jer. And he had my face. And I don't wanna look at a mean bastard with my face anymore. So I'm takin' it back and I'm gettin' away from here.
JER: You wouldn't leave me, Hughie, would you? Hughie, don't you leave me by myself. How am I gonna get my feet fixed if I'm all by myself?

> HUGH *puts an arm around his brother, who nestles, twisted, into the embrace.*

HUGH: I'll never leave you wanting, Jer. I promise you that. We're all each other's got, me and you.
JER: We go together like finger and thumb.
HUGH: I'll get your feet fixed. I will. Soon.

> *Silence.*

JER: Now what?

> *A moment of silence. Then …*

HUGH: Now we go into town. I need a drink. Go on, I'll give you a head start.

> JER *limps away.*

Rest now, Ma. I'd pray for you but … I've gotta find somethin' more.

SCENE THREE

In the town of Trafalgar, we are in the Kilker household.

In a bedroom, a young woman—MARGARET KILKER *(19) 'soft and broad'—bathes herself gently with a sponge as she wears a loosened set of stays.*

MARGARET: I'm finally a woman.

I've got mirrors all over the wall of my palatial bathroom …

When I get out, I'll put on my lovely pink—no, lilac—satin gown. And my slippers with very high heels and lots of feathers on them …

And I'll powder my nose and perfume my skin …

Then I'll meet … [*wincing slightly*] Herb Lennon at the King's Birthday Carnival and we'll—

JOSIE *(17) 'narrow and hard' suddenly appears.*

JOSIE: Who are you talking to, Margaret?

MARGARET: No-one. I just … UGH!

JOSIE *pulls tightly on the laces of her sister's stays.*

Mother of God, Josie … I'll bring up a lung! You'll pop the top off me like a daisy!

JOSIE: Serves you right for having such a big bust. You'll thank me later when Herb Lennon keeps his hands off you.

MARGARET: I'm not officially walking with Herb Lennon. He's romantic as an egg.

JOSIE: That's not what the rest of Trafalgar thinks. I heard he was going to ask you to marry him.

MARGARET: What? Who said such a thing?

JOSIE: Margaret, I'm two years younger than you and I've been walking with Noel Capper for three whole months. You should just settle for Herb Lennon to save yourself further embarrassment.

MARGARET: And why do I have to marry the first person who pays me mind?

JOSIE: He's not the first. He's the only.

MARGARET: The world's a big place, Josie. There's gotta be something more.

JOSIE: The world may be big but Trafalgar is not. You'll be married to Herb Lennon by 1921. Mark my words.
MARGARET: There's better out there than Herb Lennon. The prospect of him makes my belly heave.

> JOSIE *just pulls tighter on the stays, knocking the wind out of her older sister.*

> *Meanwhile ...* ENY *(45) and* JOHN KILKER *(55) are in the kitchen. He clips his nose hairs. She stirs a pot vigorously so that her breasts jiggle.*

ENY: Here. John. Look at this.

> JOHN *looks up as* ENY *makes her breasts jiggle even more. He can't help be turned on.*

JOHN: God in heaven, woman. Was last night not enough?
ENY: Come on, let me put me hand where it'll do the most good.

> *She places her hand down* JOHN's *pants.*

Solid as the bloody Vatican, you are, John ...

> JOHN *starts to enjoy it for a brief while. Then ...*

JOHN: Eny, no. I have to stay focused for Carnival Day.
ENY: Don't go to Carnival Day, John. Let's just send the girls off and spend the day here together. You're too old for Carnival Day anyway.
JOHN: I can handle a game of tug o' war, Eny.
ENY: Can you, though?

> *She rubs him harder. He sighs.*

JOHN: It's your lifelong insatiability that'll put me in the grave.

> *But she continues. As* JOHN *starts to enjoy it again,* JOSIE *pulls tighter on* MARGARET's *stays until the older girl screams in agony and breaks free, charging into the kitchen.* ENY *and* JOHN *separate in a hurry.*

MARGARET: Ma, she's squeezed me inside / out!
JOSIE: She won't be contained Ma!
ENY: Josie, don't be a tattle. You'll learn to love your stays, Margaret. Soon they'll feel like you're wearing nothing at all.

> *They all stare pointedly at* ENY's *jiggling, unlaced bosom. A knock at the door.*

JOSIE: That'll be the boys. For God's sake make yourselves presentable!

MARGARET, ENY *and* JOHN *do so.*

JOSIE *opens the door to* NOEL CAPPER *(19), dapper and handsome in a blazer, holding a large bunch of flowers, and* HERB LENNON *(21), scruffy and buck-toothed and carrying a euphonium.*

Good morning, Noel.

NOEL: Good morning, Josephine. Good morning, Mr Kilker. Good morning, Mrs Kilker. Good morning, Margaret.

ENY: Good morning, Noel.

JOHN: Good morning, Noel.

HERB: Good morning, Noel.

Beat. It's awkward.

I mean, good morning, Mr Kilker. Mrs Kilker. Good morning, Josephine. Good morning, Margaret.

MARGARET *gives a weak smile.*

NOEL: These are for you.

He hands JOSIE *the flowers.*

JOSIE: Well, thank you, Noel. Ma, put them in water.

She thrusts the flowers at ENY *and beams at* NOEL. MARGARET *looks expectantly at* HERB *and his euphonium.*

HERB: I'm in the brass band, if you recall.

MARGARET *nods politely and goes to touch the instrument.*

Don't touch it, please. I have a solo on 'God Save the King'. You'll have to listen out for it.

Everyone nods politely and agrees they will indeed listen out for his solo.

JOSIE: Shall we walk together?

NOEL: May we, sir?

JOHN: Not up to me, son. You'll learn that in good time.

JOHN *shows* HERB, NOEL *and* JOSIE *out.* MARGARET *trails behind. She turns back to* ENY.

MARGARET: Ma …

There's more than this. Isn't there? Something more than stays and Trafalgar and 'God Save the King'?

> ENY *smiles softly at her daughter.*

ENY: There's a full life ahead of you, Maggie. Don't be in too much of a hurry.

> *She kisses* MARGARET *on the forehead.*

Now go well, my blooming rose.

MARGARET: Pressed flower, more like.

> ENY *leaves.* MARGARET *shifts uncomfortably in her stays.*
>
> *She catches up with* HERB.

HERB: Shall we?

> *She takes his arm reluctantly.*

SCENE FOUR

As the young foursome walk, NOEL *puts his arm around* JOSIE. *She smiles and casts a pointed glance over her shoulder at* MARGARET, *who walks stiffly in her tight stays.*

HERB *struggles to put his arm around* MARGARET. *It's difficult with the euphonium in his arms.*

HERB: You haven't said anything about my moustache.

> MARGARET *stares at his face.*

I've been growing it for three weeks and four days now.

MARGARET: It's very … refined.

> *He seems happy with that.*

Do you notice anything new about me?

> NOEL *looks* MARGARET *up and down.*

HERB: Your stockings. They're new.

MARGARET: Oh … Well, yes—

HERB: You shouldn't wear them. They're vulgar.

MARGARET: They're all the rage!

HERB: Not in Trafalgar. In Trafalgar they're vulgar. Now I have to practise my solo. You can listen.

ACT ONE: MISSUS

He disentangles himself from MARGARET *and starts to parp badly.* MARGARET *trails behind as* JOSIE *casts her another glance.*

A fairground forms around them. Stalls and tents and colourful signs. As other TOWNSFOLK *fill the space ...*

FAIRGROUND ANNOUNCER: Welcome, one and all, to the King's Birthday Carnival! Take a spin on the merry-go-round! Face your fears in the House of Horrors! Under the big top, test your strength against Rusty the Boxing Kangaroo! And remember to get a slice of our special event—the monster plum duff! Four of the region's finest bakers, with the assistance of the council's brand new concrete mixer, have made a plum pudding the size of a veritable haystack! It's stuffed full of trinkets and treats as well as ... Drum roll, Bertie.

Bertie, drum roll.

A drum roll from BERTIE.

... as well as a diamond ring worth a hundred guineas!

The CROWD *gasp.*

JOSIE: Oh, Noel! Will you win me that ring?

NOEL: 'Course I will, Josie. Only the best for my girl.

JOSIE *squeals as he whisks her away.* MARGARET *smiles nervously at* HERB.

MARGARET: Do you like plum duff?

HERB: Not really. Clogs up my tubes.

MARGARET: Oh.

HERB: Come on. Brass band is about to march. Remember to cheer for my solo.

She reluctantly follows him.

As the brass band starts in the distance, JOHN *and* ENY *enter.*

ENY: I'm warning you, John. You're not young anymore. Don't try and keep up with the bairns.

JOHN: Enough, Eny.

ENY: I didn't sail halfway across the world to be left a widow before my time.

JOHN: For the love of God, woman, it's just tug o'war.

ENY: Got a feeling in my waters.
JOHN: Then go and have a piddle. I'll be fine.

He leaves her. She wanders off worriedly.

HUGH *and* JER *enter.* HUGH *is puffed up and drunk, drinking from a bottle.* JER *has trouble keeping up with him on his crutches. He carries a ukulele on his back.*

HUGH: Come on, Jer. I'll win you a prize on the strength tester.
JER: Hughie, slow down.

HUGH *takes a mallet from a little girl who runs away crying.*

He raises it, and misses the plate on the 'Test Your Strength' tower completely. He tries again. Misses again.

HUGH: Fuckin' broken!
JER: Hughie! Leave it! Come on—have a lie down.

HUGH *tries again. The mallet goes flying, just missing some* FAIR GOERS.

Please excuse my brother! He's a member of the Freak Show—they'll be on in an hour in the main ring.

He tries to grab his brother, but HUGH *is going in for a* YOUNG WOMAN*'s behind.*

HUGH: Think I pulled a muscle. My guts are all twisted.
JER: Your guts are twisted cos of the booze in your belly.

HUGH *looks green.*

Now, sit there, Hughie. I'm going to find you some food.

HUGH *sits obediently on the edge of the merry-go-round, leaning against a horse's arse, as* JER *limps away.*

The marching band passes, with HERB *parping along badly.* MARGARET *cheers, feigning excitement, as* NOEL *and* JOSIE *canoodle beside her.*

As the CROWD *moves on,* MARGARET *climbs onto the merry-go-round. Without seeing* HUGH, *she tries to sit atop a horse, but her stays are still causing her grief.*

She tries every position she can think of, but to no avail. She finally finds a halfway comfortable seating position—side

ACT ONE: MISSUS   11

>*saddle. In desperation, she reaches up her blouse and unlaces her stays. Relief. Until ... the merry-go-round jerks into rotation, its carnival music starting up and* MARGARET *is thrown from her horse. She totters on the edge of the ride before tripping over* HUGH. *They are thrown from the ride and onto the grass—* MARGARET *landing on top of* HUGH. *She smells his reeking breath.*

MARGARET: You're drunk.
HUGH: You're heavy.
MARGARET: I feel sick.
HUGH: Me too.

>*They sit and regain their composure.* HUGH *notices* MARGARET*'s loosened stays.*

You with anyone?

>*Beat.*

MARGARET: No.

>HUGH *grins.*

I'm Margaret Kilker.
HUGH: I'm Hugh Darcy.
MARGARET: I know who you are. You used to go to my school.
HUGH: Don't remember.
MARGARET: Oh.
HUGH: Not you. School.
MARGARET: Oh.

>*Beat.*

HUGH: Wanna walk around?
MARGARET: Around what?
HUGH: The carnival. With me.
MARGARET: Hugh Darcy ...

>HERB *parps in the distance. Decision made.*

MARGARET: Yes please.

>MARGARET *beams. The two of them stand and wander through the bustling festival. As* MARGARET *walks ahead,* HUGH *surreptitiously steals items from each stall and gifts them to*

her until she is laden with kewpie dolls, a coconut, paper roses, balloons and spun sugar.

They walk past JOSIE *and* NOEL. MARGARET's *stays are still loose.* JOSIE's *eyes widen.*

JOSIE: Your stays aren't stayed! Your stays aren't stayed!

MARGARET *pokes her tongue out.*

MARGARET: [*to* HUGH] Let's get out of here.

They hurry away. JER *limps his way through the crowd, holding a pie.*

JER: Hughie? Hughie! Jesus Christ …

He disappears into the throng.

Meanwhile JOHN *stretches his limbs by a long rope, ready to take on a younger man in a tug o'war.*

FAIRGROUND ANNOUNCER: Ladies and gentlemen, boys and girls, put your bets on the tug o'war! John Kilker versus Spud Taylor, on now in the main ring! Drumroll, Bertie. BERTIE! DRUMROLL!

ENY *watches in fear and calls out to his younger opponent …*

ENY: Go easy on him, boy. He's old enough to be your grandfather.

JOHN: Quiet, Eny.

FAIRGROUND ANNOUNCER: Take the strain! Three, two, one!

The two men start to pull.

JOSIE *runs up to* ENY *and whispers in her ear, gesticulating wildly about Margaret's stays.*

JOSIE: Ma! I just saw Margaret walking around with Hugh Darcy and her stays are unstayed!

ENY's *eyes widen in horror.*

ENY: Jesus, Mary, Joseph and the donkey! Which way did they go?

JOSIE: This way!

She drags her away. The tug o'war continues.

HUGH: Wanna walk with me through the House of Horrors, Margaret?

MARGARET: I'd be delighted, Hugh!

ACT ONE: MISSUS

MARGARET and HUGH *disappear into the House of Horrors.* JER *sees them and gives chase.*

JER: Hughie! Hughie!

He enters the House of Horrors, followed by ENY ...

ENY: Margaret! Margaret!

... followed by JOSIE ...

JOSIE: She's up to no good, Ma! Get her, Ma!

... followed by HERB, *who has seen the chase and run into the House of Horrors, carrying his euphonium.*

HERB: Hey! My solo! Wait for my solo!

NOEL: The tug o'war! You're missing the tug o'war! Oh hello...

He walks off with a pretty young woman.

The tug o'war continues. JOHN *grunts exhaustedly.*

After a few moments, MARGARET *and* HUGH *are chased wildly from the House of Horrors by* JER, ENY, JOSIE *and* HERB.

ENY: You get your filthy hands off my daughter!

MARGARET: Ma! We were just walking together!

JOSIE: I saw him give her a kiss you wouldn't see out of a bedroom, Ma!

MARGARET: I got jumped on by a ghoul! It was a ghoul, Ma, not Hughie.

JOSIE: Her stays are unstayed! Ma, her stays are unstayed!

HERB: Stays. I knew there was something different about you. Vulgar.

MARGARET: It wasn't him that unstayed me. I unstayed me!

JOSIE: You couldn't have. [*To* ENY] They were *really* tight.

HERB: I thought you were walking around with me, Margaret.

ENY: Josie, lace your sister.

JOSIE *does so, with relish.*

JER: Hughie, let's go home.

HUGH: What home, Jer? Margaret, keep walking with me.

He takes her arm.

HERB: She's walking around with me!

HERB *drags* MARGARET *to him.*

The tug o'war continues in the distance. JOHN *does not look well.*

ENY *pulls on* MARGARET.

ENY: Margaret, he's a Darcy.

HUGH *pulls her to him.*

HUGH: And what's wrong with that?

HERB *pulls at* MARGARET.

HERB: His ma's a mad whore.

JER: Don't you be saying that about our ma. She's in God's hands now. Hughie, let's go.

MARGARET *pulls away from them all.*

MARGARET: It was just a walk! Can't a girl just go for a damn walk in this town?!

Everyone but HUGH *is appalled by Margaret's language. The tug o' war reaches a peak—*JOHN *is beaten.*

The CROWD *applaud.* JOHN *looks around for his family, disheartened.*

ENY: You've made us miss your father's tug o' war.

HERB: I was gonna ask you to marry me, Margaret. Right after 'Click Go the Shears'.

MARGARET: You were?

HUGH: Were you just?

JER: Hughie, let's leave. Please.

HUGH: Show us the ring, then.

MARGARET: No. Don't show us the ring.

ENY: Yes. Go on, Herb. Propose.

HERB *pats at his pockets, struggling with his euphonium.*

HERB: Oh … it's here somewhere.

HUGH: Where is it, Herb?

JOSIE: Yes. Where is it?

HERB *keeps patting his pockets.*

HERB: Must have fallen out while I was marching.

The band play a fanfare.

A huge plum pudding is brought out and the TOWNSFOLK *gasp in awe.*

ACT ONE: MISSUS

FESTIVAL ANNOUNCER: And now the moment you've all been waiting for! The King's Birthday Monster Plum Duff! Who will get the lucky slice containing the bee-yoo-ti-ful diamond ring worth one hundred guineas?

Beat. HUGH *and* HERB *glare at each other. Then ...*

They both bolt for the duff, chased by MARGARET, JOSIE, ENY *and* JER.

JOSIE: Go, Herb!

ENY: Yes, hurry, Herb!

MARGARET: Herb, please don't!

JER: Hughie, no!

HUGH: I'll getcha that diamond ring, Margaret. Promise.

FESTIVAL ANNOUNCER: Competitors, take your places! And three, two, one!

They scoff slice after slice of the duff as the CROWD *cheers. The carnival is raucous.*

Apart from the crowd, JOHN, *who is mopping his brow and armpits after the tug o' war, starts to stumble. He clutches his chest and falls to the ground.*

ENY: John! *John!*

The eating comes to an end as the TOWNSFOLK *rush to* JOHN. *His family can only watch on helplessly.*

The carnival sounds come to an abrupt end—apart from the sound of a faint harp—as ENY, MARGARET *and* JOSIE *cry out ...*

ENY, MARGARET and JOSIE: John! / *John!*

MARGARET and JOSIE: Da! Da!

JOHN *is lifted and carried away, accompanied by* ENY*'s cries.*

Scene Five can form here.

JER *and a* NUN *are left onstage amidst the carnival detritus. They watch the* CROWD *hurry away with* JOHN. *The* NUN *finishes her plate of duff. She gets a ring from her mouth, looks at it with pleasant surprise.*

NUN: Praise the Lord! The diamond ring! I got the diamond ring!

She slips it onto her finger and wanders away.

JER *begins to strum softly to himself on his ukulele.*

As the world shifts, we see a middle-aged woman, ALF, *adjusting the collar of a priest,* FATHER DRISCOLL. *He stares at her with glassy eyes, a little bleary.*

The Kilker house returns as the harp echoes.

SCENE FIVE

JOHN *lays in bed, pale and lifeless.* ENY *waits worriedly beside him.*

ENY: John. Can you hear me?

No response. She forges on.

Now, you know I love you, John. And I know you've plans to leave us all soon, you bugger. But … I've a confession to make, my husband …

She leans in close and whispers in his ear.

Outside, HUGH *chops wood as* JER *stands nearby. A large pile of kindling sits beside them.* JER *waits nearby, his ukulele strapped to him. Shivering.*

JER: Cold as a dead man's tongue out here, Hughie.
HUGH: That's why I'm choppin' wood, Jer. Keeps the blood boiled.
JER: You've chopped enough wood to keep Hell hot, Hughie.
HUGH: The least we can do. That's a sick man in there.
JER: Yer just trying to get a leg over his daughter.
HUGH: What would you know about legs?

He keeps chopping.

JER: It's not the old man you should be worried about. That wife of his, she doesn't like you. I've seen the way she looks at you. Like she's sucking a lemon.

He demonstrates.

HUGH: She'll come round.
JER: She likes me. Likes my songs.

He sings.

ACT ONE: MISSUS

[*Singing*] Bryan O'Lynn was a gentleman born
His hair it was long and his whiskers unshorn,
His teeth were far out and his eyes were far in.
'I'm a thing of beauty,' said Bryan O'Lynn.

HUGH *cracks up.* JER *performs for him.*

Bryan O'Lynn was a gentleman born,
He lived at a time when no clothes were worn,
But as fashion went out, of course Bryan walked in,
'Whoo! I'll soon lead the fashions,' says Bryan O—

ENY *appears.*

ENY: You dare sing of fashion while my husband fights to stay out of his grave?

JER *stops abruptly.*

HUGH: He didn't mean anythin' by it, Mrs Kilker. He thought you might like a tune.

ENY *looks at* HUGH *like she's sucking a lemon.* JER *impersonates her behind her back to* HUGH. *'Told you so.'*

ENY: And don't think I haven't got you worked out, Hugh Darcy. I know you think I think you're doin' my family a good turn by choppin' wood. But I also know you're squattin' nearby and probably pilfering kindling for the fire I see glowin' every night amongst the scrub.

HUGH: We've taken a bundle or two of your wood. But never more than we need to get through the night. And I make sure I chop double the next time I'm back.

ENY: You'd better. I will count each stick, mark my words. You have to get up early in the mornin' to catch me out, Darcy.

HUGH: You'd have to stay up all night.

MARGARET *and* JOSIE *appear with a basket of groceries.*

MARGARET: Ma …

She sees HUGH. *Smiles awkwardly. He smiles back.* JOSIE *rolls her eyes.* ENY *watches closely.*

JOSIE: Butcher was all out of mutton.

ENY: Jesus, Mary and Joseph. How do we make a broth for your poor dying da? There's scant enough as it is with just vegetables.

HUGH: I've got meat. Some salt beef. Fresh roo.

ENY: Kangaroo? For supper? You take us for natives, boy?

HUGH: Please. Just let me cook for you.

MARGARET: What?

JOSIE: You?

ENY: Cook?

JER: Hughie's a fine cook, Mrs Kilker. He's been cookin' for us ever since Ma lost her mind.

ENY: I'm perfectly able to provide for my family, thank you very much.

HUGH: I could make you a nice Irish stew.

ENY: I'm the Irish one in this house. I'll make the stew.

HUGH: I'm Irish too.

ENY: Pffft. Irish as a feckin' wombat.

MARGARET: Ma!

HUGH: Stay by your husband. I'm sure he'll wake soon. In the meantime, let me make you a meal. Please.

> ENY *hesitates.*

ENY: Oh, alright. Penance. To make up for the stolen kindling. Josie, Margaret, get inside.

> JOSIE *heads in, casting* HUGH *a haughty look.* MARGARET *hangs back with the basket.* ENY *starts to head back inside.*

[*Turning to* JER, *glaring*] Did I say stop playing, boy?

> *He hesitantly starts again.*

JER: [*singing*] Bryan O'Lynn had no shirt to his back,
    He went to a neighbour's and borrowed a sack,
    Then he puckered the meal bag up under his chin,
    'Whoo! They'll take them for ruffles,' says Bryan O'Lynn.

> *Satisfied,* ENY *heads inside.* MARGARET *laughs at the song.* ENY *calls from inside.*

ENY: [*off*] Margaret!

> *But* MARGARET *and* HUGH *remain, staring at each other as* JER *strums his ukelele softly.*

HUGH: You ever been to Sydney?

> JER *stops playing abruptly.*

ACT ONE: MISSUS

MARGARET: No.

HUGH: No shortage of food there. Fresh fruit. Vegies. Beef and pork and chicken and duck. Fish straight out of the harbour.

> *She smiles.* JER *watches on, brooding, keeping an eye on his brother and* MARGARET.

MARGARET: And streets paved with gold, no doubt.

> *He holds the basket and watches her as she departs.*

HUGH: You don't look like a Margaret.

MARGARET: What do I look like?

HUGH: I'm not sure. I'll think on it.

ENY: [*off*] MARGARET!

> MARGARET *smiles. Heads inside.*
>
> JER *observes as he starts to strum softly.*

JER: What you cookin' up, Hughie?

HUGH: A stew. Fit for a queen.

JER: I love you, Hughie.

HUGH: I know, Jer.

JER: Despite me ankles.

HUGH: I know.

JER: Me and you. Like finger and thumb.

HUGH: Like finger and thumb. Me and you.

> *But he is still looking towards* MARGARET.
>
> *A shift.* JER *and* HUGH *move into the house.* HUGH *cooks.*
>
> JER *inhabits a chair, strumming gently.*
>
> *Scene Six can form here.*
>
> MARGARET *dances to herself in a corner.*
>
> *The two brothers are now members of the Kilker household.*
> [*Singing*] Bryan O'Lynn and his poor mad mother,
> They both went home o'er the bridge together,
> The bridge it broke down and they both tumbled in,
> 'Whoo! We'll go to hell by water,' says Bryan O'Lynn.

SCENE SIX

JOHN *still lays in bed, pale and unconscious.*
JOSIE *washes his arms.*

ALF *and* FATHER DRISCOLL *stand over him, chatting morbidly.* ALF *was flat as a stoat and yellowish too. But inside she was valiant and resolute, a majestically big woman.*

ENY *strokes* JOHN's *hair.* MARGARET *hurries in.*

ENY: I think he's looking better today, Father Driscoll.

ALF: For the love of God, Eny, it's been weeks. If he's not up by now he never will be again.

    FATHER DRISCOLL *stands over* JOHN's *frame.*

FATHER DRISCOLL: O, Holy Hosts above, I call upon Thee as a servant of Jesus Christ to sanctify our actions this day in preparation for the fulfilment of the Will of God.

    ENY *gasps and begins to weep.*

ENY: Oh, John … John …

    MARGARET, JOSIE *and* ALF *stand beside her.*

    FATHER DRISCOLL *makes the sign of the cross on* JOHN's *forehead.*

FATHER DRISCOLL: By this sign, thou art anointed with the grace of the atonement of Jesus Christ and thou art absolved of all past error.

    ENY *weeps.*

ALF: Let him go, Eny. Let him go.

FATHER DRISCOLL: Thus we give the Father Creator glory as we give you into His arms, in everlasting peace. Amen. Amen. Amen.

WOMEN: Amen.

    Silence.

JOHN: Driscoll.

    Everyone leaps with fright.

Shove your last rites up your dress.

ENY: John! You're back! He's back! Like Christ himself!
FATHER DRISCOLL: Not quite like Christ.
MARGARET: Da, we thought you were a goner!
JOSIE: You been out cold for three weeks, Da!
ENY: You see this, Alf? I'm married to Christ himself!
ALF: Christ only took three days to rise again. You've had us waiting a month.
JOHN: Come here, Eny. Not all of me's risen yet.

He drags her to him.

ALF *gasps.* FATHER DRISCOLL *looks embarrassed, as do the girls.*

ENY: No more tug o' war for you, John Kilker. We had a coffin picked for you and all. Cancel the order, Father Driscoll.
JOHN: Jesus, woman.
ENY: Had psalms picked out. Jer had a song he was going to sing on his yoo-lalla-kee.
JOHN: Jer? Who's Jer?
MARGARET: Hughie's brother.
JOHN: Hughie? Who's Hughie?
JOSIE: Margaret's beau.
JOHN: I thought Herb Lennon was your beau?
MARGARET: How many times do I have to say it? I'm not walkin' round with Herb Lennon!

ENY *slaps* JOSIE.

ENY: Josie, stop your tattling. Hughie's not her beau. Is he, Margaret?

MARGARET *shrugs.*

We needed the help, John. Wood wasn't going to chop itself, was it? The boys needed a home. We needed a hand.
ALF: Two young unmarried men living under the same roof as two young unmarried women. Scandalous.
ENY: You live with a priest, my spinster sister-in-law. Apologies, Father.

FATHER DRISCOLL *smiles nervously.*

ALF: How dare you cast aspersions on my relationship with Father Driscoll. I'm his house help.
FATHER DRISCOLL: Now, now. We needn't go into it.
ENY: What help does he need? He's in God's pocket. Apologies, Father.

FATHER DRISCOLL: Come, come, ladies. Come, come.
ALF: I starch his collar.
ENY: If he can assist God with transubstantiation, he's more than capable of starching his own collar. Apologies, Father.
FATHER DRISCOLL: No, no … no, no …
ALF: And I fix him his meals while he's preparing sermons.
ENY: Aye! Like a wife! Apologies, Father.
FATHER DRISCOLL: It's fine, now. It's fine.
ALF: And I put him to bed when he's had too much wine.

An awkward silence.

FATHER DRISCOLL: Sometimes I have to drink the holy sacrament when it's vinegarised. 'Tis sinful to waste God's blood.

Beat.

ALF: And it's sinful to take in two young men when you've got two young girls at their ripest.
ENY: Safer for me to have them all here under the one roof so I can keep an eye on things.
ALF: I pray for their souls nightly.
ENY: Well, don't. I've got it covered.
ALF: That's a fine way to talk after your husband's just been absolved of all his sins.
JOHN: Got a clean slate, have I? That's a stroke of luck. Come here, Eny!

He goes for ENY *again.*

JER and HUGH appear. HUGH carries a large pile of wood. JER holds a couple of twigs.

JOHN pulls himself up.

JER and HUGH remove their hats.

JOHN pulls back the sheets and sits on the edge of the bed. He's dizzy. The women hurry to him.

Just a rush of blood. Leave me be.

They do. JOHN *turns to the boys.*

You're Darcy's boys.
HUGH: We are, sir. I'm Hugh.
MARGARET: Hughie.

ACT ONE: MISSUS

HUGH: This is my brother Jer.
JER: Short for Jeremiah. [*To* FATHER DRISCOLL] The weeping prophet.
ALF: [*looking at his twisted legs*] I'm sure.
JOHN: That's quite a load you've brought in there.
JER: There's plenty more where that came from, sir. We've been keeping your trade going while you been poorly.
MARGARET: And he cooks. [HUGH] And he sings. [JER]
JOHN: I see.

> *He looks up at* FATHER DRISCOLL.

Thank you for your time, Father Driscoll. I'll not be needing you for the next little while.
FATHER DRISCOLL: I'll continue to pray for you, John.
ALF: [*to* ENY] As will I, for *you*.

> ALF *and* FATHER DRISCOLL *leave.*

JOHN: Margaret. Josie. Stay.

> MARGARET *and* JOSIE *obey.* JOHN *turns to* HUGH *and* JER.

Why are you not working your own property?
JER: Ma drowned. Da threw us out. I got twisted ankles and my skin's a funny colour.
JOHN: I see.
JER: I'm saving up for an operation. For my ankles. So people know that I'm able to love.
JOHN: How'd you mean, son?
HUGH: You love, Jer. You do.

> JOHN *looks at the boy, confused.*

JER: You know the saying?
'May those that love us, love us
And those that don't love us,
May God turn their hearts.
And if he can't turn their hearts,
May he turn their ankles
So we'll know them by their limping.'
> God turned my ankles. So maybe I haven't loved enough.
> So maybe if I get an operation, I can turn my ankles back, and love like everyone else does.

He smiles at JOSIE. *She scowls back.*

JOHN: [*to* HUGH] Your da threw you out too?
HUGH: He's my brother. Where he goes, I go.
JER: We go together like finger and thumb.

    JOHN *nods.*

JOHN: So in the three weeks I've been sleeping, you've come into my house, taken over my business and romanced my girls.
MARGARET: No, / Da!
JOSIE: Da, / no!
ENY: What kind of mother do you take me for, John Kilker?
MARGARET: They sleep on the verandah!
JOSIE: He can't love anyway—God told us by his twisted ankles!
HUGH: No, sir. No. I would never take anything from you that you weren't willing to part with.

    An awkward beat.

Mr Kilker, may I have a word alone, please?
ENY: No.
JOHN: Outside, girls. Eny.
ENY: John!
JOSIE: She's taken by Herb Lennon, you know.
MARGARET: Shut up, Josie. [*To* HUGH] I'm not.
ENY: She is.
JOHN: I said outside.

    The girls go, along with a reluctant ENY.

Eny.

    ENY *finally begins to slink away.*

HUGH: And you, Jer.
JER: What? But where you go, I go, Hughie.
HUGH: No. Where you go, I go. There's a difference.

    Beat. JER *limps out.* ENY *turns back.*

ENY: John … Did you hear what I whispered to you? While you were sleeping all this time? Do you remember?

    JOHN *thinks.*

JOHN: No, Eny. Why?

ACT ONE: MISSUS 25

She smiles, relieved.

ENY: No reason.

ENY *casts a worried glance at* HUGH, *then leaves.*

SCENE SEVEN

JOHN *and* HUGH *face each other.* MARGARET, JOSIE, ENY *and* JER *listen through the door.*

HUGH: I've not taken a penny from your business, sir. I just wanted to help out is all.
JOHN: Why?
HUGH: I wanna go to Sydney. The Hills. There's work goin' there. Factories.
JOHN: What's that to do with me?
HUGH: If Jer could stay here with you, I could go, save up some money for his operation, then send for him to join me in the city.

Outside the door ...

JER: What? Hughie, no ...
JOSIE: Shush, Jeremiah!

ENY *belts her across the head.*

Inside the door ...

JOHN: You want me to keep your brother for you? Isn't that what your da's for?
HUGH: Da hates him. He'd rather see him dead.

Outside, JER *sits on the ground, bereft.*

Inside ...

JOHN: Because the boy can't love?
HUGH: He loves. Too much, sometimes. God twisted the wrong ankles with that one.
JOHN: And what would I do with a cripple?
HUGH: He's good around the house. Decent cook. Makes a lovely pudding.

Outside ...

ENY: My puddin' is lovely enough.

Inside ...

HUGH: And he's a great storyteller. Singer. Tells a funny joke.

Outside ...

MARGARET: He's right, Jer. You do tell a funny joke.

JER *just sits with his head in his hands.*

Inside ...

JOHN: But his ankles are turned.
HUGH: We'll get that fixed.
JOHN: And?

Beat.

HUGH: In return ... I'll marry your daughter.

Outside, JOSIE *and* ENY *gasp in horror.*

Inside ...

JOHN: Which one?
HUGH: Margaret.

Outside, MARGARET *squeals.* ENY *looks faint.*

Inside ...

JOHN: She's not a trade-off, Hughie.
HUGH: No, no, no—I *want* to marry your daughter.
JOHN: Why?
HUGH: Because I believe we belong together.

Outside ...

JOSIE: Why does *he* get to say who belongs with who? When I marry Noel Capper, *I'll* be the one sayin' where *he* belongs.

Inside ...

HUGH: There's a place for women in Surry Hills, Mr Kilker. More than Trafalgar. What's the best she's gonna get here? Married to Herb Lennon, listening to him blow his own trumpet for the rest of her life?

JOHN, JOSIE, MARGARET and ENY: [*together*] Euphonium.

HUGH: She deserves somethin' more. And there's promise in Surry Hills, sir. There's hope.

ACT ONE: MISSUS

JOSIE: Pffft. Hope.
MARGARET: Hope …
JOHN: Hope?

> *Beat.*

> JOHN *gets to his feet.*

My family has starved to be here, Hugh Darcy. We spent six months in a boat, Eny and I, escaping the only home we'd ever known, seasick and sideways—till we landed on this unknowable fuckin' soil. Nothin' in our bellies but hope. I don't want my Maggie marrying no caterpillar-lipped euphonium player. But I don't want her to be the wife of the kind of Irish we were escapin' neither.
There's no fuckin' hope in that.

HUGH: I understand, Mr Kilker.
JOHN: Does she love you, my daughter?
HUGH: I believe so.

> *Outside,* JER, ENY *and* JOSIE *look to* MARGARET. *She ignores them.*

> *Inside,* JOHN *contemplates.*

JOHN: Your brother can stay till you've saved the money for his operation.

> JER *buries himself back into a ball.*

Till then, you make my daughter happy, you hear? We came from nothing and I fear there's nothing coming after this life is through. So you make sure you give her everything now.

> *He pauses.*

If, of course, that's what she wants.
I'm off to the woodpile. Sorry for the colourful language.

> *Outside the door, everyone scatters.*

> JOHN *picks up the wood.* HUGH *opens the door for him and* JOHN *exits.*

> *A moment of* HUGH *alone.*

> MARGARET *enters.*

MARGARET: Hello.
HUGH: I've been talking to your da.

MARGARET *nods.*

I think you should know ...
    You ... you make me grow six inches and put on four stone and feel like I'm in a uniform of red and gold instead of ... well, this.

MARGARET: I like ... that.

HUGH: You ... make me feel like there's trumpets and kettledrums inside me, Margaret. In here. And in here. Like they're ... heralding something.

MARGARET: Goodness. Must be noisy in there.

HUGH: I'd like to take you to the city, Margaret. To the Hills. Where the streets aren't gold, but at least they're paved—and there's big factories and dress shops and bathtubs and marketplaces. I want to give you the life you deserve. Full. And fantastic. I may have been too young to fight in the Great War like your brothers, but I'll fight for you. I will. I'd kill anyone who hurt you.

She waits.

Because there's gotta be something more, yes? Than this? Trafalgar?

She smiles.

MARGARET: I hope so.

HUGH: [*beaming*] Then let's go get it. Me and you. Hughie and ... I still don't reckon you're a 'Margaret'.

MARGARET: What am I then?

HUGH: Dunno. I'll keep thinking on it.

They kiss. Then ...

JER *bursts into the room. Watches until the kiss ends.*

I'll send for you, Jer. I promise. Then we'll have a dance, hey?

    HUGH *beams at* MARGARET.

In the Hills of Sydney. All of us. Together.

MARGARET *and* HUGH *lean into each other and kiss again.* JER *is left to the side, forlorn and alone.*

A shift.

The harp plays gently ...

SCENE EIGHT

ALF, JOSIE, MAUREEN, BETSY *and* ENID *enter calling across the space in a woman's song as they gather flowers.*

They sing 'Siúil a Rún' throughout Scene Eight.

WOMEN: I wish I was on yonder hill
        'Tis there I'd sit and cry my fill
        Until every tear would turn a mill
        Is go dté tú mo mhúirnín slán
        Siúil go sochair agus siúil go ciúin
        Siúil go doras agus éalaigh liom
        Is go dté tú mo mhúirnín slán

As the song is sung, JER *tries to dance. Alone. But his feet won't move right.*

Meanwhile, HUGH *and* MARGARET *drop slowly to the ground.*

HUGH *fumbles at her dress.*

MARGARET *goes stiff as a board.*

HUGH: *You alright?*

MARGARET: Yes.
HUGH: I won't hurt you.
MARGARET: Yes.

HUGH *continues.*

The WOMEN *keep singing.* JER *keeps dancing his mother's dance alone.*

WOMEN: I'll sell my rock, I'll sell my reel
        I'll sell my only spinning wheel
        To buy my love a sword of steel
        Is go dté tú mo mhúirnín slán
        I'll dye my petticoats, I'll dye them red
        And 'round the world I'll beg my bread
        Until my parents shall wish me dead
        Is go dté tú mo mhúirnín slán

MARGARET *is still stiff as a board. She stops him suddenly.*

MARGARET: Tell me where we're going, Hughie.
HUGH: We're going where we'll begin.

> HUGH *holds her face gently as he gazes into her eyes ...*

It's alright. I promise. You're mine and I'm yours. You're mine and I'm yours. You're mine and I'm yours.

> MARGARET *joins the soft chant.*

MARGARET and HUGH: [*chanting together*] You're mine and I'm yours. You're mine and I'm yours. You're mine and I'm yours.

> *They say it together as the* WOMEN *sing on ...*

WOMEN: Siúil, siúil, siúil a rún
      Siúil go sochair agus siúil go ciúin
      Siúil go doras agus éalaigh liom
      Is go dté tú mo mhúirnín slán

> MARGARET *relaxes as* HUGH *removes her dress.* JER *gives up his dance and limps away. Alone.*

SCENE NINE

Outside, ALF, JOSIE *and the other* WOMENFOLK *are searching for flowers, still singing.*

> MARGARET *stands on a chair in her slip.*

> ALF *sneezes incessantly.*

MARGARET: Quick, Ma! I'll turn red as the devil himself soon!
ALF: These weeds will be the death of me. Look at 'em! Whiskers for petals. Wire for stems. Thorns where there should be leaves.

> *She sneezes.* JOSIE *pricks herself on a stem.*

JOSIE: Ow! Why did we have to pick them anyway? They're just gonna end up dead and trampled on some Sydney street.
MARGARET: Ma! I'm roasting!

> ALF *sniffs at a flower.*

ALF: They don't even smell! Wax and gum is all I get. Monstrous things.
MARGARET: Ma!
ALF: If we were back home, there'd be no shortage of flowers, would there, ladies?

ACT ONE: MISSUS

WOMEN: Aye. Aye.
ALF: Beautiful, delicate, fragrant flora. Honeysuckles and irises.
MAUREEN: Fairy foxgloves.
ELSPETH: Primroses.
BETSY: Wild angelicas.
ENID: Bogbeans.
> *They all glance at* ENID, *then continue.*

ALF: Willowherb.
MAUREEN: Periwinkles.
BETSY: Summer snowflakes.
ELSPETH: Bramble and blinks.
ENID: Toadflax.
> *They glance at her again.*

ALF: Bilberries, forget-me-nots—
ELSPETH: Grass of Parnassus—
MAUREEN: Sundew, sweet briar—
BETSY: Early purples and—
ENID: Wort. More wort than you could poke a stick at.
> Waterwort, Saint John's wort, ragwort, pennywort, woundwort, dropwort, figwort, gipsywort, sandwort, butterwort, milkwort, lousewort, mudwort, bladderwort, squincywort, glasswort, pepperwort, marshwort, toothwort, nipplewort, barrenwort, hogwart …

ALF: All of them, perfect for an Irish wedding veil. God must've been workin' with leftovers the day he made these.
> *She sneezes.*
> ENY *hurries out carrying a wedding dress and veil.*

ENY: Here it is! Put it on! Quick!
> *She calls inside as* MARGARET *tries on the dress.*

> Don't peek, Hugh Darcy! Bad luck to see the bride in her dress!
> Here, ladies—the veil …
WOMEN: Ooooh!
> *The* WOMEN *take the veil. They all work to attach the flowers to it.* ENY *keeps working on* MARGARET'*s hem.*

ENY: Stay still now. Help me here, Josie.

> MARGARET *calls out to the ladies.*

MARGARET: Hughie told me that in Sydney they're about to build a bridge that goes right across the water, from one side of the harbour to the other!

WOMEN: Ooooh …

JOSIE: Who needs bridges when there's boats?

MARGARET: He reckons we're gonna get a house right near the bridge. On a hill. Overlooking all of Sydney.

WOMEN: Ooooh …

ENY: Don't wriggle, Margaret, or I'll pin your ankle.

MARGARET: Hughie reckons he's gonna get us a big enough house that you can all come and holiday with us. We can go to Boondy Beach and have picnics.

WOMEN: Ooooh …

JOSIE: It's pronounced Bondi. And it's full of sharks and shysters, apparently.

ENY: Josie. Be nice to your sister.

JOSIE: Why? She's done nothing but boast since that ring got put on her finger. Not even a real ruby. Looks like a rat's eye.

WOMEN: Tch tch tch.

ENY: Josie! Shut it!

> JOSIE *scowls and goes back to pinning the frock.*

Now, Maggie … there was a man, long ago, who captured my heart the way Hugh has caught yours. Not your father.

> MARGARET *gasps.*

MARGARET: Ma!

WOMEN: Tch tch tch.

ENY: A man in a town a little way from here.

> *The* WOMEN *all whisper 'Stevie' to one another scandalously.*

It's hard to believe now, Maggie, but I was a beauty then. Wasn't I, ladies?

WOMEN: Aye. Aye.

ENY: Skin like a petal. Waist as small as a whippet's. Red mane down my back like bushfire. But this man … Stevie.

ACT ONE: MISSUS

The WOMEN *cross themselves.*

This man didn't know a good thing when he had it. When he wasn't all fists he was all hands with women who should know better.

WOMEN: Tch tch tch. Aye. Aye.

MARGARET: Did you ever … lay with him, Ma?

The WOMEN *lean in to listen.*

ENY: I loved him deeply. The way you love that Darcy boy.

MARGARET: I haven't laid with Hughie, Ma. But I love him the way Mother Mary must've loved Saint Joseph.

WOMEN: Amen. Amen.

JOSIE: I can't let the waist out any further, Ma.

ENY: Josie. Go help the ladies with the veil.

JOSIE: But—

ENY *sticks her with a pin.*

Ow!

ENY *speaks gently to* MARGARET *as* JOSIE *walks to* ALF.

ENY: Now, Margaret … I wasn't in love with your father when I married him.

MARGARET: Ma!

ENY: When I said the words, 'With my body I thee worship', I was screaming inside. My chest burning with yearning for another.

MARGARET: Sweet Jesus, Ma …

ENY: But I married your father anyway. And within two, three years, I loved him. Despite the fact he wasn't the first to … have my heart.

MARGARET *stares down at her mother.*

It's part of being Irish, Maggie. Lost love is a bleak reality, isn't it, ladies?

WOMEN: Aye. Aye.

MARGARET: I'm not Irish.

WOMEN: Tch, tch, tch.

ENY: Then what are you?

MARGARET: I … don't know.

WOMEN: Whist-a-whist. Whist-a-whist.

ENY *continues.*

ENY: We women have to find our place in the world, Maggie.
 That's why we marry. We become wives and mothers and grandmothers.
 Some poor souls lose their way. They fall through the cracks and become spinsters.
ALF: There's nothing wrong with being an unmarried woman, Rowena. Especially if you give your life to serving God.
ENY: You're not serving God, Alfreda. You're a *servant* of one of God's *servants*. Quite the difference in class there.
ALF: I've fallen through no cracks.
ENY: You wash the whiskey-stenched sweat stains from the armpits of Father Driscoll's vestment and sleep on a wheat mattress in his vestibule. That's a crack if I ever saw one, woman.

> *Beat.*

What I'm saying is, there's not much choice as a woman, my Maggie.
 So if you get to make one—a choice—make it worth makin'.
 Are you wasting your choice on a Stevie when you might find yourself a John Kilker?
MARGARET: I'm sure, Ma.
ENY: I'd rather give cherries to a pig than advice to a fool, Margaret.
MARGARET: I know, Ma.

> ENY *nods solemnly.*

ENY: Veil, ladies?

> ALF *and the* WOMEN *approach, chattering excitedly, and go to place the veil of flowers on* MARGARET. ALF *puts her hands on* MARGARET*'s belly. Her smile fades. The other women realise ...*

Say something happy. For the bride.

> ALF *clears her throat.*

ALF: Marry in blue, love won't be true,
Marry in pink, your spirit will sink,
Marry in grey, you'll live far away,
Marry in brown, live out of town,
Marry in black, you'll wish you were back ...

> *Elation deflates by the second ...*

Marry in green, ashamed to be seen,
Marry in yellow, ashamed of your fellow,
Marry in red, you'll wish you were dead,
Marry in white …

She presents the veil of wildflowers. Sneezes.

… everything will be right.

ALF *places the veil on* MARGARET's *head and kisses her hand tenderly.*

MARGARET: Thank you, Aunty Alf. Thank you, ladies.

They depart. She calls after them.

After the wedding I'm going to press the flowers and take them with me to Sydney so I'll remember each and every one of you forever!

They leave.

JOSIE: I'll try and find a sash for that waist.

JOSIE *and* ALF *leave* ENY *and* MARGARET *alone.*

ENY: You look beautiful, my darling girl.

MARGARET: Ma. I lied. I have laid with Hughie.

ENY: I know.

MARGARET: This is the beginning of something big, Ma. I can feel it. In here.

She places her hand on her belly and beams at a worried ENY.

ENY: Is go dté tú mo mhúirnín slán.

She embraces her daughter tenderly.

And may you go safely, my darling.

She kisses MARGARET's *belly.*

JER *watches on, unseen.*

SCENE TEN

As we shift …

Church bells. A CONGREGATION *gathers. They sing.*

ALL: [*singing*] 'Tis the last rose of summer,

> Left blooming alone;
> All her lovely companions
> Are faded and gone …

MARGARET *walks up the aisle, beaming.* JOHN *is at her side.*

> No flower of her kindred,
> No rosebud is nigh,
> To reflect back her blushes,
> Or give sigh for sigh.

FATHER DRISCOLL *stands before the couple. Their hands are bound with white cloth.*

HUGH *looks around for* JER. *He is not there. Because ...* JER *is at the dam on his father's farm.*

> I'll not leave thee, thou lone one!
> To pine on the stem;
> Since the lovely are sleeping,
> Go, sleep thou with them.

At the church, MARGARET *and* HUGH *kiss. The* CONGREGATION *throws rice.*

> Thus kindly I scatter,
> Thy leaves o'er the bed,
> Where thy mates of the garden
> Lie scentless and dead.
> So soon may I follow,
> When friendships decay,
> And from love's shining circle
> The gems drop away.

The CONGREGATION *departs as* MARGARET *and* HUGH *head to their new life.*

At the dam, JER *sings softly, accompanied by a ghostly harp.*

JER: [*singing*] When true hearts lie withered,
> And fond ones are flown,
> Oh! who would inhabit
> This bleak world alone?

At the dam, JER *leaps into the black water. The harp echoes.*

SCENE ELEVEN

MARGARET *and* HUGH *stand on Plymouth Street, Surry Hills, as a slum of dilapidated houses and shops form around them.* MARGARET *holds a baby in her arms.*

The sounds of the street.

Voices calling, bells. A nearby rail line.

They take it all in. Wide-eyed. Terrified. Exultant.

Finally, a dilapidated house appears. It towers above them as they look up at it. It is 12 1/2 Plymouth Street.

It is home.

HUGH: This is it.
MARGARET: Twelve-and-a-half Plymouth Street.
HUGH: Surry Hills.
MARGARET: Sydney.

She looks around.

Pretty flat for a hill.
HUGH: We'll see more from the roof.
MARGARET: Where are the markets?
HUGH: Sure they'll be round here somewhere.
MARGARET: Where's the bridge?
HUGH: Not finished yet. But soon.

They take it all in.

MARGARET: So this is where we begin.

HUGH *puts down his suitcase and puts an arm around* MARGARET.

HUGH: It is. Me. You. This one—young Thady Darcy.
And Jer, when he gets here.
MARGARET: Will we survive, do you think?
HUGH: We'll survive, Missus.
MARGARET: Missus?
HUGH: Yeah. Missus.
MARGARET: [*trying it out*] Missus.

Beat.

HUGH: Wanna walk through the House of Horrors with me, Missus?

She smiles.

MARGARET: I'd be delighted, Hughie.

They stand there for a while as the street noises become louder and louder.

The younger HUGH *and* MARGARET *are replaced by older versions.*

An eight-year-old boy replaces the baby. He is THADY.

HUGH *and* MARGARET *embrace.*

HUGH: Missus.

MARGARET: Hughie.

She calls THADY *to her.*

Thady …

She gives him a bag of marbles and they all head inside.

The door is left open.

Plymouth Street becomes a hubbub of noise and activity.

THADY *comes back outside. He is clutching his bag of marbles in his hand. He steps into the busy street and is swept away before our very eyes. All that is left behind are the marbles.*

MARGARET *hurries outside.*

Thady?

She picks up the marbles. HUGH *follows.*

HUGH: Thady?

MARGARET *looks around desperately for the boy.*

MARGARET: Thady?!

Her panic grows.

HUGH: *Thady?!*

They hurry down the street, looking for THADY.

HUGH and MARGARET: *Thady?!*

ACT ONE: MISSUS

The harp echoes.
Silence.
Blackout.

END OF ACT ONE

A short interval.

Jack Ruwald and Heather Mitchell in Sydney Theatre Company's
The Harp in the South, Part One and Part Two, *2018.*
(Photo: Daniel Boud)

ACT TWO: THE HARP IN THE SOUTH

SCENE ONE

Plymouth Street, Surry Hills, 1948. A world of dilapidated houses and shops.

A thirteen-year-old girl, DOLOUR, *appears in a grubby dress and bare feet. She watches the street as it comes to life.*

DOLOUR: The hills are full of Irish. When their grandfathers and great-grandfathers arrived in Sydney, they came to this shanty town. Not because they were dirty or lazy, though many of them were that, but because they were poor.

The street starts to fill with LOCALS. *Movement and colour.*

People from all walks of life—SHOPKEEPERS, PROSTITUTES, NUNS *and* DRUNKS—*fill the street.*

Scene Two can form here.

There are Brodies and Caseys and Murphys and O'Briens, Grogans, Maloneys and Kells... And although here and there you'll find a Sciuto or a Katsopoulis, a Jewish shopkeeper or a Chinese laundryman, most of us here are Irish.

Hugh Darcy had brought his Missus from Trafalgar to this street a little way into the century when everything was hopeful. Long before 1948.

Long before Mamma's bones ached and her bunions burst through her shoes.

In front of her house ...

This is the place the Darcys live, in an unlucky house on Plymouth Street, Surry Hills, that the landlord renumbered from thirteen to twelve-and-a-half.

A little boy, THADY, *wanders past.*

This is the house that many years ago, my little big brother Thady wandered out of with his bag of marbles and his red braces ...

ACT TWO: THE HARP IN THE SOUTH

THADY *disappears.*

… and was never seen again.

SCENE TWO

Music plays, loud and raucous.

PHYLLIS *and* FLO *lounge on the balcony of Delie Stock's brothel as they watch over their turf below.* KIDGER *lurks beside them.* 'Kidger was an alcoholic who nightly slept with snakes. A tall, emaciated creature, he was so bowed by his indulgences that he was bent in the middle like a fish-hook, with a face as stony as a turbot's. Kidger drank plonk, plink, metho, bombo … This protégé and employee of Delie Stock was never known to eat.'

MEN *swill beer on the verandah of a pub.*

A THIRSTY WOMAN *and her* HUSBAND *approach. He goes in, she waits outside next to an* ABORIGINAL MAN *in a tattered World War II army uniform.*

A beer is passed out the window to her and she swills it.

A CHINESE MAN *paints 'LICK JIMMY' on the front of his house.* 'He was a small, neat, compact creature with polished shoes and eyes as glossy as jet.'

FLO *and* PHYLLIS *call down to him.*

FLO: Is that an invitation, Jimmy?

PHYLLIS: Where exactly shall we lick, Jimmy?

> LICK JIMMY *just smiles and waves and goes on to write 'FRUITERER'.* PHYLLIS *and* FLO *giggle.*
>
> DELIE STOCK *appears.*

DELIE: Flo, Phyllis—get ready. Swill's nearly up. Kidger, open some bombo.

> *Below, in the pub …*

PUBLICAN: Last drinks! Last drinks!

> *He rings a bell. The* MEN *in the bar clamour, waving their money*

in the air, haggling to be served. A cacophony of desperate testosterone.

The THIRSTY WOMAN *outside yells through the window ...*

THIRSTY WOMAN: Get me a pony! Artie! Get me a pony!

DOLOUR *runs to the front letterbox to check the mail. She looks disappointed.* LICK JIMMY *appears.*

LICK JIMMY: Hello, Dolour.

DOLOUR: Ni hao, Lick.

LICK JIMMY: Letter come yet?

DOLOUR: Nah, Jimmy. Not yet. Soon, I reckon. Yours?

LICK JIMMY: Not yet. Soon, I reckon.

DOLOUR: S'that?

LICK JIMMY: Poor man's orange.

He gives it to her.

DOLOUR: It's ugly. Can I have a bit?

He takes it back.

LICK JIMMY: Not ready yet.

The pub bell chimes.

A voice from the pub ...

PUBLICAN: Swill's over! Go home to your wives!

A general ruckus. Not happy.

Swill's over! *Out!*

The pub doors burst open and MEN *filter out, drunk as skunks. They step over the* ABORIGINAL SOLDIER.

DOLOUR: Da will be home soon. I better warn Mamma. Zai jian, Lick!

LICK JIMMY: See you later, Dolour!

Inside 12½ Plymouth Street, Dolour's older sister ROIE *(18) is in the kitchen with* MARGARET *who is poking a Puffing Billy stove aggressively.*

MARGARET: Goddlemighty. I don't know how many meals Puffing Billy's got left in him, Roie. Don't know how many I've got either. I'm all out of inspiration. [*Beat*] Maybe sausages. And a baked potato?

ACT TWO: THE HARP IN THE SOUTH

DOLOUR *skulks in with the mail.*

DOLOUR: Didn't come.
ROIE: Never mind, Dolour. I'm sure it's on its way.
DOLOUR: You ever tried a poor man's orange?
ROIE: Nope.
DOLOUR: Lick Jimmy showed me one. But he wouldn't let me eat it.
MARGARET: Don't know what's going on with the neighbourhood. Won't last, that fruit shop. No-one likes dealing with Orientals.
DOLOUR: I like it. The way he puts the potatoes and the cherries and the apples all together. Like a big garden. And his abacus.
MARGARET: His what?
DOLOUR: It's a counting machine! Oh, here's the mail, Mamma.

She likes saying the word.

Abacus. Abacus. Lick's teaching me to count on his abacus.

MARGARET *sorts through the mail, sighing with each bill.*

There's one from Trafalgar! Who's it from? Granny Eny? Aunty Alf?

MARGARET *hurriedly tucks the letter away, turning her attention back to* DOLOUR.

MARGARET: Nothing. No-one. What didn't come for you, Dolour?
DOLOUR: My application to be on the 'Junior Information Quiz' on 2MB.
MARGARET: Oh. Think you're clever enough to be on the wireless, do you?
DOLOUR: Yes! I can answer things all those posh kids on there can't. Last week they asked who the patron saint of mad people was, and I screamed down the wireless, 'Dymphna! It's Saint Bloody Dymphna, yer dingbats!'
MARGARET: Language, Dolour.
ROIE: Dolour, how on earth do you know that?
DOLOUR: She was Irish, like Granny Eny. Her mother died and her da went mad. He tried to marry her because she looked so much like her dead mother, but Dymphna refused because he was her da so he chopped off her head and then she became saint of all the loonies.
MARGARET: Why did she become saint of all the loonies when it was her father that was the mad one?
DOLOUR: There's worse things you can be saint of. Saint Appolonia is

the patron saint of sore teeth. Saint Gummarus is the patron saint of barren women and divorcees. Saint Bibiana is the patron saint of drunkenness …

She is reminded ...

Oh, Da's on his way home from the swill.

MARGARET: Well, he can leave Saint Bibiana on the front doorstep.

A middle-aged man has entered, his face stern. MR DIAMOND *stands with one hand in his grubby waistcoat. 'Mr Diamond did not have a soul in the world to care whether he lived, died or berated Catholics about pope-worshipping.'*

MR DIAMOND: Tch. Teaching your children to bow and scrape to heathen idols and taking wilful pleasure in scarlet mummery.

MARGARET: Good evening, Mr Diamond. Happy Saint Patrick's Day.

ROIE: Good evening, Mr Diamond.

DOLOUR: Saint Patrick. Patron saint of the Irish.

MR DIAMOND: Not this Patrick.

Puffing Billy spews and shudders. MARGARET *calls upstairs.*

MARGARET: Will you be joining us for dinner tonight, Mr Diamond?

MR DIAMOND: No. I just came down to pay the rent. I retreat to my room away from these vulgar celebrations.

DOLOUR: What *are* we celebrating?

MR DIAMOND: *You're* celebrating a filthy pagan saint of separatism who doesn't deserve a moment of memory. *I'm* commiserating the shame of my countrymen trying to cut the umbilical cord of proud British history.

DOLOUR: Huh?

MARGARET: We're Catholic, he's Protestant.

MR DIAMOND: I'm loyal. You're traitors.

DOLOUR: But we're all Irish?

MARGARET: Apparently. We may as well just stand in a field and throw potatoes at each other.

She calls upstairs.

Johnny, darling! Would you like some apple charlotte?

ACT TWO: THE HARP IN THE SOUTH

JOHNNY SHEILY *comes downstairs, yelling,*

JOHNNY: Charlotte's apples! Charlotte's apples!

He was 'a poor unfortunate with his crooked back and great square box of a head, a bewildered brain that peopled the air around him with butterflies and other things that needed to be snatched at.'

HUGH *enters, singing, 'The Minstrel Boy' by Thomas Moore.*

HUGH: The Minstrel Boy to the war is gone
In the ranks of death you will find him ...
His father's sword / he hath girded on,
And his wild harp slung behind him ...

MR DIAMOND: Wild harp, my orange arse.

MR DIAMOND *suddenly breaks into a vehemently competitive song— 'The Sash My Father Wore'.*

Sure it's old, but it is beautiful
And the colors they are fine –
It was worn at Derry, Aughrim,
Enniskillen, and the Boyne.

HUGH: Then bugger off back there.

MR DIAMOND: Sure my father wore it when a youth
In the bygone days of yore,
And it's on the twelfth I love to wear
The sash my father wore.

HUGH: The sash your father wore.

HUGH *is peeved. He sings louder.*

HUGH: 'Land of Song!' said the warrior bard,
'Tho' all the world betrays thee,
One sword, at least, thy rights shall guard,
One faithful harp shall praise thee!'

MR DIAMOND *cuts him off, singing at the top of his lungs.* ROIE, DOLOUR *and* MARGARET *cover their ears as the men sing on, yelling at them to be quiet.*

MR DIAMOND: Oh, when I'm going to leave you all
Oh, good luck to you I'll say

> As I cross the raging sea, my boys,
> Surely the orange flute I'll play.

MARGARET: Keep an eye on Johnny, Dolour.
DOLOUR: Yes, Mamma.

JOHNNY dances awkwardly as the men continue to compete.

MARGARET and DOLOUR call to JOHNNY as the song continues ...

MARGARET & DOLOUR: Johnny, be careful! Johnny, where's your ma? Johnny, you funny sausage!

The song is absolutely raucous now, as the men sing over the top of one another ...

Suddenly ... silence. Puffing Billy farts out a cloud of smoke as HUGH and MR DIAMOND face off.

MARGARET: You two done?
HUGH: Diamond.
MR DIAMOND: Darcy.
HUGH: Happy Saint Patrick's Day.
MR DIAMOND: Your rent.

He hands HUGH money.

HUGH: Why weren't you down the pub? Missed the swill.
MR DIAMOND: Had other things to do.
HUGH: Really? Well, let's have a drink now.

He pulls out a bottle. The women roll their eyes. JOHNNY claps his hands.

MR DIAMOND: I will not.

But it's clear he wants to.

HUGH: Oh, come on, Pat. We always have a nightcap. Come on.
MR DIAMOND: Has it got holy water in it, Darcy? Does it cure you of your DTs? Or just wash away the guilt of your poor twisted brother, roamin' the earth alone?
MARGARET: That's enough, Mr Diamond.
HUGH: Yer stinkin' old Prod-hopper. Jer will be walkin' through that door any day now. Mark my words.
MR DIAMOND: Doesn't take twenty-five years to walk from Trafalgar to

ACT TWO: THE HARP IN THE SOUTH 47

Surry Hills, twisted ankles or not. Only took me four months to get here from Belfast.

HUGH: And I wish you'd bugger off back there, you Orange bastard.

MR DIAMOND: I might! An Irish bog would be a damn sight cleaner than this boarding house, I can tell yer, yer dirty feckin' rock-chopper.

MARGARET runs at MR DIAMOND with a potato masher.

MARGARET: You dare comment on my housekeepering? Go on! Get out of here, you old bastard, or I'll use your head as a broom!

MR DIAMOND wrestles with MARGARET as she tries to beat him with the masher. HUGH jumps on MR DIAMOND's back. It's raucous. JOHNNY laughs and claps as ROIE and DOLOUR yell over one another.

ROIE: Da! Leave him be!

DOLOUR: Do you want the coppers to come round?

JOHNNY: Pleeceman! Pleeceman! Pleeceman!

During the battle, a woman appears and watches: MISS SHEILY. *'Miss Sheily was a tiny thin woman, as bitter as a draught of alum water, with a parchment face and subtle black eyes ...'*

JOHNNY: *Mamma!*

MISS SHEILY: Caesar's ghost!

The kitchen falls silent. MARGARET *lowers the potato masher and smoothes her hair, embarrassed.* HUGH *is still on* MR DIAMOND's *back.*

I've come to pay my rent.

JOHNNY *grins.*

JOHNNY: Mamma! Mamma! You find the hills?

MISS SHEILY: There's no hills. Upstairs, Johnny.

MARGARET: Would he like some apple charlotte, Miss Sheily?

JOHNNY: Charlotte's apples! Charlotte's apples!

MISS SHEILY: No. There's my rent.

She puts it on the table and looks at them disapprovingly.

I'd appreciate it if you kept the noise down. Johnny has to sleep.

She leaves, dragging JOHNNY *behind her, and heads to her room upstairs.*

MARGARET: [*softly, to herself*] I wonder what her name is, that woman. I think something refined. Like Stella. Or Glenys.

ROIE: She's no lady, Mamma. She signs her name 'Miss' Sheily, remember? You're more of a lady than her.

DOLOUR: [*whispering to* ROIE] Mamma called the Prod-hopper a bastard.

> *She giggles but is walloped by* MARGARET.

MARGARET: Don't you be using such words, Dolour.

DOLOUR: Prod-hopper?

MARGARET: The other one.

DOLOUR: *You* did!

MARGARET: I did no such thing.

> HUGH *slides off* MR DIAMOND's *back. Puffing Billy belches smoke.*

MR DIAMOND: Well. Goodnight.

> *He starts to leave and then turns back to* HUGH.

At one minute past twelve, when it is no longer the seventeenth of March, I will have a nightcap with you, Darcy.

> HUGH *nods politely.* MR DIAMOND *goes to leave.*

DOLOUR: Mr Diamond …

> *He turns back.*

Did you know Saint Patrick was actually born in England?

> HUGH *gasps.*

HUGH: What?! Bullshit!

> MR DIAMOND *breaks into a victorious beam.*

MR DIAMOND: *Ha!*

> MR DIAMOND *leaves.*

DOLOUR: The posh kids got that one wrong too. On 'Junior Information Quiz'. On 2MB.

> *Puffing Billy spits smoke.*

ROIE: The apple charlotte's burned.

> MARGARET *stares at her husband through the smoky kitchen.*

MARGARET: Hughie.
HUGH: Missus.

> *He wobbles, drunk.*

MARGARET: I think this year he might come home.
HUGH: Jer?
MARGARET: Thady.
HUGH: Oh.
MARGARET: I can feel it. Saint Patrick told me. Our Thady. He's coming.

> *We shift ... as a song from* JOHNNY *comes from upstairs.*
>
> *He sings 'The Laughing Policeman' raucously, his voice echoing through the house.*

JOHNNY: I know a fat ol 'pleeceman
    He always on our street
    A fat and jolly red-faced man
    He really is a treat.
    He laugh upon point duty
    He laugh upon his beat.
    He laugh at ev'rybody
    When he's walkin' in the street.
    Oh ho ho ho ho ho ho.
    Ha ha ha ha ha ha.
    Hohohohohohoho.
    Hahahahahaha.

SCENE THREE

DOLOUR *and* ROIE *sit on a single bed in a room as they listen to Johnny's song. They rub talcum powder on each other.*

MR DIAMOND *drinks alone in his room.*

As JOHNNY *sings on,* MISS SHEILY *covers her ears in their shared bedroom. In the girls' room ...*

DOLOUR: What's wrong with Johnny?
ROIE: God struck him like wild lightning strikes a tree, I suppose. No-one knows why. Could just as easily be one of us with a harelip or a strawberry for a nose. We should be kind to him. Because Miss Sheily hates him.

DOLOUR: She couldn't have hated him when he was a little weenie baby.
ROIE: He's still a baby. And she still hates him. But she must have loved someone to end up with him.
DOLOUR: Do you think Mamma and Da love each other?
ROIE: I've never given it much thought.
DOLOUR: Have you ever been in love, Roie?
ROIE: No. Never at all.
DOLOUR: I'm never going to get married. Except to God.
ROIE: You want to be a nun?
DOLOUR: Yes. I like the way they walk.

She gets out of bed.

I've been practising, Roie. Look.

She walks serenely.

Just like Sister Theophilus, don't you reckon?
ROIE: Very like. Now, come on, Sister Dolour. Prayers.

They kneel and pray.

DOLOUR: Dear God. Thank you for this day. I hope you had a nice one too. Could you please call upon Saint Thomas of Aquinas to hear my prayer? I'll wait a moment while you get him.

Hello, Saint Thomas. Just wanted to ask you to please pour forth your brilliance upon my dense intellect so that I may be the smartest kid in all of Surry Hills so that I can get onto the 2MB 'Junior Information Quiz' before I become a nun.

Thank you. Could you get God again, please, Saint Thomas. I'll wait.

God, I hope you have a nice day tomorrow. Send my hellos to Jesus and Mother Mary. We pray Thady will come home safe and sound. Amen.

DOLOUR looks to her sister who is also praying silently. DOLOUR climbs into bed and strokes ROIE's long hair as she prays.

I reckon they love each other. Mamma and Da. 'Course they do.

And we shift through each room as they extinguish their lamps ... to Margaret and Hugh's room.

MARGARET *kneels in prayer by the bed in an old tattered*

ACT TWO: THE HARP IN THE SOUTH 51

nightgown as HUGH *snores on the bed in a singlet and underwear and holey socks.*

MARGARET: Eighteen years, six months and nineteen days since I held Thady's hand. Amen.

She crosses herself and begins the laborious task of moving HUGH *into position so that she may get into bed.*

She finally succeeds.

HUGH: Missus ...

MARGARET: Yes, Hughie.

HUGH: My Missus ...

MARGARET: Your Missus.

HUGH: Take that nightgown off and let me show you how I love you.

He paws at her.

MARGARET: [*grinning*] You dirty old coot.

She wriggles out of her nightgown and HUGH *snuggles in close ...*

I got a letter, Hughie. There's some news. From Trafalgar.

But he has fallen asleep on her breasts.

Goodnight, my darling.

Darkness.

The harp echoes ...

From the silence ... screams from Miss Sheily and Johnny's room. The sound of whipping.

*The full house converges on the landing—*HUGH, MARGARET, DOLOUR, ROIE *and* MR DIAMOND—*as the screams continue from behind the locked door. They call out,*

RESIDENTS: Miss Sheily! Miss Sheily! Johnny? Miss Sheily!

JOHNNY: No! Mamma! Mamma!

MR DIAMOND: She's killing the wretched creature!

HUGH: Open the door or I'll kick it in!

The screams and thudding continue.

MARGARET *takes a key from around her neck and shoves everyone out of the way.*

MARGARET: Miss Sheily, I'm coming in!

>She unlocks the door.

>They hurry in and everyone gasps. ROIE covers DOLOUR's eyes.

>Inside the room are piles of unwashed clothes. Uneaten food. Open tins. In a corner, his hands tied to the bedhead, is JOHNNY, naked, his back whipped red. MISS SHEILY stands nearby, quivering, holding a piece of electrical wire.

JOHNNY: Mamma … Mamma no …
MISS SHEILY: This is trespassing. I'll see you jailed.
MARGARET: What have you done to the poor little devil?

>She hurries to JOHNNY and unties him.

MISS SHEILY: He keeps getting out. He's too strong for me now.
HUGH: The Red Cross will be hearing about this. And the RSPCA, you old vulture.

>MISS SHEILY suddenly howls.

MISS SHEILY: I'm sick of him! I'm sick of the look of him! Every time I remember he's mine I want to cut my throat!
MARGARET: You don't deserve a child.
MISS SHEILY: I didn't want him! I tried every way I knew to get rid of him before he was born!
JOHNNY: Mamma … Mamma … Where the hills?
MISS SHEILY: *There's no damn hills, Johnny!*
MR DIAMOND: Why don't you put him in an orphanage if you feel that way?
MISS SHEILY: Because I don't want to!
HUGH: Because she gets a pretty pension for him, don't you, Miss Sheily?
MISS SHEILY: How dare you! How *dare* you?

>She runs at HUGH, fists flailing.

I don't hear you complaining about my 'pretty pension' when you hand my rent over to the publican of an afternoon!

>HUGH *tries to stop her punches.*

JOHNNY: Don't hurt Mamma!

>JOHNNY *knocks* HUGH *to the ground and sits on top of him, drooling and bleeding, his fist raised high above* HUGH's *face.*

Don't hurt Mamma!
MISS SHEILY: [*quietly*] That's enough, Johnny.
HUGH: Ah, God in Heaven.
JOHNNY: *Don't! Hurt! Mamma!*
MISS SHEILY: Johnny.

> *Beat.* JOHNNY *lowers his fist and climbs off* HUGH. *He goes to* MISS SHEILY *and stands beside her obediently.*
>
> HUGH *gets to his feet.*

HUGH: If I hear one more cry from this room, I'll report you.
MARGARET: And to think you'd judge a Republican and an Orangeman for having a little tiff when this is what you do up here to your own son.
MISS SHEILY: It was just the once.
MARGARET: For shame, Miss Sheily.

> *They file out, one by one.*

JOHNNY: Bye-bye. Bye-bye. Bye-bye.

> *He starts to sing his song again as* MISS SHEILY *breaks down and cries.*
>> I know a fat ol' pleeceman
>> He always on our street.
>> A fat and jolly red-faced man
>> He really is a treat.
>
> MISS SHEILY *weeps as she strokes and kisses* JOHNNY's *hair.*

MISS SHEILY: I love you, Johnny. I love you.
JOHNNY: He never can stop laughin'
>> He says he'd never try.
>> But once he did arrest a man
>> And laughed until he cried!
>> Oh ho ho ho ho ho ho. Ha ha ha ha ha ha.
>> Hohohohohoho. Hahahahahaha.

SCENE FOUR

Day.

Silence.

MARGARET *sits at the kitchen table alone, as Puffing Billy smokes beside her.*

She reaches into her apron pocket and gets out the envelope she'd secreted earlier.

She opens it up and reads it, tracing her fingers across the handwriting delicately.

THADY *enters.*

MARGARET *sees him.*

MARGARET: Hello, Thady. Can I hold your hand?

> THADY *smiles and comes closer.*
>
> *Puffing Billy groans loudly and spits, startling* MARGARET.

[*To the stove*] Goddlemighty, keep your trap shut. None of your business anyway.

> THADY *draws away.*
>
> MARGARET *puts away the letter as* ROIE *enters with* DOLOUR.

What are you doing home so early?

ROIE: Machine broke down at the factory. We got liberated for the afternoon.

DOLOUR: She was waiting for me at the school gate, Mamma!

MARGARET: That's nice.

ROIE: Need help with dinner, Mamma?

> MARGARET *looks flustered.*

MARGARET: Dinner. Yes. Ah, God in Heaven, I've run out of all inspiration.

> *Puffing Billy snorts.*

No thanks to you, you little …

> I s'pose we could have sausages again. With a baked potato?
>
> *She gets out a purse.*

ACT TWO: THE HARP IN THE SOUTH

Here. Go and get me some potatoes from Paddy's Markets.

DOLOUR: Paddy's Markets! Oh my stars! I've never been to Paddy's Markets!

ROIE: Mamma, that's miles away. We can just go to Lick Jimmy's next door!

DOLOUR: Oh, please, Roie! Please can we go to Paddy's Markets? I've heard so much about it!

MARGARET: I'd rather have my potatoes from Paddy's than the Oriental's, Roie. Go on. And here's a little something extra for your birthday next week.

ROIE: Mamma …

MARGARET: Go on, love. Please.

ROIE nods reluctantly and takes the proffered cash.

Close the door on the way out!

DOLOUR: We're goin' to Paddy's Markets! We're goin' to Paddy's Markets! [*Calling up the stairs*] Johnny! Guess what?! We're goin' to Paddy's Markets!

JOHNNY appears at the top of the stairs and claps.

JOHNNY: You go find the hills? Find the hills!

The girls grab a sugar bag and leave the house as MARGARET once again gets the letter from her apron and opens it, wiping her brow worriedly as Puffing Billy spits.

SCENE FIVE

ROIE *and* DOLOUR *pass Lick Jimmy's. He waves at them.*

LICK JIMMY: Where you going, girls?

ROIE: Down to—

DOLOUR: Just a stroll to Darling Harbour, Lick Jimmy! Lovely day for it!

She hurries ROIE *away, shamefully.*

The girls pass the pub, quivering with loud male voices.

Oy! Is my dadda in there?

BARFLY: Oy! Hughie!

HUGH *appears from amid the throng, slightly sozzled.*

HUGH: There's my girls! Oy! There's my girls! Where youse off to, my girls?

DOLOUR: We're goin' to Paddy's Markets, Dadda! Can you believe it?! *Paddy's Markets!* Don't tell Lick Jimmy.

The girls walk on as their father calls out after them ...

HUGH: Thass my girls ... thass *my* beautiful girls! See 'em? Look at 'em! See 'em? *I made them.*

They pass Delie Stock's place. DELIE *fans herself on the balcony with* PHYLLIS *and* FLO *and* KIDGER, *who peer down at the passing sisters.*

ROIE: Don't look at them. Don't look at them.

DELIE: Where you off to, girlies?

ROIE: Don't say anything. Don't say anything.

DOLOUR: Off to Paddy's Markets, Miss Stock!

DELIE: That right?

DOLOUR: I ain't never been to Paddy's Markets before!

DELIE: Never?

DOLOUR: Nup! Not the zoo, the museum, the circus ... But today I get to go to Paddy's Markets!

DELIE: Well, lah-di-dah, my darling. You have fun.

DOLOUR: Will do, Miss Stock!

She walks on, then hurries back.

Don't tell Lick Jimmy!

ROIE *drags her sister away as* DELIE *watches, intrigued.*

What do they *do* all day?

ROIE: Their hair.

They walk on, leaving the street.

Meanwhile, JOHNNY *makes his way out of 12 1/2 Plymouth Street.*

JOHNNY: I find the hills! I climb the hills! I find the hills! I climb the hills!

He disappears. Meanwhile ...

BARROWMEN *pass the girls with laden wagons.*

ACT TWO: THE HARP IN THE SOUTH

The sounds of STALLHOLDERS *touting their wares fills the space as the wide-open doors of Paddy's Market lets forth a surf of sound.*

DOLOUR: What do they sell?

ROIE: Everything.

They walk through the marketplace. DOLOUR *is wide-eyed as* STALLHOLDERS *of all ethnicities swarm the stage, touting their wares.*

STALLHOLDERS: Barley! Pure golden barley, straight from the crop!
Dried octopus! Get your dried octopus!
Seaweed for your budgerigars!
Blackfish straight from the harbour!
Chrysanthemums! Begonias! Gladdies!
Nanny goats! Give your baby the best milk there is! Nanny goats! Nanny goats!
Strapless brassieres and waist pinchers! As used by Rita Hayworth!
American candy! Off the boat from the Big Apple! Get yer yankee candy!
Antique books! Mended and fumigated! Mended and fumigated antique books!

DOLOUR picks up a book from the stall and looks at it with awe.

DOLOUR: William Shakespeare. Cripes, look at the dome on him.

BOOKSELLER: Oy. You buying?

DOLOUR stammers silently.

ROIE: Needs more fumigating.

ROIE puts the book down and turns haughtily.

Come on, we gotta get the potatoes. Down the back.

They move past another stall—a jumble of exotic clothes. Dainty, scuffed heels, Russian boots, a velveteen fez ... DOLOUR *can't get enough of it. And then,* ROIE *stops.*

Dolour, look …

Her eye has been caught by a fringed red silk shawl, embossed with green flowers. It is the same shawl we have seen before—around the throat of Frances Darcy.

ROIE *strokes the shawl gently.* DOLOUR *is as transfixed by her sister's face as* ROIE *is with the shawl.*

The stallholder, a CLOTHES SELLER, *comes forward.*

CLOTHES SELLER: Pretty, ain't it? Bin in the family for years. My sister wore it on her back for ten years 'fore she got diseased in the Epidemic. So it's special, see?

She looks them up and down, somewhat disapprovingly.

DOLOUR: [*firmly*] How much?

CLOTHES SELLER: Ten shillings.

ROIE: I ... I only got five.

DOLOUR: There's the other five Mamma gave us for the potatoes.

CLOTHES SELLER: Ten bob. Take it or leave it.

DOLOUR: Lick'll take care of us. Go on, Roie.

ROIE *reluctantly hands over the money. The* CLOTHES SELLER *takes it and shoves it in her coat. She's all smiles now.*

ROIE *drapes it over her head and loops the fringe over her shoulders.*

CLOTHES SELLER: Aw. Look how loverly yer look.

The CLOTHES SELLER *shoves a mirror in her face and* ROIE *stares at her reflection, transfixed.*

DOLOUR: Roie ... you could be straight out of one of William Shakespeare's stories ...

TOMMY: Oh, rose of all the world ...

ROIE *is shaken from her reverie as a man appears beside her in the reflection. She gasps and turns to see a young man with black hair and a thin, pale face.* TOMMY *is 20. 'He had the marks of three boils on his neck. He had a gay green-printed tie, and a tweed suit which seemed too cumbrous and important for his slender boyish body.'*

ROIE *takes the shawl from her head, embarrassed.*

ROIE: Shut yer big mouth.

She goes to drag DOLOUR *away.*

TOMMY: I've seen you before. In Coronation Street.
ROIE: So?

She goes to hurry away again.

TOMMY: What's your hurry? Scared I'll bite? Come and visit my stall!

He gestures to a nearby stall that says 'JOSEPH MENDEL. LICENSED VENDOR OF OLD WARES'.

DOLOUR: Mendel? You ain't old Joseph Mendel! You know Mr Mendel's on Coronation Street, Roie?

TOMMY: I'm not old Mendel. I'm his nephew Tommy. I work for him sometimes. I sell stuff here he can't sell there.

ROIE: Sorry if I was rude. You just got my goat when you laughed at me.

TOMMY: Hell, I didn't laugh at you. You looked pretty as a picture, that's all.

ROIE: Oh.

An awkward silence. ROIE *and* TOMMY *stare at each other.*

DOLOUR: She's Rowena Darcy and I'm Dolour Darcy.

Another awkward silence as ROIE *and* TOMMY *stare at each other.*

What's on your neck? Are they boils?

The romantic interlude is broken.

TOMMY: No!
ROIE: Dolour!
DOLOUR: What? He's got three!
ROIE: Sorry.
TOMMY: S'alright.

Beat.

Hey, can I come round and take you to the flicks some time? There's a cowboy pitcher on at the Palace.

ROIE: I'm not really into cowboys.
TOMMY: He's a *singin'* cowboy.

She ponders.

ROIE: Alright then. S'pose.
TOMMY: Can I come tonight?
ROIE: I'm not doing anything.

TOMMY: Whacko.
ROIE: I live at twelve-and-a-half Plymouth Street.
TOMMY: Whacko.
DOLOUR: What's wrong with your shoe?
TOMMY: What?
ROIE: Dolour, what?
DOLOUR: He's got one shoe taller than the other one!
ROIE: Dolour! Sorry …
TOMMY: S'alright. Now's your cue to say you ain't goin' to be seen with no hop-and-go-fetch-it.
ROIE: Don't be silly. I don't mind if you're a bit wonky.
TOMMY: Whacko. Well, see you tonight?
ROIE: Yes.

> ROIE *walks away with* DOLOUR *through the markets as* TOMMY *watches them go.*

DOLOUR: He didn't say what time he was gonna come get you. [*Calling back*] Hey! You didn't say what time you was—!

> ROIE *grabs her sister firmly.*

ROIE: He's not a boob. He'll be around at quarter past seven. You'll see.

SCENE SIX

They walk on as the neighbourhood starts to shift. DOLOUR *walks ahead, pretending to be a nun.*

DOLOUR: He's handsome, isn't he? 'Cept for the boils.
ROIE: We've all had boils, Dolour. Now hurry into Lick Jimmy's and work your magic.

> DOLOUR *hurries in as* ROIE *wraps her shawl around her head again and sings as she fingers the embroidered flowers. As she does, we see* JOHNNY *on the busy Surry Hills street.*

> [*Singing*] 'Tis the last rose of summer,
> Left blooming alone;
> All her lovely companions
> Are faded and gone;

ACT TWO: THE HARP IN THE SOUTH

> No flower of her kindred,
> No rosebud is nigh,
> To reflect back her blushes,
> Or give sigh for sigh.

DOLOUR exits Lick Jimmy's.

DOLOUR: Lick gave us his leftovers, Roie! They're a bit coloured but Mamma won't mind, I'm sure.

Neighbourhood CHILDREN *swarm around* JOHNNY.

JOHNNY: Where the hills? Where the hills?

CHILDREN: Lookut the loony! Lookut the loony! Lookut the loony!

The CHILDREN *copy him meanly.*

DOLOUR: Sweet Jesus, Roie! Johnny's got outside! Miss Sheily will belt the daylights out of him!

ROIE: Johnny! Johnny!

She runs.

The CHILDREN *keep teasing him.*

CHILDREN: Lookut the loony! Lookut the loony!

JOHNNY *realises they're teasing him. He covers his ears and tries to get away from them.* DOLOUR *tries to cross the road to him, but it is filled with traffic.*

DOLOUR: Johnny! Stay off the road! Johnny!

ROIE: Careful, Johnny!

DOLOUR: Johnny! *Johnny! No!*

As JOHNNY *steps into the middle of the road, there is a squeal of tyres. The crowded street falls silent.*

As the crowds part, we see JOHNNY, *mangled and twisted on the road. Blood spews from his head.*

DOLOUR *walks to him slowly.* ROIE *covers her face with the shawl.* DOLOUR *squats down beside* JOHNNY *and stares at his corpse, stunned. From inside 121/2 Plymouth Street,* MISS SHEILY's *voice* …

MISS SHEILY: Johnny? Has anyone seen Johnny? Johnny?

She arrives outside. Sees. Screams.

Blackout.

The harp echoes.

SCENE SEVEN

Inside 12 1/2 Plymouth Street.

MARGARET, DOLOUR, ROIE, MR DIAMOND *and* HUGH *sit in the lounge room, numb.* ROIE *is weeping softly.*

MISS SHEILY *sits in her room, stunned still. A long silence, filled only by* ROIE *weeping.*

DOLOUR: [*whispering to* MARGARET] We saw it happen. Johnny's squashed melon on the road. His teeth all scattered like corn.

    ROIE *weeps more.*

We saw it happen.

    ROIE *murmurs softly as she weeps.*

ROIE: Did we leave the door open?

MARGARET: He got out all by himself. Weren't your fault, Roie.

HUGH: It's probably for the best.

MR DIAMOND: Aye.

HUGH: Who'd want to go on living like that, anyway, all minced up since birth?

ROIE: He went looking for the hills and they don't even bloody exist!

    She weeps.

DOLOUR: I'll bet Miss Sheily's glad.

MARGARET: Dolour. Shush.

DOLOUR: She always hated him! She beat him till he bled! No wonder he wanted to escape!

MARGARET: She kept him inside to keep him safe. She always fed him. Tucked him in. Can't have been easy for her.

DOLOUR: She tied him up like a dog!

MARGARET: Enough.

    ROIE *weeps more.*

    Silence.

ACT TWO: THE HARP IN THE SOUTH

Then ...

TOMMY: Excuse me? Hello? Anybody home?

    TOMMY *is there.*

  Sorry. I knocked, but ...

    He limps in further.

    HUGH *stares at him strangely.*

MARGARET: Can I help you, young man?

TOMMY: I'm Tommy Mendel. I've come to take Roie to the pitchers. Is ... is everything alright?

MR DIAMOND: Excuse us, boy. There's been a terrible accident. We're all a bit out of sorts.

TOMMY: Oh, yeah. Heard about that. Loony crossing the road.

    ROIE *weeps.*

DOLOUR: We saw it happen.

ROIE: I'm sorry, Tommy. I can't go out.

    ROIE *runs upstairs, leaving* TOMMY *downstairs with the others.*

TOMMY: Crook business. Kids are always getting run over in these streets. Not enough room for everyone, is there?

    HUGH *is still staring strangely at* TOMMY.

  Is there something wrong, sir?

HUGH: Sorry, fella. You got a lean to yer. Reminded me of me brother Jer. We went together like ...

    He gestures.

TOMMY: Oh. Yeah. I got trod on by a policeman's horse a few years back. Down Riley Street. Snapped me leg in two. Grew back a bit short.

    The family sit morosely.

  Please ... can I go and see if I can do anything for her? Poor thing.

    HUGH *doesn't answer. Just stares at the boy.*

MARGARET: I wish to heaven you would. Thank you.

    TOMMY *limps upstairs as* HUGH *watches wide-eyed.*

    Scene Eight can form here.

HUGH: Reminded me of Jer. For a moment there … I thought Jer had come home.

MARGARET: He's not Jer, Hughie. And even if he was, we still can't afford that damn operation.

  HUGH *crumples, as* MR DIAMOND *passes him a drink.*

SCENE EIGHT

Upstairs, in Roie and Dolour's room, ROIE *weeps on the bed.* TOMMY *knocks on the door and enters.*

ROIE: Go away, please.

TOMMY: Just forget it, kid.

  ROIE *looks at him furiously.*

ROIE: Forget it? How can you say that? He died. Johnny died! He'd hardly lived and then he died!

TOMMY: Accidents happen, Roie. I should know. [*Pointing at his boot*] Hit by an Acme 125 when I was a kid. Just round the corner from here. That's a motorcycle. A really fast one.

ROIE: Gee, Tommy. You're so brave.

TOMMY: I know. Just … don't blame yourself, Roie. Blame these streets.

ROIE: Alright. Thank you.

  He puts the shawl around ROIE*'s shoulders.*

TOMMY: Can I still take you to the pitchers sometime? See a singin' cowboy?

ROIE: [*smiling at him*] Yes.

TOMMY: I'll make sure you get across the street safe and sound.

  A shift. The harp plays softly …

  As we move, we see MISS SHEILY *kneeling, her back to us. She removes her dress. Raises the electrical wire.*

  Blackout.

  The harp echoes …

SCENE NINE

In the darkness ...

CHILDREN'S VOICES: [*in unison*] One times eleven is eleven. Two times eleven is twenty-two. Three times eleven is thirty-three. Four times eleven is forty-four. Five times eleven is fifty-five.

A schoolroom. Catholic icons line the walls, as do Christmas decorations.

A nun, SISTER THEOPHILUS, *stands at the front. 'She is a poised young woman with a warm, friendly face. She wears her brown habit rolled up at the sleeves.'*

SISTER THEOPHILUS *accompanies the* CHILDREN ...

Six times eleven is sixty-six. Seven times eleven is seventy-seven. Eight times eleven is eighty-eight. Nine times eleven is ninety-nine.

The voices peter off as the sums get higher, except DOLOUR *who speaks loud and proud.*

Ten times eleven is a hundred and ten. Eleven times eleven is a hundred and twenty-one.

By now it is just DOLOUR *and the teacher.*

DOLOUR and SISTER THEOPHILUS: [*together*] Twelve times eleven is a hundred and thirty-two!

SISTER THEOPHILUS: Well done, Dolour. You can draw the Christmas tree on the blackboard.

She passes DOLOUR *some chalk.* DOLOUR *starts to draw.*

DELIE STOCK *enters the room.*

CHILDREN: [*whispering excitedly*] Crumbs! It's Delie Stock! Delie Stock! Delie Stock's right here! She's more famous than jam!

SISTER THEOPHILUS: Children. Enough. Write the story of the Three Wise Men in your books for me, please. Best handwriting for Jesus.

She approaches DELIE, *who stands nervously in her expensive stained coat and hat. 'Sister's own eyes, fascinated, kept returning to Delie's, as to a window through which could be seen some mysterious and appalling scene.'*

How do you do? Do you wish to see me?
DELIE: I'm Delie Stock. Mrs Delie Stock.
CHILDREN: [*whispering excitedly*] Told you … Said so, din't I? Delie Stock! My dad knows her.
>SISTER THEOPHILUS *bows slightly and offers her hand.*
SISTER THEOPHILUS: Sister Theophilus.
>DELIE *looks shocked. She shakes the nun's hand uncertainly. Spies* HARRY DRUMMY.
DELIE: Harry Drummy. Don't think I don't know it was you that bunged a goolie through my window this morning.
>HARRY *looks mortified. The other* CHILDREN *stare at him wide-eyed …*
CHILDREN: [*whispering*] Um-ahhh!
>*… then back to* DELIE.
SISTER THEOPHILUS: How can I help you, Mrs Stock?
DELIE: Well, it's this way, Sister. I was thinkin' of the kids the other day. All the kids here. The Drummys. The Stevenses. The Brodies.
>DOLOUR *smiles and waves at* DELIE *from behind the Sister.*
The Darcys.
And I said to meself, I said, 'Delie, it's time you did something about them poor little dirty-nosed bastards. Give 'em a bit of fun.' You know, Sister?
>SISTER THEOPHILUS *smiles quizzically.*
So. I'm gonna give 'em a picnic, see? The whole shebang. Hire a bus.
CHILDREN: [*gasping throughout the following*] A bus! Ice-cream! The beach! A magician!
DELIE: Two buses. Whatever you need. Ice-cream. Baskets of tucker. Beach and everythink. And maybe we can get a magician or somethink. Give 'em the works. How many kids in this school, Sister Theoctopus?
SISTER THEOPHILUS: Uh … there's … over two hundred.
DELIE: Here then.
>DELIE *opens her purse and takes out a wad of scrunched-up notes.*

ACT TWO: THE HARP IN THE SOUTH

The CHILDREN *gasp in awe.*

SISTER THEOPHILUS: Holy Mary, Mother of God.

DELIE: Gawn. There's a hundred and thirty there. Gawn.

SISTER THEOPHILUS *stands gaping.*

Hang on.

She reaches into her blouse and pulls out another note.

There's another tenner.

The CHILDREN *gasp in awe again.*

SISTER THEOPHILUS: Oh, Mrs Stock. Crumbs! We could take them to Dee Why, perhaps? Or Collaroy? They could make forts! Get some beach sand in their britches instead of bloody worms!

They laugh.

Mrs Stock, I just can't thank you enough! What a thoughtful act!

SISTER BEATRIX *appears and claps sharply.* FATHER COOLEY *stands behind her.*

CHILDREN: [*in chorus*] Good afternoon, Father Cooley and may God bless you!

FATHER COOLEY: Oh, pardon me, Sister. I didn't know you had a visitor.

He sees the money.

Oh! The Lord look down on us!

SISTER THEOPHILUS: Isn't it wonderful, Father? Sister Beatrix? Mrs Stock has donated all this money for the children! For a Christmas picnic!

DELIE: Ice-cream for the poor little bastards. Buggers. Beggars.

SISTER THEOPHILUS: I thought perhaps Collaroy.

CHILDREN: [*whispering throughout the following*] Collaroy! Where's Collaroy? Collaroy's over the bridge!

SISTER THEOPHILUS: I went there once for a holiday. It's a lovely beach. A nice bus ride. The children can—

FATHER COOLEY: I'm sorry, Mrs Stock, but we cannot accept it.

The CHILDREN *fall quiet.*

SISTER THEOPHILUS: Oh, Father!

FATHER COOLEY: Your generosity will be long remembered by us, but I'm afraid that what you suggest would be quite impossible.

DELIE: So you ain't taking me money, is that it? Tainted, is it? There's a hundred and forty good quids there that you're keeping from those kids, you mangy Bible-banger.

The CHILDREN *gasp quietly.*

FATHER COOLEY: I am afraid it would be against my principles to take this money. It is tantamount to stolen property.

DELIE: Stolen from who?

FATHER COOLEY: Stolen from the wives and children of the men who spend it in your foul place of pleasure.

DELIE: Places. I own six establishments.

FATHER COOLEY: Shameful.

DELIE: When Mary Magdalene came along to Jesus, did he tell her to take her precious hair oil somewhere else? Gawn. Answer that, you old stinkin' buffalo. I'm an honest businesswoman.

FATHER COOLEY: You are no Magdalene. You're a dope peddler. You sell liquor brewed in your own backyard laced with fuel and tobacco. Liquor that fills the brains of men with madness and murder.

He points at the CHILDREN.

Their fathers!

The CHILDREN *squirm, a little alarmed.*

DELIE: Yeah, I'm the worst woman in the district. Everyone says so. I'm not ashamed to repeat it. But who comes across with fifty quid when there's a funeral, hey? When Johnny Sheily got hit by a truck—

DOLOUR: I saw that happen! He lived in my house!

DELIE: —who gave his ma enough dough to give him a nice headstone? Delie Stock. That's who.

FATHER COOLEY: To square your conscience.

Beat.

DELIE: Let me tell you somethink, Father Cooley. I didn't set out for this life. It found me. Would've starved on the streets if I hadn't got into a house up on Murphy Street run by old Ruthie Nairn. No customers allowed after midnight!

She turns to the CHILDREN.

ACT TWO: THE HARP IN THE SOUTH

Can you believe it?
CHILDREN: [*together*] No.

> FATHER COOLEY *glares at* SISTER THEOPHILUS.

DELIE: Well, when Ruthie died, she left the house to me. It's been hard work, but it's good business brains that done it. Six houses and forty girls I got.
SISTER BEATRIX: That's even more than King Herod!
DELIE: All taken care of well and good. I feed 'em. I clothe 'em. I make sure they're healthy and have a good place to sleep. Where would they be otherwise? Would you take 'em in, Father? Would you give 'em your bed?

> *He looks mortified.*

Didn't reckon. So you've got no call to be looking down at me, Cooley.
FATHER COOLEY: You've started them all on a road to Hell.
DELIE: Well, yer gotta make the most of what yer got. Make the most of the few choices yer actually given.

> *She looks at the* CHILDREN, *who watch on with eyes like saucers. She shakes her head sorrowfully.*

Poor little bastards. Buggers. Beggars.

> *She turns back to* FATHER COOLEY.

Look … if it'll ease your conscience … that money was won in the lottery. Me numbers came in a couple of weeks ago. Was in the papers and everythink. Cross me heart and spit.

> FATHER COOLEY *eyes the money.*

FATHER COOLEY: The lottery, you say? Well … if the government condones it …

> *He takes the money.*

We'll pray for you and your girls, Mrs Stock.

> FATHER COOLEY *leaves.*

> *The* CHILDREN *glance at each other, excitedly.*

DELIE: Don't bother. We got the devil lookin' after us just fine.

> *She turns back to* SISTER THEOPHILUS.

Give 'em a good picnic. Might be the only one they ever get.

The CHILDREN*'s excitement increases.*

SISTER THEOPHILUS: Thank you, Mrs Stock. Oh! I've been saying ejaculations under my breath the whole time!

DELIE: Well, we've all been there.

She points at HARRY.

Stop bungin' goolies through me windows, Drummy.

HARRY *looks mortified again. The* CHILDREN *look at him wide-eyed, then back to* DELIE. *She nods at the* SISTERS.

Sister Beatrix. Sister Theoctopus.

DELIE *saunters out.*

SISTER THEOPHILUS *turns to her classroom excitedly.*

SISTER THEOPHILUS: Children! Sister Beatrix! We're going on a picnic! We're going on a bloody picnic!

The CHILDREN *cheer excitedly.*

We shift ...

SCENE TEN

... to Plymouth Street, where DELIE *and* KIDGER *watch from their balcony as the* CHILDREN *chant ...*

CHILDREN: [*in chorus*] We're goin' to Collaroy! We're goin' to Collaroy!

DELIE: Have fun, you little buggers! If someone gets stung, piss on 'em. Works a treat.

DOLOUR *appears in swimmers that are too big for her.*
MARGARET *pins them as* DOLOUR *wriggles excitedly.*

SISTER THEOPHILUS *and* SISTER BEATRIX *appear.*

MARGARET: Now, don't be goin' too far out. Them sharks.

SISTER THEOPHILUS: They'll only be allowed in the baths where it's perfectly safe, Mrs Darcy. Don't you worry.

A PHOTOGRAPHER *appears.*

ACT TWO: THE HARP IN THE SOUTH

PHOTOGRAPHER: Mind if I get a pic of the bairn, miss? She'll be right under the headline 'Santa Claus comes to Surry Hills'.
HUGH: More like 'Look what the cat dragged out'.
MARGARET: Hughie.
DOLOUR: 'Course you can take my pic. Like my swimmers? They're my sister Roie's.

She poses excitedly.

Do I look like Betty Grable? Dadda, do I look like Betty Grable?
HUGH: Not really, love.
MARGARET: Dolour! Contain yourself!
SISTER THEOPHILUS: Alright, everybody. On the bus! Give a wave to Mrs Stock and say thank you!

The CHILDREN *get in formation. As they depart, they wave.*

CHILDREN: Bye, Mrs Stock! Thank you!

DELIE *poses on her balcony as the* PHOTOGRAPHER *takes snaps.* KIDGER *lurks.*

DELIE: Get outta me frame, Kidger.

The CHILDREN *depart excitedly.*

CHILDREN: [*chanting as they go*] We're going to Collaroy! We're going to Collaroy!

Their voices fade away and the street goes very still. HUGH *and* MARGARET *are left alone.*

HUGH: At last. Some peace and quiet.

He puts his arms around MARGARET.

Come here, Missus.

He pulls a sprig of frangipani from his pocket and holds it above her head.

A bit of a kiss under the mistletoe? What do you reckon?

He kisses her. She fights him off.

MARGARET: Hughie.
HUGH: Come on. When do we ever get a morning to ourselves?
MARGARET: Get off me.

HUGH: Wanna come and sit outside the pub? I'll sneak you a sherry.

She shoves him away. Pulls the letter from her pocket and gives it to him.

S'this?

MARGARET: I bin tryin' to tell yer. It's a letter from Trafalgar. There's news.

HUGH *looks stunned.*

HUGH: Is it from Jer?

He opens it hurriedly and reads. His face falls in shock.

MARGARET: I bin meaning to tell yer.

HUGH *deflates, the frangipani drops.*

An old woman enters, unseen by them. It's ENY, *smaller and shrunken now.*

There's just nowhere else for her to go.

HUGH: When … when does she get here?

ENY: She gets here now.

HUGH *practically leaps out of his skin.*

HUGH: Christ, Missus.

MARGARET: Ma!

ENY: Hello, my Maggie.

HUGH: Why can't she stay with Josie in Trafalgar?

ENY: Josie's husband lost all their money on the horses. She's divorcing him. And her arches have fallen. Margaret's turn now. Get me coat, Margaret.

MARGARET *helps* ENY *with her coat.*

MARGARET: Was yer trip alright, Ma? Do yer need to rest?

ENY: Whist-a-whist. Come here, me Maggie.

They embrace.

MARGARET: Ma! You've shrunk!

ENY: And you've spread!

HUGH *looks at* MARGARET *incredulously.*

HUGH: Where will she sleep? House is full to the brim!

ENY: I'll sleep with Margaret. You can take the couch.
HUGH: No. No. No. It's not right. Not by no manner of means. A man shouldn't be separated from his wife. Send her back to your sister.
MARGARET: Hughie. She's Ma.
HUGH: She'll be breathin' fire at me every time I come home with more than one drink in me.
ENY: I've never seen you with less than one drink in you.
MARGARET: Hughie. She's Ma. And while I live she won't be turned out onto the street.
HUGH: Ahhhh. I might've known this was me unlucky day. Metho in me booze last night, mother-in-law in me bed this mornin'.

He paces, perturbed.

Tell you what. I'll strike you a deal. We'll take Johnny's stretcher from Miss Sheily.
ENY: Johnny? Who's Johnny?
MARGARET: No-one, Ma.
HUGH: We'll hang a sheet across the bedroom. Us on one side in our marriage bed, as it should be, Eny on the other on Johnny's stretcher.
ENY: Johnny? Who's Johnny?
MARGARET: No-one, Ma. I'll go and set up the beds.

They head inside.

ENY: You got old, Hugh Darcy.
HUGH: With any luck I'll be dead by bedtime, mother-in-law.

SCENE ELEVEN

The sounds of screaming children as the children of Saint Brandan's frolic in the sand. Sandcastles are being built and children splash in the shallow water of the Collaroy baths.

SISTER THEOPHILUS *and* SISTER BEATRIX *watch on, smiling.* SISTER THEOPHILUS *raises her skirt and paddles into the water as* SISTER BEATRIX *waits nearby.* DOLOUR *watches on, transfixed, as she makes a fort with* HARRY DRUMMY.

DOLOUR: Blimey, Harry! I didn't expect that!
HARRY: What?
DOLOUR: Look. Sister Theophilus. She's got ankles.

HARRY: 'Course she's got ankles. How would she walk without ankles?
DOLOUR: I always thought they just, sort of … floated. The nuns.
HARRY: You're a dingbat, Dolour.

He squashes her head into the sand.

Say it! 'I'm a dingbat!' 'Dolour, the dingbat!'

She screams furiously, her face muffled by the sand.

SISTER THEOPHILUS: Harry Drummy, that's *quite* enough.

HARRY *lets* DOLOUR *go. She lifts her head and spits sand out angrily.*

Go and play with the boys, please. Dolour come here, and let me clean you up.

As HARRY *runs off,* DOLOUR *angrily stomps to* SISTER THEOPHILUS, *who starts to clean her face of sand.*

DOLOUR: I didn't do anything, Sister.
SISTER THEOPHILUS: I'm sure you didn't, Dolour. Boys will be boys. That's how God made them. All part of His very mysterious plan.
DOLOUR: Well, I reckon He might've got the recipe wrong with Harry Drummy, Sister. He's a right squib.
SISTER THEOPHILUS: He is a bit.
DOLOUR: One day I want to be a nun. Just like you, Sister Theophilus.
SISTER THEOPHILUS: Really? Why?
DOLOUR: To get away from boys. And drunk old men. So I can float. And so I can have just one special friend that takes care of me, that I take care of back.
SISTER THEOPHILUS: You mean God?
DOLOUR: No. Sister Beatrix.

SISTER THEOPHILUS *looks taken aback. She glances at* SISTER BEATRIX *who blushes a little behind her.*

But God too, of course. I can have two friends. As long as He doesn't make me eat sand.
SISTER THEOPHILUS: Sister Beatrix is indeed a good friend, Dolour.

Beat.

As is God.

She glances at SISTER BEATRIX.

As is God.

A moment of strange silence.

Now come on. Let's go for a paddle, shall we? Can't send you home covered in sand.

DOLOUR *hurries off excitedly.*

DOLOUR: Oy! Last one to the baths is a rotten egg!

The two SISTERS *exchange a secret smile ...*

The sounds of the children's squeals and shouts are replaced by the furious arguing of HUGH *and* ENY ...

SCENE TWELVE

... fighting over a mixing bowl.

HUGH: I'm tellin' you, woman! Dates, prunes, cherries, sultanas and currants! So many you couldn't spit between 'em! That's a Darcy puddin'!

ENY: Currants! Wasted space! That's nothin' but a heathen cake you're makin', Hugh Darcy. Yer mullet-headed sheeny.

HUGH: Eny, I tell you, I been a shearers' cook in my youth and I know how to boil a puddin'. Shearers demand only the best on Christmas Day, woman!

ENY: I bin cookin' puddin's every year since I was eleven years old and living with me da in Faroe Street, Cookstown, *Ireland*. Heard of it? No, I didn't think so.

HUGH: Don't you question my blood, woman. This will be as Irish a pudding as there ever was.

ENY: You've taken leave of your seven small senses, Hugh Darcy, if you think yourself more Irish than me! Out of my way.

She snatches the bowl from him.

HUGH: Get out of my kitchen, woman!
ENY: My kitchen now! Currants. Ugh.

She sniffs the cup of currants and suddenly quietens. Her voice softens to a melodic sweetness.

Ooooh. Is that brandy, Hugh Darcy?

HUGH: It is, Eny. I always soak my currants in brandy.
ENY: Ooooh. Where'd you get the brandy, Hughie?
HUGH: A friend.

> ENY *inhales the aroma of the currants deeply.*

ENY: Ooooh. Can I have the cup after you've finished with it, Hughie?
HUGH: Will yer keep outta me kitchen if I give you a sip?
ENY: Or two.
HUGH: Shut yer eyes.

> *He gets out a bottle of brandy secreted nearby and pours her a tiny amount. She peers into it, her smile fades.*

ENY: Call yourself an Irishman! Not enough there to warm a kitten! Ah, it'll be a glorious day for me when you're old and aching and knobbly in every joint and some tight-fisted Jeremiah of a son-in-law deprives you of yer wee sup of brandy!

> MARGARET *enters with a sugarbag of groceries.*

HUGH: What did you say, Eny?
ENY: *Jer*-e-mi-ah!
MARGARET: Ma! Don't you / speak of Jer!
HUGH: You leave Jer out of this. He'll be back.
ENY: Jer? Who's Jer?
HUGH: My poor broken brother! You remember, old woman! He used to live in yer damn house! Sing you songs!
ENY: Oh, yes. Jer and his yoo-lalla-kee. Disappeared on your wedding day, didn't he?
MARGARET: Ma, enough!
HUGH: He'll come walkin' through the door any day now.
ENY: With young Thady on his shoulders, no doubt. What is it with people just disappearin' from this family?
HUGH: I'm warnin' you, / woman.
MARGARET: Ma, please.
ENY: Prob'ly you, Hugh Darcy. You've got the manner of a pig under a bed.

> *She grabs the bowl and puts her hands inside it to knead the dough.*

HUGH: Get your hands off me pudding!

ACT TWO: THE HARP IN THE SOUTH

He grabs it back.

She hits him with a wooden spoon on the head.

He raises his hand to her.

MARGARET: *Hughie!*

ENY: Go on now! Hit an old woman, Hugh Darcy! Show what sort of a man you really are. No different to your father.

MARGARET: Ma, there's no call / for—

HUGH: You leave my father out of this, Eny Kilker.

ENY: He drove his wife to madness, didn't he? You'll do the same to my daughter, I'll bet.

HUGH: Me? It's her that drives me to madness! All of you women drive us fellas to madness!

ENY grabs a handful of flour and throws it at him.

HUGH throws a handful back.

They have a brutal flour fight in the kitchen.

MARGARET: [*admonishing as she watches*] Ma, stop! *Hughie*, she's Ma! Both of you, behave! You're acting like children! Hughie, be careful!

MARGARET cops a fistful of flour in the face.

The fight ends.

Silence.

HUGH: I'm goin'.

MARGARET: But the pudding, Hughie …

HUGH storms out.

ENY: I'm makin' the puddin' this year.

She gets out the brandy as MARGARET stands forlornly in the flour-covered kitchen.

SCENE THIRTEEN

ROIE *and* TOMMY *sit in Centennial Park. He holds a present, looking shocked.*

ROIE: I know we haven't been seeing each other long, Tommy. And I know presents aren't really the spirit of Christmas. But I got you something anyway. For being so nice. It's not much. I don't make much of a wage at the factory. But I wanted to get you something. To say thank you. And ... Merry Christmas.

He unwraps the gift. It's a green pullover.

Too hot for it now, of course. But when winter comes, it'll be lovely and warm. Don't you reckon? Tommy?

Silence.

TOMMY: [*softly*] I've never gotten a Christmas present before, Roie. I've never had any kinda gift since my parents were alive.

ROIE: Oh, Tommy. I'm sorry. We can wrap it back up.

TOMMY: No! Bugger the heat. I want to wear it now.

He puts on the pullover.

Fits perfectly, Ro.

He kisses her on the cheek, awkwardly. She blushes.

One day, when I have enough money and I'm not livin' in some dirty little attic in Haymarket, I'm gonna take you to the races, Roie. You'll wear a slinky black dress and a great big hat with lace round the brim and a string of green beads. And I'll give you a big wad of cash to bet with. On any horse you like. And we'll walk out of there even richer than when we walked in. That'll show 'em.

ROIE: Who?

TOMMY: All of 'em.

Beat.

Bet you thought I wasn't gonna get you anything.

ROIE: Oh, Tommy, I ... I never thought about it. Much.

He fishes around in his pockets as ROIE *waits expectantly. He finally pulls out a small, shabby gift.*

ROIE *unwraps it gently, her hands shaking.*

It's ... soap.

TOMMY: And a flannel.

ROIE *is momentarily thrown.*

ROIE: [*forcing a smile*] Gee, Tommy ... it's awfully ... useful. I mean ...

ACT TWO: THE HARP IN THE SOUTH

everyone needs soap. And the flannel is awful pretty. Pink, I mean. I like pink things. Thank you so much.

TOMMY: Thought you could use it.

He nestles his head into her lap. She gives her armpit a surreptitious sniff.

I know I've got a gammy foot. And I don't make much money. But I will take you to the races one day, Ro. I will.

ROIE *kisses his face.*

ROIE: I love soap, Tommy. I love soap. And I love you with all my heart.

She gasps and covers her mouth. TOMMY *looks stunned.*

TOMMY: Do you mean that, Ro?
ROIE: I do. I know it's only been a couple of months, but …
TOMMY: I love you too, Roie.

He is suddenly on top of her, kissing her roughly. She giggles.

ROIE: Tommy … my dress … my hair … Tommy, don't! Don't!

He takes the pullover off and throws it aside.

TOMMY: Let me touch you.
ROIE: What do you mean?

He starts to put his hand up her dress.

TOMMY: Don't play hard to get.

She pushes his hand away.

ROIE: I'm not like that. I don't go in for maulings.
TOMMY: But I'm different. You know that.

ROIE *sits up, crossly.*

ROIE: I don't like it.
TOMMY: So you don't love me, then.
ROIE: What? No …
TOMMY: It's my foot, isn't it? Puts you off. Not my fault my mother didn't nourish me in the womb.
ROIE: I thought it was an Acme 125 motorcycle?
TOMMY: It was both. You can't blame me for wantin' to get close to you. You're not like all the other sheilas in Surry Hills.
ROIE: You don't have to be a rat just because you live in a hole.

Beat.

TOMMY *sulks miserably.*

ROIE: Tommy? Darling?

She awkwardly places his hand on her breast.

Maybe I wouldn't mind it if it was you that did it. But not tonight. Just this tonight. Maybe … maybe next year.

TOMMY: Next year starts next week, Roie.

She nods reluctantly.

Whacko.

He squeezes her breast.

The sounds of singing fill the space ...

SCENE FOURTEEN

Inside 12 1/2 Plymouth Street, Puffing Billy spits smoke as MARGARET *bustles around the kitchen preparing Christmas lunch.*

ENY, HUGH, DOLOUR *and* ROIE *sit around the kitchen table.* ENY *and* HUGH *are quite drunk already. They sing ...*

HUGH and ENY: [*together, singing*]
    Bryan O'Lynn had no stockings to wear,
    He bought a rat's skin to make him a pair,
    He then drew them over his manly shin,
    'Whoo! They're elegant wear,' says Bryan O'Lynn.

HUGH: Hear this, Eny! The old goat remembers Jer's song! Yer remember Jer's song?!

HUGH and ENY: [*together, singing*]
    Bryan O'Lynn to his house had no door,
    He'd the sky for a roof and the bog for a floor,
    He'd a way to jump out, and a way to swim in,
    'Whoo! It's very convenient,' says Bryan O'Lynn.

ENY: Why'd you stay here, Margaret?

HUGH: Missus.

ENY: Why'd you not come back to Trafalgar? To your ma and your sister Josie and your dear ol' da.

ACT TWO: THE HARP IN THE SOUTH

HUGH: I promised her somethin' more! Thass why.
ENY: Oh, yes? And when's it arriving?
MARGARET: Ma. It's a good life. God has blessed us this Christmas Day. And last night I dreamt of Dagda's harp. Playing all by itself! Surely a sign of good things to come.
DOLOUR: Who's Dagda?
MARGARET: Dagda was the first of the Irish warriors … Wasn't he, Ma?
ENY: Aye. Aye.
MARGARET: And he always carried his magical harp with him.
ENY: Made of oak and jewels and gold. Aye.
MARGARET: And just by plucking its strings, Dagda could call his men to battle with a single chord.

HUGH burps.

ENY: Aye, my Maggie. Keep going. Keep going.
MARGARET: And when the battles were over, Dagda would play his harp, and the music would soothe any wounds inflicted upon his soldiers. The men forgot their injuries and their sorrows. The harp's music reminded them of their loved ones at home—their wives and children. They thought not of the brutality of the fight, but of the honour of it.

Silence.

That was Thady's favourite story. Last night I dreamed of the harp.

She beams.

MISS SHEILY *enters.*

MISS SHEILY: Good evening.
MARGARET: Merry Christmas, Miss Sheily. Will you be joining us for Christmas dinner?
MISS SHEILY: I will not. I'll be having a sandwich in my room. I'd ask that you keep it down to a quiet riot this year, please.
HUGH: Come and join us, Miss Sheily. You can sit on my lap.
MARGARET: Hughie! Enough!
HUGH: Or you can sit on the stove. Might warm you up a bit.
MISS SHEILY: Caesar's ghost, man.
ROIE: Da, that's enough.
HUGH: What? Stinking hot in here and she's colder than a penguin's tail.
ROIE: Please feel free to join us, Miss Sheily.

MISS SHEILY: Thank you, Rowena. But no.

    MR DIAMOND *has appeared.*

MR DIAMOND: I also won't be joining you.

HUGH: Who asked you, you Prod-hopper?

DOLOUR: Prod-hopper.

ENY: Prod-hopper!

MARGARET: Dolour, don't use that word on Christmas Day. Are you sure you won't join us, Mr Diamond?

MR DIAMOND: I'll not eat with pope-worshippers.

HUGH: Hasn't stopped you any other time, Diamond.

MR DIAMOND: 'Course, if there's any leftovers, just leave them on a plate by my door. Thank you.

    MR DIAMOND *leaves.*

MISS SHEILY: May the Lord find blessings for you all.

    She leaves.

    MARGARET *plonks a tray of food on the table.*

MARGARET: Chook and potatoes.

DOLOUR: Big as a football, that chook, Mamma.

MARGARET: Was bigger before Puffing Billy got to it. Shrunk it somehow.

HUGH: Gravy?

MARGARET: Not enough flour.

    HUGH *and* ENY *exchange a guilty look.*

HUGH: Shall I carve it up, Margaret?

MARGARET: By all means.

    HUGH *carves the chicken. As he does,* MARGARET *sits down wearily and* ENY *gets a bottle from inside her dress skirts.*

ENY: Merry Christmas from me.

HUGH: Eny Kilker, you sly cat. Here I was thinking we were all out of grog and you've got a brewery up your dress.

ENY: That's a port. I think. Oh, wait, no. This one is.

    She brings out another bottle from underneath her skirts.

MARGARET: Here's your presents from me and Hughie, girls.

    She puts two parcels on the table. The girls open them.

ACT TWO: THE HARP IN THE SOUTH

DOLOUR: A book of saints! Thank you, Mamma! Look at them all! I'll be in here one day!
MARGARET: What will you be the patron saint of, Dolour?
DOLOUR: I'm not sure. I'll have to ruminate.
ROIE: Oh, Mamma! Lace gloves? Thank you.
MARGARET: To keep your hands soft when you're not working them to the bone, Roie.
DOLOUR: Thank you, Da!
ROIE: Thank you, Da.
DOLOUR: I made you a shell bracelet, Mamma!
MARGARET: Thank you, Dolour!
ROIE: I got you a scarf, Mamma. And one for you too, Da. And some new underpants for you, Grandma.
ENY: Thank you.

The presents are opened and admired. Except for one, which remains on the table unopened.

Whose is that one?
MARGARET: No-one here.

They fall silent and stare at it. DOLOUR *breaks the silence.*

DOLOUR: Mamma, shall I say grace? I've been practising.
MARGARET: Of course, Dolour.

They all sit and close their eyes.

DOLOUR: Dear God. Thank you for the chook and potatoes. Thank you for dying for us terribly.

ENY *drinks from the port surreptitiously.*

Thank you for the gift of each other. For keeping us together and safe on this special day. We hope Thady is safe too, wherever he is, and that he comes home soon.

HUGH *drinks from the port surreptitiously.*

We hope you have a lovely day up there. Happy birthday to Jesus from all of us. Amen.
ALL: Amen.
HUGH: If I may speak now.

He gets to his feet.

An Irish proverb on this Christmas Day.
May the roof above our heads never fall in,
And those gathered beneath it never fall out.

> ENY *rolls her eyes.* HUGH *sits.*

> ENY *stands.*

ENY: Let's have a real Irish proverb, shall we? On this Christmas Day.

> HUGH *glares at her.*

May we all live as long as we want
And never want as long as we live.
And as we slide down the banister of life
May the splinters always point the other way.

> *She sits.* HUGH *stands.*

HUGH: May the most you wish for be the least you get,
And misfortune follow you the rest of your life, but never catch up.

> *He sits.* ENY *stands.*

ENY: May all your ups and downs be beneath the sheets.

> *She sits.* HUGH *stands.*

HUGH: May you be half an hour in Heaven before the Devil knows you're dead.

> *He looks pointedly at* ENY. *He sits.*

> *They start to eat.* ENY *stands.*

ENY: May those that love us love us
And those that don't love us,
May God turn their hearts.
And if he doesn't turn their hearts,
May he turn their ankles
So we'll know them by their limping.

> *She looks pointedly at* HUGH. *He stands, seething.*

HUGH: May your troubles be as far between as my mother-in-law's tits.

> *This sets off a raucous argument.*

ENY: That's not a real Irish proverb, Hugh Darcy / and you know it!
HUGH: Don't you tell me what's Irish! I'm as Irish as a fuckin' harp!

ENY: You wouldn't know an Irish harp if it popped out of yer trousers and played a feckin' jig!

> MARGARET *sits weeping, cradling the unopened present. They all fall quiet as she begins to wail.*

MARGARET: Nineteen years, three months and twenty-eight days since I held his hand.
Thady … Thady …
Thady …

ROIE: Oh, Mamma …

> *She runs to her mother and wraps her arms around her.*

MARGARET: I stay here, Ma, because … What if he comes back? I need to be here when he comes back …

> *She cradles the gift and weeps.*

ROIE: Here, Mamma.

> *She takes the gift from* MARGARET.

I'll put it in the cupboard with the others.

> *She opens a cupboard to reveal several more unopened presents. She places it gently inside and closes the door.*

ENY: I lost a boy once. Stevie.

HUGH: Eny! Not now.

ENY: We've all lost, is all. We've all lost.

> ROIE *gets a gift from her pocket.*

ROIE: Look! I got another gift. It's from Tommy Mendel. He gave it to me last night.

> MARGARET*'s tears abate.*

HUGH: Is it, just?

ENY: Who's Tommy?

DOLOUR: Roie's beau. He's got three boils.

ENY: Jesus, Mary and Joseph.

> ENY *crosses herself and takes a swig of port.*

DOLOUR: Open it, Roie!

MARGARET: Go on, Roie.

They all watch in anticipation as ROIE *opens the gift. It's a brooch. They all murmur approvingly.*

ROIE: It's a brooch!
DOLOUR: Looks expensive!
MARGARET: Oh, Roie. It's beautiful!
HUGH: Put it on, Roie.

ROIE pins it to her chest.

DOLOUR: Are those rubies? They're rubies!
ENY: Redder than the one you gave my Margaret, Hugh Darcy. The one that looked like a rat's eye.
HUGH: Well, it can't be that cheap, Eny, because every time we've hocked it, it's given us at least a few bob.
ROIE: He shouldn't have. Dear Tommy.
DOLOUR: He must really love you, Roie.
ROIE: He says he does.
DOLOUR: Rubies are red. Red means love.
MARGARET: He said he loves you?
HUGH: Love, he said?

ROIE nods.

ENY: Whist-a-whist! Whist-a-whist...
HUGH: You sure?
ROIE: He gave me a brooch, didn't he?

HUGH pours port.

HUGH: Well, then. To love.
ALL: To love.

ROIE smiles nervously as her father gulps his port.

MARGARET: And to Thady.
ALL: To Thady.
HUGH: And to Jer.
ALL EXCEPT MARGARET: To Jer.

They drink.

Christmas CAROLLERS *pass as the family dines. They sing 'A Kerry Christmas Carol'.* MARGARET *does not eat. Just waits for everyone to finish and clears away the plates.*

ROIE *moves to the bathroom ...*

She undresses to her undergarments and steps into the laundry tub. Steam rises as she washes herself with the pink flannel and soap that TOMMY *gave her.*

MARGARET *lights candles in the window as her daughter bathes and the* CAROLLERS *sing.*

CAROLLERS: Brush the floor and clean the hearth,
And set the fire to keep,
For they might visit us tonight
When all the world's asleep!
Don't blow the tall white candle out
But leave it burning bright,
So that they'll know they're welcome here
This holy Christmas night!
Leave out the bread and meat for them,
And sweet milk for the Child,
And they will bless the fire, that baked
And, too, the hands that toiled.
Leave the door upon the latch,
And set the fire to keep,
And pray they'll rest with us tonight
When all the world's asleep.

The CAROLLERS *become an excited mob, who collect wood and scraps and place them in a large pile in the street, in preparation for New Year's Eve.*

DELIE STOCK, KIDGER *and her* GIRLS *hang a sign on their balcony: 'HAPPY NEW YEAR—1949'.*

SCENE FIFTEEN

In the kitchen, MARGARET *and* ENY *gather scraps of newspaper and wood.*

MARGARET: Come on, Ma. Let's get a good spot.
ENY: Help me with me potatoes.
HUGH: Where'd you get all those, Eny?
ENY: A woman never tells.

MARGARET: She's made friends with Lick Jimmy.
HUGH: Will wonders never cease?

> *He enters the bathroom as* ENY *and* MARGARET *leave.*

I'll grab that broken stool.
ROIE: Da! I'm naked as a baby!
HUGH: Christ in a sidecar.

> *He departs hurriedly and calls through the door.*

How long you gonna be?! The bonfire will be lit soon, Roie!
ROIE: I've only just got in!
HUGH: Bring the broken stool with you when you come out.
DOLOUR: [*calling up the stairs excitedly*] Mr Diamond! Miss Sheily! Have you got anything for the New Year's Eve bonfire?!

> *A crash as a chair is thrown down the staircase.*

MISS SHEILY: Disgusting! Take the foul thing and burn it! Riddled with bugs. Caesar's ghost, a woman can't even sit down in this house for fear of getting her bottom bitten!
DOLOUR: Thanks Miss Sheily! That'll do nicely!

> *She hurries with it outside.*
>
> MR DIAMOND *comes down the stairs.*

HUGH: You're looking dapper, Diamond.
MR DIAMOND: I feel lucky, Darcy. Like I might find meself a wife tonight. Start 1949 with a lady on my arm.
HUGH: You'll still be up for a drink later though?
MR DIAMOND: Of course.

> *As the* CROWD *gathers outside,* ROIE *stares at herself in the bathtub in the reflection of a broken mirror.*
>
> *A man outside,* MR GUNNARSON, *arrives with a barrel organ in a pram. He starts to play a jangling melody and* ENY *dances beside him.*
>
> *He encourages* MISS SHEILY *to join in.*

MR GUNNARSON: Dance, Miss Sheily! Dance.
MISS SHEILY: Caesar's ghost, no.

> LICK JIMMY *runs to the bonfire with boxes.*

ACT TWO: THE HARP IN THE SOUTH

LICK JIMMY: Look! Boxes! Lots and lots of boxes.

He piles them onto the mound.

And here! Sparkles! Lots and lots of sparkles! Here, Dolour! Share!

He and DOLOUR *pass the sparklers around the gathering* CROWD.

DELIE *and her* GIRLS *loiter nearby on their balcony, posing provocatively.* KIDGER *lurks.*

A very pregnant MRS SICILIANO *approaches* MARGARET.

MRS SICILIANO: Hello, Mrs Darcia.

MARGARET: Hello, Mrs Siciliano. How many will this make?

MRS SICILIANO counts on her fingers.

MRS SICILIANO: Antonetta, Rosina, Amelia, Grazia, Maria, Violetta, Giacomo … Otto. Eight.

She gestures to her belly.

And this one. Finito.

ENY: Jesus. Even the Irish are worn out at eight.

MRS SICILIANO: That's why we have to sell my beautiful brooch to Roie!

MARGARET: What?

MRS SICILIANO: Only thirty bob. Bargain! Roie said she was going to give it to someone who had not a present. She's a good girl. Look! They are going to light the fire!

ROIE *hurries out of the tub and starts dressing.* DOLOUR *is with* HUGH …

DOLOUR: What's your New Year's resolution, Da?

HUGH: I'll keep off the plonk. Except Saturdays. Does no harm for a man to have a bit of a gee-up now and again.

DOLOUR: I'm gonna get on the 'Junior Information Quiz' on 2MB if it's the last thing I do. What about you, Mamma?

MARGARET: I'm not ready for a New Year's resolution. This year hasn't delivered all it was supposed to yet.

DOLOUR: Still got a few minutes, Mamma. Anything could happen.

MARGARET *looks around the* CROWD *for her long-lost son.*

MARGARET: I don't think so.

DOLOUR: What about you, Granny? What's your resolution for the New Year?
ENY: I'm just going to try and make it to tomorrow.
DOLOUR: Where's Roie? She's gonna miss the bonfire! I wonder what her New Year's resolution is?

In the bathroom, ROIE *stands, dressed and ready.*

ROIE: Tommy.

A match is struck outside ...

LICK JIMMY *starts to light fireworks ...*

LICK JIMMY: Fireworks! All the way from Shanghai!

As the CROWD *starts to count down,* ROIE *hurries through the house.*

ALL: Ten ... nine ... eight ... seven ... six ... five ... four ... three ... two ... one!

ROIE *runs out of the house, smack bang into the arms of* TOMMY.

Happy New Year!

The fireworks whizz and crackle. The CROWD *kiss and celebrate.*

TOMMY *kisses* ROIE, HUGH *kisses* MARGARET, ENY *cuddles* DOLOUR, MR DIAMOND *and* MR GUNNARSON *both try to kiss* MISS SHEILY, DELIE'S GIRLS *kiss each other.* KIDGER *lurks, lonely.*

TOMMY: Let's go for a walk. I'm sick of these yammering boneheads.
ROIE: Okay.

As they depart, the sounds of wailing sirens. POLICE OFFICERS *arrive.*

POLICE OFFICER 1: Move along. Move along there. Break it up.
HUGH: It's just a little celebration! We do it every year!
POLICE OFFICER 2: All fires forbidden after midnight in the Hills area. You read it in the newspapers and it's posted up around the streets.
CROWD MEMBER 1: Brass-hatted bastards!
CROWD MEMBER 2: Go home, you wet blankets.
CROWD MEMBER 3: Trust the coppers to break up some innocent fun.

ACT TWO: THE HARP IN THE SOUTH

DELIE: Would you like to come inside, Sergeant Rogers? Bed's still warm from last time!

The CROWD *laughs raucously at the* POLICE OFFICER.

POLICE OFFICER 1: That's enough! You're all drunkards! Oy! That's enough! Party's over!

The POLICE OFFICERS *start to put out the fire with bags and blankets and buckets of water.*

ENY: Ye feckin' eejit peelers! May the devil use yer spine as a ladder and take a burnin' shite in yer hat!

The CROWD *cheers wildly.*

Scene Sixteen can form here.

The POLICE OFFICERS *turn their bags, blankets and buckets on the crowd. Mayhem ensues.*

MARGARET *tries to drag a ranting* ENY *inside.*

MR DIAMOND *and* HUGH *end up on top of each other.* LICK JIMMY *tries to protect* DOLOUR.

MISS SHEILY *is flattened, her dress around her ears.*

MR GUNNARSON *tries to help her but she shoves him away.*

DELIE *and her* GIRLS *watch on from the balcony, laughing.* KIDGER *lurks.*

Finally, the crowd is silent ...

Except for the puffing of MRS SICILIANO.

MRS SICILIANO: The constable broke my waters! Dio mio! The constable's broke my waters!

She hurries away.

HUGH: Didjer manage to find yerself a wife, Diamond?

MR DIAMOND: Not this time, Darcy. Next year, for sure. Now how about another cup of kindness before bed?

They go in.

SCENE SIXTEEN

ROIE *and* TOMMY *kiss passionately in a park, lit by moonlight.*

TOMMY *starts to unbutton her blouse, and* ROIE *pushes his hand away gently. He tries instead to put his hand up her skirt and she pushes him away again. He lowers her to the ground and starts to unbutton his trousers.*

ROIE: No. No, I can't. Not here.

> *He starts to pull at her stockings.*
>
> Tommy …
> > Please …
> > No!
>
> *He stops.*

TOMMY: I wish you were a man. Just for a minute. So you could feel how I feel. Then you wouldn't say no to me again, ever.

ROIE: Tommy, you do love me, don't you?

TOMMY: Roie, would I be doing this if I didn't? Come on, Ro. Only once. I swear I'll never ask you again. Just let me have it once. Just once, Ro. Once.

> *She lays down reluctantly.*
>
> You smell so good. Did you use that soap I got you?
>
> *She nods.*

ROIE: Yes. I did. Thank you, Tom—

> TOMMY *takes his chance.* ROIE *gasps in pain.*
>
> *As* TOMMY *rapes,* ROIE *lays stunned.*
>
> *The lights fade as the faint sound of 'Auld Lang Syne' drifts across the Hills.*

VOICES: [*singing*] Should old acquaintance be forgot
> And never brought to mind?
> Should old acquaintance be forgot
> And auld lang syne?

> DELIE *and her* GIRLS *take down the New Year sign …*

For auld lang syne, my dear,
For auld lang syne,
We'll take a cup of kindness yet
For old lang syne.

SCENE SEVENTEEN

Back in the Darcy house, MR DIAMOND *and* HUGH *are at the table, drinking and singing, completely plastered.*

MR DIAMOND and HUGH: [*singing together*]
And surely you'll buy your pint cup
And surely I'll buy mine
And we'll take a cup o' kindness yet
For auld lang syne …

As they continue to sing, ROIE *makes her way softly up the stairs. She sits on the landing and cries as the men sing on.*

For auld lang syne, my dear,
For auld lang syne …

They pass out, plastered.

MISS SHEILY: [*singing*] We'll take a cup of kindness yet
For the sake of auld lang syne …

She raises her wire.

Johnny … Johnny … Johnny …

In Margaret's room, as she prays, THADY *appears and watches her.*

MARGARET *lifts her head from her prayer. She holds out her hand to* THADY.

MARGARET: Thady … Thady … Thady …

The harp echoes …

ACT THREE: THE HARP IN THE SOUTH

SCENE ONE

A new year. 1949.

MARGARET *and* ENY *sit on the balcony, watching the street life go by, as* MARGARET *darns underwear.*

MR GUNNARSON *passes. He has a barrel organ in a pram.*

MR GUNNARSON: Hello, Mrs Darcy! Mrs Kilker!
ENY: Oh, what yer got fer us today, Mr Gunnarson?
MR GUNNARSON: Today, 'Swannee River'!

> *His organ starts to play and he does a little dance in the street for them.* ENY *gets to her feet and dances too.*

ENY: Watch how fast me feet go! You can barely see 'em, can yer? Look at 'em go! Look at 'em go!

> MISS SHEILY *appears.*

MISS SHEILY: Cut that earbashing. Caesar's ghost.
MR GUNNARSON: Good afternoon, Miss Sheily!
MISS SHEILY: What's good about it? There's a kraut on the street making a racket.
MARGARET: It's only a bit of fun, Miss Sheily.
MISS SHEILY: I can make my own fun, thank you very much.

> *She glares at* MR GUNNARSON *and heads inside.*

MR GUNNARSON: She is so wonderful. Hej då!

> *He walks on up the street, beaming.*

MARGARET: Have a good day, Mr Gunnarson. I still haven't worked out Miss Sheily's first name yet. Probably something elegant. Like Olga. Or Cornelia.
ENY: There'll be potatoes aplenty when the circus is over.
MARGARET: What's that, Ma?
ENY: Your stays were loose, that's what got you into this mess.

ACT THREE: THE HARP IN THE SOUTH

MARGARET: You feeling poorly, Ma?
ENY: I'm fine, Josie.
MARGARET: Margaret, Ma. Josie's back in Trafalgar.
ENY: I know who you are. Came out of my nethers now, didn't you?

>DOLOUR *runs past with a kite.*

DOLOUR: Ma, look! Grandma!

>LICK JIMMY *watches from his own balcony.*

LICK JIMMY: Hold high, Dolour! Catch the wind! Catch the wind!

>*He waves and smiles at* MARGARET *and* ENY.

Hello, Missus! Hello, other Missus!
ENY: What did he call us?
MARGARET: Missuses.

>*A woman,* LOLLY MOLLY, *waits on a street corner, her skirt hitched slightly.*

ENY: Who's that? Who's that?
MARGARET: That's Lolly Molly, Ma.
ENY: Tch, tch, tch.
MARGARET: She's got a nerve showin' her face down this way. She's from Darlinghurst, not the Hills.

>MEN *wander the streets surreptitiously, dipping their hats at* LOLLY MOLLY *as they look her up and down from afar.*

MAN: G'day, darlin'.
LOLLY MOLLY: Lookin' for love, fella?
MARGARET: Look at 'em sniffin' her out. Like dogs. That's one thing I'll say for my Hughie. He won't look twice at another woman.
ENY: Aye. Not even you.
MARGARET: She'll wanna be careful. Someone stabbed a Dutch sailor down the corner the other night. Showing off his cash and had his throat cut ear to ear. Bet he was on his way to Delie Stock's.

>ROIE *wanders onto the balcony.*

MARGARET: Hello, Ro darlin'. Finished for the day?
ROIE: Yes.
ENY: Yer lookin' peaky, Roie.

ROIE: I'm just tired. And I got into a muddle at the factory today. And the foreman told me off. I ... I just need a rest.

> ROIE *heads inside.*

ENY: Looky here. Looky here. Oooh, this'll be good. Looky here.

> *At Delie Stock's house,* PHYLLIS *and* FLO *see* LOLLY MOLLY *from the balcony.* PHYLLIS *hurries inside and exits with* DELIE. KIDGER *loiters behind.* DELIE *directs the* GIRLS *downstairs and they exit onto Plymouth Street.*

> 'They were a strange pair. Phyllis was very young, about sixteen, with an oblong, solid face lined and grimed with guilt. She had been a prostitute since she was ten. Flo was a tall, slender, elderly woman with a face painted into the semblance of gentility. She wore a tight black costume, and her hair was set with steely rigidity into the most elegant of afternoon-tea coiffures. She even wore gloves.'

MARGARET: I reckon we're in for some trouble, Ma. Come on. Inside.

ENY: Get your hands off me. This is better than the pitchers!

> *As* LOLLY MOLLY *chats with a* MAN, PHYLLIS *and* FLO *make their way across the street towards her.* KIDGER *lurks along behind.* DELIE *watches from her balcony.*

PHYLLIS: Oy. Molly, you dirty little scrub.

> *The* MAN *turns to see* DELIE *and* KIDGER *watching from afar.* DELIE *glares at him.*

MAN: Sorry, Delie! Sorry, Kidger!

> *He hurries away as the two girls corner* LOLLY MOLLY.

FLO: You put the coppers onto Delie's dope peddlin'?

LOLLY MOLLY: I didn't! It weren't me!

PHYLLIS: Coppers told Delie it was you. Told her you made fifty bob out of it.

FLO: You got a hide showin' your arse in the Hills after you dobbed in Delie.

LOLLY MOLLY: I didn't dob in Delie!

> *She sees* DELIE *watching.*

I didn't dob on you, Delie!

ACT THREE: THE HARP IN THE SOUTH

PHYLLIS and FLO close in as ONLOOKERS stare from all corners of the street.

Get away from me, you bitches! You touch me and I'll tell the coppers!
PHYLLIS: You think yer gonna have a tongue left in yer head after we're done with yer?

LOLLY MOLLY tries to run but FLO trips her up. She falls hard and is pounced on by PHYLLIS. 'Phyllis punched Molly in the teeth a dozen times.'

LOLLY MOLLY: Help! Help! Someone, please!

The ONLOOKERS keep watching, including ENY and MARGARET. DOLOUR and LICK JIMMY arrive back with the kite. DOLOUR stops still and the kite falls to the ground as the sickening thuds of LOLLY MOLLY being kicked in the stomach fill the street.

Thud. Thud. Thud.

ENY: She should be on the football field, that one.
MARGARET: They'll kill her. They will.

But they cannot look away.

FLO takes off her gloves and hands them to KIDGER. Then, smiling ever so slightly, she gouges LOLLY MOLLY's eyes.

LOLLY MOLLY *screams.*

LICK JIMMY turns DOLOUR away from the sight and blocks her ears. Finally, KIDGER stops the two women from their massacre.

FLO puts her gloves back on. They leave LOLLY MOLLY for dead.

DELIE: She still breathing?
PHYLLIS: Yes, Delie.
DELIE: Good girls. While you're down there, you might as well drum up some work.
FLO: Will do, Delie.
DELIE: Kidger. Take her back to Darlinghurst. Leave her on Liverpool Street so everyone can see her.

DELIE goes back inside.

KIDGER drags LOLLY MOLLY away.

MARGARET: These streets ... these godawful mean streets. How do we survive 'em, Ma?
ENY: Whist-a-whist ... whist-a-whist ... whist-a-whist ...
MARGARET: Dolour! Get home please!

> DOLOUR *is still being shielded by* LICK JIMMY, *but she has seen it all. Stunned.*

LICK JIMMY: Dolour. Pick a piece of fruit?

> DOLOUR *peruses his stall, shaken.*

DOLOUR: Can I have a poor man's orange, Lick?
LICK JIMMY: No. Not ready. Take a peach instead.

> *She does.*

SCENE TWO

Night.

The residents of the house get ready for bed.

MARGARET *tucks* ENY *into bed. She snores behind the sheet partition.*

MARGARET *kneels and prays by her own bed where* HUGH *is passed out.*

DOLOUR *hangs pictures of movie stars by her bed, impersonating their poses.* ROIE *is nearby, looking poorly.*

MR DIAMOND *in his room, hugging a pillow close.* MISS SHEILY *sits in a chair, preparing her electrical wire.*

MARGARET: Nineteen years, seven months and six days since I held his hand. Amen.

> *She climbs into bed beside* HUGH.

Hughie ...

> *He doesn't wake. She kicks him and he wakes with a start.*

HUGH: Jesus, what is it?
MARGARET: Hello.
HUGH: What, Missus?
MARGARET: Hello. I'm Margaret Kilker.

> HUGH *sits up.*

HUGH: [*smiling*] I'm Hugh Darcy.

ACT THREE: THE HARP IN THE SOUTH

MARGARET: I know who you are. You used to go to my school.
HUGH: Don't remember.
MARGARET: Oh.
HUGH: Not you. School.

> MARGARET *smiles.*

Wanna walk through the House of Horrors with me?

> MARGARET *starts to weep.*

MARGARET: Ah, Hughie. All I want is to hold his little hand.

> *She weeps.*

HUGH: Shhh … shhh …

> *In Dolour and Roie's room, the two girls lay in their shared bed.* DOLOUR *wriggles wildly.*

DOLOUR: Ugh.

> *Beat.*
>
> *She wriggles violently.*

Ugh! Blasted critters!

> *She sits up furiously.*

Are you not getting eaten alive, Roie? They're savage tonight.
ROIE: You should be used to it by now, Dolour.

> DOLOUR *flops back in bed. She tries to cuddle in close to her sister.*

Don't.
DOLOUR: I'm cold, Roie. There's a nip in the air at last. You're so warm.
ROIE: I'm not here to warm you. Get off.
DOLOUR: Fine, I'll just cuddle up to the bed bugs, shall I?

> *They lay in the darkness together.* DOLOUR *shivers dramatically. Grunts as she's bitten by bugs.*
>
> *In Margaret and Hugh's room,* MARGARET *takes off her dressing-gown and hitches up her nightdress.*

MARGARET: Comfort me, Hughie.
HUGH: Missus.
MARGARET: Margaret. Comfort me. Please.

> *She weeps.*

Please, Hughie. [*Whispering*] Remember. You're mine and I'm yours. You're mine and I'm yours …

He joins in, kisses her deeply and they disappear under the sheets as ENY *snores behind the curtain.*

In Roie and Dolour's room, DOLOUR *wriggles with itching.*

ROIE: Oh, come here, Dolour.

DOLOUR snuggles into her sister.

I'm sorry. I'm just a bit … out of sorts.

DOLOUR: It's all that overtime you're doin' at the factory. What you savin' up for, Roie? A winter coat?

ROIE: Just a rainy day.

DOLOUR: Why doesn't Tommy come round anymore, Ro? Did you have a fight?

ROIE: He's moved to Leichhardt.

DOLOUR: Oh. Do you miss him?

ROIE: No.

DOLOUR: You're so warm, Roie.

Scene Twenty can begin here.

As DOLOUR *cuddles her sister tight,* ROIE *lays awake in the shadowy room.*

In Margaret and Hugh's room, MARGARET *prays softly to herself as* HUGH *and* ENY *snore beside her.*

MARGARET: God bless Thady, God bless Roie, God bless Dolour, God bless Hughie, God bless Ma, God bless Josie, God bless Thady, God bless Roie, God bless Dolour, God bless Hughie, God bless Ma, God bless Josie, God bless Thady, God bless Jer … God bless Jer …

She stops.

God bless Thady, God bless Roie, God bless Dolour, God bless Hughie, God bless Ma, God bless Josie, God bless Thady …

Night darkens.

SCENE THREE

DELIE STOCK *sings as she arrives home.* KIDGER *lurks behind her.*

DELIE: The snow is snowing
    The wind is blowing
    But I can weather the storm
    Why do I care how much it may storm
    I've got my love to keep me warm

ROIE crawls from bed and dresses herself quietly.

    I can't remember
    A worse December
    Just watch those icicles form
    What do I care if icicles form
    I've got my love to keep me warm

ROIE *sneaks down the stairs and out the front door onto Plymouth Street. She tries to avoid* DELIE*'s stare as she passes beneath the brothel balcony.*

    Off with my overcoat
    Off with my gloves
    I need no overcoat
    I'm burning with love
    My heart's on fire
    The flame grows higher
    So, I will weather the storm
    What do I care how much it may storm
    I've got my love to keep me warm

ROIE *reads from a slip of paper as she stands in front of an old, dilapidated yellow house with a row of ferns and vines curtaining its windows.*

    I've got my love, I've got my love
    I've got my love to keep me warm.

ROIE *knocks on the door of 17 Murphy Street. A woman opens the door a crack.*

MRS X: Feeling bad, dearie?

ROIE: Is this where the …? I mean … does the …?
MRS X: Yes, dearie. It's here. And he does.

> *Beat.*

Yer comin' in?

> ROIE *hesitates, then nods. And we are inside the house* ...
>
> MRS X *and* ROIE *sit in a waiting room. Another young woman,* LYNETTE, *sits nearby.*

How far are yer?
ROIE: Four months.
MRS X: Tch. Y'oughta come earlier. Three months is bad enough. But four!
ROIE: I had to save up the money. It took longer than there was time for.

> *Beat.*

But … I suppose you know that.

> *Beat.*

MRS X: [*smiling*] Men. What's yer name, love?
ROIE: Beryl Graham.
MRS X: It's an improvement on Smith or Jones.
ROIE: Will it … will it hurt?
MRS X: The doctor's a good'un. Good as any of those Macquarie Street lot. He's got a kind heart and just wants to help out you poor girls who get into trouble. Don't hurt more than a toothache if you don't move. It'll be twelve pounds.
ROIE: Twelve?! I was told ten! I only saved up ten!
MRS X: [*not impressed*] I'll have to speak to the doctor.
ROIE: Oh, you must make him. Please make him help me.
MRS X: Ho! Mighty snooty, you are. The doctor won't be *made* to do anything by no dirty little tart who made herself do everything!
ROIE: I'm sorry. I didn't mean to … I'm just … so scared.
MRS X: Wait here. With Lynette.

> *As* MRS X *disappears,* ROIE *sits with* LYNETTE. *'A dark, oily-skinned girl with bold Italian eyes and an old food-stained coat pulled around her already prominent stomach.'*

LYNETTE: It's not so bad when it comes to the point. You've always got more guts than you thought.

ACT THREE: THE HARP IN THE SOUTH

ROIE: How ... how far are you?

LYNETTE: Four-and-a-half. I got stuck into the dope but it didn't work. So now I'm here again.

ROIE: You've been here before?

LYNETTE: Cripes, this is me fourth miss, if it comes off. Somehow I'm always falling in. 'Course, I'm married, so I don't have much say in things.

Beat.

But don't you be afraid, love. Just put yer hanky in yer mouth and bite on it. Say 'Mary help, Jesus save', then try to think of something else.

She shrugs.

It's getting home that's the worst.

ROIE: Why?

LYNETTE: Things sometimes happen on the way.

MRS X *reappears.*

MRS X: Lynette.

LYNETTE *smiles at* ROIE.

LYNETTE: That's not even a made-up name. Nice to meet yer, Beryl. Might see you again in a few months.

She winks.

MRS X: You're next.

ROIE *nods nervously as they leave. She sits in the dark room.*

Sounds from the next room. ROIE *listens through the door. A man's voice mutters.*

Metal clinking on china.

A horrible gagged scream.

Gurgling moans. Running feet.

The hiss and pop of gas. Trickling.

Another hoarse shriek, suddenly gagged.

ROIE *can take no more. She struggles with the lock and runs out of the house onto Murphy Street and along the shadowed road. She runs and runs.*

And then ...

Men appear from the shadows. SAILORS *in Dutch sailor outfits.*

The SAILORS *chant as they spin* ROIE *and touch her roughly and prod and poke at her, tossing her from one to the other.*

MEN: Good efening … Good efening … Good efening …
Yer out late, girly …
Where you going, girly?
Show us around, girly …
Why you play so hard, girly?
Pretty girly …

ROIE: No … no, please. I'm on my way home. I'm going to have a baby! Please let me go home. Mamma! *Mamma! Mamma!*

But the SAILORS *pile onto her, tearing at her clothes as she struggles against them wildly.*

Help! Please! Someone! Mamma!

One of the men kicks her in the belly, hard. Suddenly, DELIE *appears with* KIDGER.

DELIE: Oy! You lot! Clear out or I'll call the vice squad! *Oy!* Get off 'er!

KIDGER *pulls a knife out and holds it to one of the* SAILORS' *crotch.*

It was me that got yer mate the other night. Left me best knife in his Adam's apple. I can do the same now, if you like.

The SAILORS *retreat and back away into the shadows.* ROIE *is laying on the ground. Blood on her dress.*

What are yer doin' here, dear?

ROIE: Did you really kill that man the other night?

DELIE: Nah. Wouldn't waste a good knife on a Dutchman. Come on, darlin'.

ROIE: I'm going to have a baby.

DELIE: Never you mind about that now. Come on. Kidger. Lift her.

SCENE FOUR

KIDGER *carries* ROIE *to Plymouth Street.* DELIE *knocks on the door.* HUGH *answers.*

DELIE: Mr Darcy.
HUGH: Miss Stock …? Who's that?
DELIE: It's your eldest. She got cornered by some sailors.
HUGH: Jesus … Where are they? I'll kill 'em!
DELIE: Forget 'em.
> KIDGER *passes a barely-conscious* ROIE *to* HUGH.

Get her a doctor. Not a quack. Here.
> *She gives* HUGH *a wad of cash.*

And in the meantime, give her this.
> *She hands over a bottle of brandy.*

It's my best stuff. It'll help ease her mind. Ease the pain. She won't need much.
> HUGH *takes it, hesitantly.*

See she gets it?
HUGH: Yes, Miss Stock.
> *She turns to go.*

Thank you for bringing my little girl home.
DELIE: Look after her.
> *She goes to leave.*

HUGH: I always have.
> DELIE *smiles.*

DELIE: 'Course. Kidger.
> KIDGER *follows* DELIE.
>
> HUGH *is left on the doorstep, holding* ROIE. MARGARET *appears.*

MARGARET: Roie? Oh, Roie …
ROIE: Mamma! Mamma! Mamma! Mamma!
> *Her hysterical screams build as the* TENANTS *of Plymouth Street peer out of their doorways.*

DOLOUR *runs downstairs, followed by* ENY.

DOLOUR: What happened? Roie! Roie!

ROIE sinks to the floor, a bloody mess.

ENY: Fetch water and a cloth, Dolour. There's a good girl.

DOLOUR hurries off.

HUGH: She's bleedin' everywhere. Where's it comin' from? She's bleedin'!

Beat as MARGARET *looks at her daughter.*

MARGARET: She's losing a baby, Hughie.

She strokes ROIE*'s head as she lays on the floor.*

There, there, Roie. Let it go. Let it go, now. Let it go.

ROIE: *Mamma! Mamma! Mamma!*

HUGH *stands over the women as they take* ROIE *to her bed.*

DOLOUR *re-enters and hurries after them.*

Scene Five can form here.

The harp echoes ...

HUGH *looks to the brandy in his hand. He stumbles out the front door ...*

And walks away from his house, cradling the brandy like a baby, and shoving the cash in his pocket.

SCENE FIVE

ROIE *lays in her bed as* DOLOUR, ENY *and* MARGARET *stand around her in dim candlelight.*

DOLOUR: Is Roie going to die?

MARGARET: Don't be silly. Them sailors knocked her down, is all. She'll get back up again. Now go downstairs and sleep on the couch. Yer been up all night. And take yer rosary with you and say a Pater-n-Ave for my intention.

DOLOUR leaves.

You too, Ma.

ENY: What? I'm her grandmother. I got every right to be here.

ACT THREE: THE HARP IN THE SOUTH

MARGARET: Ma. Please. Go.

> ENY *strokes* ROIE*'s hair. She kisses* MARGARET *on the forehead and leaves.* ROIE *stares up from the bed.*

ROIE: Mamma, you know about me? My secret?
MARGARET: Yes, darling.
ROIE: What's going to happen?
MARGARET: You're going to be alright. Everything's going to be alright.
ROIE: [*panicked*] What about my baby?! You haven't said anything about my baby!

> MARGARET *restrains her daughter.*

MARGARET: There isn't any baby now, Roie. Shhh. Shhh. No baby, now.
ROIE: I killed it.
MARGARET: No, darling. The sailors killed it. And it wasn't alive. It didn't miss anything of life.
ROIE: I killed it. I killed it because I didn't want it. That's why God's punishing me this way!
MARGARET: You didn't kill it, Ro. I promise you.
ROIE: Mamma, I went to that place in Murphy Street. The one with curtains that are always closed. I went there tonight.

> MARGARET *looks horrified.*

MARGARET: Roie … did they touch you?
ROIE: I ran away, Mamma. I couldn't do it. But God knew what was in my heart and He saw it happen anyway. He sent those sailors to find me. I deserved everything I got.

> MARGARET *stands over* ROIE, *mortified. A long moment.*

MARGARET: Such thoughts do nothing but harm, Roie love. You're a good girl, and whatever's happened, it's over now and nothing to you but the past.

> '*She pressed Roie's head close to her breast, and the poignant pain which had been hers when first she had felt Roie's little downy head at her birth went through her again, and she knew that her feeling was no different.*'
>
> *We move to downstairs, where* DOLOUR *lays on the couch with* ENY.

DOLOUR: Will she be alright, Grandma?
ENY: Not for a long while, Dolour. But she will. She will.

> *Beat.*

DOLOUR: Are you gettin' bitten, Grandma?
ENY: Aye.
DOLOUR: This house is filthy.
ENY: Aye.

> *Beat.*

When I was a little girl in Ireland, I lived in a house with a fine shaggy roof on it. Our house was right in the middle of the shaky-quaky bog, and there were pools of brown water, for all the world like coffee, right at the back door. When you stamped very hard on our front door sill the whole bog shivered all over. It did so. But one day when I was digging with a stick in the mud I found a golden coin shaped like a shell with a strange lady's face on it.

DOLOUR: Was it a sovereign, Grandma?
ENY: Pffft. It was not. It was a coin of the fairy times, long before any people at all came to Ireland. They was great goldsmiths, the fairy people. And my dadda took the coin into the town, and he came back with a brown pony and a little wagon with red spokes to the wheel that I could run through the muddy bog to my heart's content. And it was called 'Eny's cart', that cart, for my name is Eny, though the dear Lord knows what use it is to me now, as I've always been Ma and Grandma for sixty wearisome years.

DOLOUR: Would you like me to call you Eny, Grandma? Grandma? Eny?

ENY: Sometimes the fairy people would visit us. Secretly. They'd wander through the house, leaving their muddy footsteps. I'd follow those footsteps until they disappeared to nothing.

> *She looks at* DOLOUR *strangely.*

They're tricksters, the fairy people. They're all around us. Pretending to be someone we know. Someone we knew.

> *A man,* STEVIE, *has appeared. As if from out of nowhere. He strokes* ENY*'s hair.* ENY *sees him, but* DOLOUR *cannot.*

Stevie, it's wicked, you are. You're wicked, Stevie.

ACT THREE: THE HARP IN THE SOUTH

DOLOUR: I'm Dolour, Grandma. Who's Stevie? Grandma?
ENY: Red hair down me back like bushfire. Waist like a whippet's.

She stands up.

Let me undo me stays, Stevie. You're all thumbs …

DOLOUR *watches, shocked, as* ENY *takes off her nightgown.* STEVIE *watches.*

We won't tell John, now will we, Stevie? We won't tell John … There's hellfire under me feet, but I love you, my Stevie.

DOLOUR *gently helps her grandmother into bed.* STEVIE *disappears from whence he came.*

I always followed the fairy footprints, Dolour.
DOLOUR: Let's get you to bed, Grandma.

ENY *sleeps.*

As MARGARET *rocks* ROIE *upstairs, downstairs* DOLOUR *strokes* ENY*'s grey hair back from her face …*

… while MR DIAMOND *listens in, wide-eyed and lonely in his room …*

… and MISS SHEILY *quietly cleans up the blood by the front door.*

SCENE SIX

Night. HUGH *wanders the street with* MR DIAMOND.

MR DIAMOND: Can I have some more of that, Darcy? Just to warm me up a little.

HUGH *passes him* DELIE'S *bottle.*

HUGH: I'll find that Mendel bastard. I'll beat him till he bleeds as much as Roie did.
MR DIAMOND: And so will I, Hughie.
HUGH: He ruined her, Diamond.

HUGH *stops and weeps.*

She's my little girl, see. My beautiful girl. I made her.
He cries. MR DIAMOND *tries to hold* HUGH.
MR DIAMOND: Come here, Hughie.
HUGHIE *turns from him slightly, trying to hide his tears.*
Come here. Just to warm you up a little.
DIAMOND *wraps his arms around* HUGH.
HUGH: I made her…
DIAMOND *rocks* HUGH *as he weeps.*
I made her …

SCENE SEVEN

LICK JIMMY *sings 'Ye Shanghai' (Shanghai Nights) as he plays a ukulele.* DOLOUR *dances beside him. She joins in his song.*

LICK JIMMY: Yè shànghǎi yè shànghǎi
   Nǐ shìgè búyèchéng huádēng qǐ yuè shēngxiǎng gēwǔ shēngpíng
   Zhǐjiàn tā xiàoliǎn yíng shuí zhī tā nèixīn kǔmèn yèshēnghuó dōu wèile yīshízhùxíng
   Jiǔ bù zuìrén rén zì zuì hú tiān hú de cuōtuóle qīngchūn xiǎo sè ménglóng juàn yǎn
   Xīngsōng dàjiā guī qù
LICK/DOLOUR: Xīnlíng er suízhe zhuǎndòng de chēlún huàn yī huàn xīntiāndì
   Bié yǒu yīgè xīn huánjìng
   Huíwèizhe yèshēnghuó rú mèng chū xǐng
   Night in Shanghai, night in Shanghai,
   Chang da te bei hao!
   He beams.
DOLOUR: What's that song about, Lick?
LICK JIMMY: About Shanghai at night. About the lights. And the cars. About people getting drunk. About waking up with a sore head in the morning and doing it all over again night after night after night.
DOLOUR: Shanghai nights sound like every day in Surry Hills.

ACT THREE: THE HARP IN THE SOUTH

LICK JIMMY: I like it when you sing, Dolour. Remind me of my daughter.
DOLOUR: You got a daughter, Lick?
LICK JIMMY: Two daughters, one tall, one small. Mai-Lin has a scar here on her nose—where she had chicken pox. Very pretty. Zhi-An—she can blow bubbles with her tongue! One son. He's fat and soft. I call him Roger. So that when he gets here, he fits in.
DOLOUR: Roger.
LICK JIMMY: I have a wife. Shu Wei. Very beautiful. She has big feet. And I have a mother and a father and grandparents. Old and wrinkled and no teeth. They smile like this.

He demonstrates. DOLOUR *laughs.*

DOLOUR: Why aren't they here with you?
LICK JIMMY: Too much war in China. And too many rules in Australia. But for now, they are in here. And in here. [*He gestures to his head and his heart. Then gesturing to his Surry Hills*] And soon they will be here.

DOLOUR *kisses his hand.*

DOLOUR: Postie been today, Lick?
LICK JIMMY: [*shaking his head*] Haven't seen him, Dolour. No letters for us today.
DOLOUR: I handed in my application to the 'Junior Information' Quiz nearly a year ago. *Still* no reply.

SISTER THEOPHILUS *and* SISTER BEATRIX *float up the street.*

Cripes! It's the sisters! They must've heard about Roie! [*Yelling upstairs*] Mamma! Mamma, the sisters are here! *Mamma!*

MARGARET *peers over the balcony.*

MARGARET: What?!

She sees SISTER THEOPHILUS *and* SISTER BEATRIX *approaching.*

Oh, Jesus, Mary, Joseph and the donkey … Don't let them in, Dolour! The house is a sty!

She hurries around the house, cleaning up, as DOLOUR *greets the* SISTERS *on the front doorstep.*

DOLOUR: Hello, Sister Theophilus. Good morning, Sister Beatrix.

SISTER THEOPHILUS: We've come to see if there's anything we can do for you, Dolour. You've been very quiet at school. How is Roie?

ENY appears at the door.

ENY: Have you come for me? I'm not ready.
SISTER THEOPHILUS: Pardon?
ENY: You tell that man upstairs that Eny Kilker is not ready. Tell him.
SISTER THEOPHILUS: Oh, no, Mrs Kilker—
DOLOUR: She's Grandma. She's eighty-one!
SISTER THEOPHILUS: Eighty-one! That's quite an innings! You're almost as good as Bradman, Mrs Kilker.
ENY: I never did like a bone in yer skin, yer crooked ould disciples!
DOLOUR: She's so old, she speaks proper Irish!
ENY: Yer breakin' my heart into three halves, you devils. Three halves!
DOLOUR: Hahaha. Grandma, you funny old thing!
ENY: I'll not go with you! Do you hear me? Don't invite them in, Dolour! They've come for me! Don't invite them in!

She is dragged aside by MARGARET.

MARGARET: Sister Theophilus. Sister Beatrix. Do come in. Do come in.

ENY *shrieks and hides behind the door.*

Grandma! Enough!

She smiles sweetly again at the SISTERS.

Come in. Come in. Come in.

The SISTERS *enter the house. The door is left open.*

Outside, STEVIE *tips his hat to* ENY.

ENY: Stevie!

She smiles, hitches her dress and follows, unseen by all ...

Meanwhile ...

MARGARET *and* DOLOUR *lead the* SISTERS *into the kitchen where* ROIE *is sitting, pale.*

MARGARET: Please excuse the mess. We weren't expecting such holy company.

ROIE *is embarrassed.* MARGARET *offers a chair to* SISTER

ACT THREE: THE HARP IN THE SOUTH

BEATRIX. *She sits, and the chair creaks and leans to one side. Everyone does their best to ignore it.*

SISTER THEOPHILUS: May I sit here, Roie?

ROIE *nods weakly.* SISTER THEOPHILUS *sits beside her. She sees the red shawl nearby.*

What a truly beautiful shawl! Is this your handiwork, Roie?

DOLOUR: She got it from Paddy's Markets.

ROIE *starts to weep.*

MARGARET: She's not herself yet. Not quite.

An awkward silence as ROIE *cries.*

SISTER BEATRIX *shuffles* SISTER THEOPHILUS *out of the way. She holds* ROIE *close, firmly.*

SISTER BEATRIX: God has his own ways of giving us experience, Rowena. Don't regret all the pain. You will learn in the long run that it gave you wisdom of strength. Lift up your heart and be glad that God thought you worthy to go through this trial. You are worthy, young woman. You are worthy.

ROIE*'s tears abate. She holds* SISTER BEATRIX *tight. The* SISTERS *stand.*

SISTER THEOPHILUS: If you need us at all, just ask.

MARGARET: Oh, thank you, Sister Theophilus. Thank you, Sister Beatrix. Thank you. Thank you. I'll say a pater and ave for my intention. And a Hail Mary. And a Holy Father…

MARGARET *leads the* SISTERS *out of the house.* DOLOUR *follows, impersonating their walk.*

MARGARET *closes the door. Turns.*

Silence.

It's too quiet.

Beat. DOLOUR *is still walking around like a nun.*

Dolour, where's Grandma?

DOLOUR: I think when I'm a nun, I'll be Sister Anne. After Saint Anne. The grandmother of Jesus himself.

MARGARET: Grandma?
>   *She starts to panic.*

Ma!
>   *She calls upstairs.*

Ma?
>   HUGH *and* MR DIAMOND *enter, drunk.*

Hughie! Ma's gone.
>   *They look around groggily.*

HUGHIE: What?! Eny!
DOLOUR: Grandma!
MARGARET: *Ma! Ma!*

SCENE EIGHT

The harp echoes ...
ENY *walks the streets of Surry Hills, following Stevie ...*
She chats away to herself as she wanders, lost, wearing a nightgown and bare feet.

ENY: You hear that? It's the harp callin' me, Stevie. Calling me back.
>   *She searches.*

I came out on the *Fair Isle,* I did. In eighteen eighty-eight ... Eighteen eighty-eight.
Stevie. Stevie ... wait till I undo me stays ...
>   JOHN KILKER *appears.*

Oh, Johnny! John Kilker was the finest man in Trafalgar. He could win a tug o' war against a team of fifty. Just him. By himself. My Johnny.
Do you hear the harp? Do you?
>   *She clutches her head. Looks around. Lost. She falls.*

>   FRANCES DARCY *appears.*

I remember you, Frances Darcy. You and yer songs.
>   [*Singing*] 'Tis the last rose of summer

ACT THREE: THE HARP IN THE SOUTH

    Left blooming alone;
    All her lovely companions
    Are faded and gone.

JER *appears.*

[*Spoken*] There ye are, Jer. Tell me a joke. Sing me a song.
    [*Singing*] No flower of her kindred,
    No rosebud is nigh,
    To reflect back her blushes,
    Or give sigh for sigh.

THADY *appears next.*

[*Spoken*] Hello there, little Thady. I'm yer Grandma Eny. Yer ma's worried fer ye. Ye ought to get home, child.

MARGARET, HUGH and DOLOUR: [*off*] Ma! Eny! Grandma! *Ma?!*

ENY: [*spoken*] We all ought to … we all ought to just go home.

    She turns back momentarily. Confused.

    [*Singing*] I'll not leave thee, thou lone one,
    To pine on the stem;
    Since the lovely are sleeping,
    Go, sleep thou with them.

The dead wander away. Except THADY.

He takes ENY *by the hand.*

MARGARET, HUGH and DOLOUR: [*off*] Ma! Eny! Grandma! *Ma?!*

THADY: Grandma was nowhere, nowhere at all.

    The harp fades.

    The street falls silent as THADY *leads* ENY *away.*

SCENE NINE

The RESIDENTS *of Plymouth Saint assemble in black as* HUGHIE, MR DIAMOND *and* LICK JIMMY *carry a coffin from the house and onto Plymouth Street.*

MARGARET *weeps, alongside an ashen* ROIE *and a miserable* DOLOUR. MISS SHEILY *is there too, along with* SISTER THEOPHILUS *and* SISTER BEATRIX. FATHER COOLEY *leads the procession.*

DELIE *watches from the balcony with her girls.*

As the procession passes, MR DIAMOND *sings from the shadows ...*

MR DIAMOND: Siúil, siúil, siúil a rún
I wish I was on yonder hill
'Tis there I'd sit and cry my fill
Until every tear would turn a mill
Is go dté tú mo mhúirnín slán
Siúil go sochair agus siúil go ciúin
Siúil go doras agus éalaigh liom
Is go dté tú mo mhúirnín slán

The song continues softly throughout ... ROIE *is left behind. She sits weakly on the doorstep.* DELIE *comes down from her balcony, but doesn't follow the procession. The song continues throughout ...*

I'll dye my petticoats, I'll dye them red
And 'round the world I'll beg my bread
Until my parents shall wish me dead
Is go dté tú mo mhúirnín slán

ALL: Siúil, siúil, siúil a rún
Siúil go sochair agus siúil go ciúin
Siúil go doras agus éalaigh liom
Is go dté tú mo mhúirnín slán

MR DIAMOND: I wish, I wish, I wish in vain
I wish I had my heart again
And vainly think I'd not complain
Is go dté tú mo mhúirnín slán

On the street ...

DELIE: How yer feelin', lovey?
ROIE: Alright.

DELIE *nods. She goes to walk away.*

Miss Stock.

DELIE *turns.*

I know it was you who saved me that night. I remember what you did.

ACT THREE: THE HARP IN THE SOUTH

DELIE *nods.*

I wish you hadn't.

DELIE: Beg yours?

ROIE: I didn't deserve to be saved. 'Specially not now.

DELIE: Whatcha mean?

ROIE: If I hadn't have kissed Tommy, I wouldn't have got in trouble, which means I wouldn't have got beaten up, which means I wouldn't have got poorly, which means we would have taken better care of Grandma, which means she wouldn't have died alone in a Surry Hills gutter, which means she wouldn't be in that damn box you paid for.

DELIE: Ah, I see. Playin' the woman's part, are yer? Wrappin' yerself in guilt like yer nicked someone's rib?

ROIE *shrugs.*

Let me tell yer somethin', Roie. Kissin' a boy doesn't kill an old woman. 'Specially not the likes of your granny. She would've died whether that Mendel bloke knocked you up or not. She would've died whether you fought off them sailors or not. She would've died whether you even existed or not. Cos yer got things all back to front, see? You don't lead to her. She leads to you. Yer wouldn't be here without her. So you gotta get up and keep things goin'. Who knows what it'll lead to.

DELIE *goes to leave again.*

ROIE: Miss Stock. Do you have kids?

DELIE: I got me girls.

ROIE: What do you do in there all day? When you're not … you know.

Beat.

DELIE: We dream.

The procession starts to return.

I gotta get back. Business always picks up after a funeral.

She turns back to ROIE.

[*Smiling*] Don't worry, love. In no time at all you'll have four kids, cystitis, and never a spare moment to brood on past ambitions.

ROIE *blushes and heads inside.*

As the CONGREGATION *makes their way into their respective abodes,* MR GUNNARSON *starts to turn his barrel organ. 'Pop Goes the Weasel' plays.* DOLOUR *rifles through the mail forlornly.*

MISS SHEILY *appears.*

MISS SHEILY: A fine time to be playing a barrel organ. At a funeral! Caesar's ghost!

MR GUNNARSON: I liked the old lady. She always danced to my tunes.

MISS SHEILY: Well, there'll be no more of that now.

She goes to head inside.

MR GUNNARSON: Miss Sheily?

MISS SHEILY: Yes. What?

MR GUNNARSON: I like you. You are a lovely lady. Not married. I'd like to come and see you then and now.

MISS SHEILY: You dirty man. Using a funeral to pick up a woman. It's ghoulish, that's what it is, you disgraceful creature. Get away from here, at once!

MR GUNNARSON: I do not try to pick you up. I am a good man. And I am not dirty. I wash my hands many times a day. Look. And I have a good business. Here is my bank book. Look.

He shows her.

MISS SHEILY: Caesar's ghost!

MR GUNNARSON: I like when you say that. You have kick in you, Miss Sheily. Fire. I like that.

MISS SHEILY: I'll show you how much 'kick' I have in me. Right in the bottom. In. The. Bottom.

MISS SHEILY *hurries inside, passing* DOLOUR *as she exits the house.* MR GUNNARSON *beams.*

MR GUNNARSON: Hej då! I'm going to marry that lady, Dolour! Mark my words!

MR GUNNARSON *lopes away, playing 'Pop Goes the Weasel' on his barrel organ.* DOLOUR *stops rifling suddenly.*

DOLOUR: Oh, my stars.

She rips open a letter. Reads.

Oh, my stars! Mamma! Da! Roie!

ACT THREE: THE HARP IN THE SOUTH

I'm gonna be on the wireless! Oy! Surry Hills! *I'm gonna be on the wireless!*

SCENE TEN

The radio theatre.

A CROWD *gathers excitedly and takes their seats in an auditorium.*

MARGARET, HUGH *and* ROIE *take their seats amid the throng. They are overdressed for themselves, but underdressed for the event. They talk over the noise.*

HUGH: Jesus. Look at all the toffs here. We shouldn't be here, Missus.

MARGARET: We got every right to be here, Hughie. Our Dolour is doing us proud.

HUGH: She'll make fools of us further. With the whole world listenin' in. Jesus.

MARGARET: You alright, Ro?

ROIE: I'm fine. Just not used to being out.

HUGH: Jesus, what are we doin' here?

> *Loud music, applause and excited fanfare as a presenter,* BILL BRIGGS, *steps up to a microphone before the studio* AUDIENCE. *'He was a glittering individual in a white dinner jacket; his spectacles flashed semaphore messages of hope and cheer to the farthest corners of the theatre. Hugh hated him on the spot.'*

BILL BRIGGS: Hello, and welcome to the 'Junior Information, Please' quiz session on 2MB, brought to you by Ivory Soap.

> *The* AUDIENCE *applauds excitedly.*

I'm your compere, Bill Briggs.

> *The* AUDIENCE *applauds excitedly.*

Thank you. I know. I know. Thank you.

> *He quiets the* AUDIENCE *down.*

Now, a little housekeeping. I know you're all very excited to be here, but do try and keep silent during the show, unless the lovely Lyndall over there holds up this sign.

> *A* TRIO *of three singers—*LYNDALL, BERNICE *and* DENISE—

stands to the side in front of a microphone. LYNDALL *holds an 'APPLAUSE' sign.*

Shall we have a go?
Ready?
One ... two ... three ...

LYNDALL *holds up the sign. The* AUDIENCE *applauds.*

Good. Let's get started then, shall we?
And shhhhh.
Three ... two ... one ...

A fanfare of music. The TRIO *sing.*

TRIO: 'Junior ... Junior ... Junior Information, Please'! On 2MB ...

LYNDALL *holds up the applause sign.*

BILL: Welcome, welcome, to 'Junior Information, Please' on 2MB, brought to you by Ivory Soap.

LYNDALL *holds up the applause sign. The* AUDIENCE *obeys. Except* HUGH.

Are your rough hands snagging your stockings, ladies?
BERNICE and DENISE: [*together*] They sure are.
DENISE: It's all the dishwashing I do. My husband won't hold my hand at the pictures anymore.
BILL: No, no, ladies. Dishwashing isn't what hurts and ages your hands.
BERNICE: Isn't it?
DENISE: It isn't?
BILL: Of course not. It's the kind of soap you use.
BERNICE and DENISE: [*together*] Ohhh!
BILL: Strong soap is the villain of the dishpan. But if you use Pure Ivory, you've got as nice and gentle a soap as you'd use at your washbowl. Naturally, your hands will thank you. Soon they'll look like lady-of-leisure hands!
BERNICE and DENISE: [*together*] So no more snagged stockings?
BILL: That's right.
BERNICE and DENISE: [*together*] Ohhh!
BILL: And your husband will be proud to hold your hand.

HUGH *glances at* MARGARET'*s hands. She hides them from view.*

ACT THREE: THE HARP IN THE SOUTH

Pure Ivory Soap. For perfectly smooth hands that your dishes will love.

> LYNDALL *holds up the applause sign. The* AUDIENCE *obeys.*

Alright, let's get into it, shall we?
Our contestants today are Ernest Blainey from Potts Point.

> LYNDALL *holds up the applause sign. The* AUDIENCE *obeys. A primly-dressed boy,* ERNEST, *steps up to the microphone.*

Welcome, Ernie.

ERNEST: It's Ernest, Bill.

> *The* AUDIENCE *laughs.*

BILL: Well, my apologies, young man.
And Dolour Darcy from Surry Hills.

> *He has mispronounced her name.*

> LYNDALL *holds up the applause sign. The* AUDIENCE *obeys.*

> DOLOUR *steps up to the microphone and bumps her face into it.*

DOLOUR: It's Dolour, Bill.

> *The* AUDIENCE *laughs.*

HUGH: Jesus. Look at her. She's gonna make a fool of the lot of us.

BILL: Ernest, your first of three questions. Name all four of the Presidents who have recently been sculpted into the side of a mountain in America.

> *A clock ticks ...*

ERNEST: George Washington. Thomas Jefferson. Abraham Lincoln and Theodore Roosevelt.

BILL: Correct!

> LYNDALL *holds up the applause sign. The* AUDIENCE *obeys.*

ERNEST: The artist was Gutzon Borglum, Bill.

HUGH: Well, he didn't ask that, did he?

> DOLOUR *glares at her father from the stage as an* USHER *shines a torch on him crossly.*

What? That shouldn't count!

BILL: Hahahaha. Good work, Ernest. Right. Dolour.

He mispronounces Dolour's name throughout.

DOLOUR: Dolour.

BILL: Your first question. Which horse won the 1934 Melbourne Cup?

The clock ticks.

HUGH: Jesus. She doesn't know anything about betting. Who'd ask a little girl a question like that?

The torch shines on him again.

ROIE: Da. Shhh.

DOLOUR: Um … was it … was it Peter Pan?

BILL: Peter Pan is correct!

LYNDALL *holds up the applause sign. The* AUDIENCE *obeys.*

DOLOUR: He also won in 1932.

HUGH: Christ on a bike, I'm takin' her down the bookies with me next time.

BILL: Ernest, your next question. What creature died in 1936 in Hobart Zoo?

A clock ticks.

ERNEST: The last Tasmanian Tiger.

BILL: I'll need the scientific name, please, Ernest.

ERNEST *pauses.*

ERNEST: Tha … thal … thylacine?

BILL: Correct!

LYNDALL *holds up the applause sign. The* AUDIENCE *obeys.*

Thought we'd stumped you for a moment there, Ernie.

ERNEST: Ernest.

BILL: Dolour …

DOLOUR: Dolour.

BILL: … your second of three questions. What colour is a ten-pound note?

ERNEST: Oh, what?

DOLOUR *looks bewildered as the clock ticks.*

DOLOUR: Ten pounds?

BILL: Yes, Dolour.

ROIE: Dolour!

MARGARET: Well, that's not fair. She's never seen that amount of money in her life.

HUGH: Nor have I.

> DOLOUR *looks around worriedly.*

DOLOUR: Um ...

> *She picks at her red cardigan distractedly.*

Um ...

> ERNEST *sniggers.*

Is it ...
Red?

> *Beat.*

BILL: *Correct!*

> LYNDALL *holds up the applause sign. The* AUDIENCE *obeys.*

DOLOUR: I saw a tenner once! Delie Stock came to our school and pulled one right out of her bosom!

BILL: Hahaha. Did she? And now for your final question, Ernie.

ERNEST: Ernest.

BILL: When were women given the right to vote in the state of New South Wales?

> ERNEST *is immediately stumped. The clock ticks.*

ERNEST: Who?

BILL: Women, Ernie.

ERNEST: Women?

> *Beat.*

Women?

> DOLOUR *bites her lip expectantly.*

I ... don't know.

> *The* AUDIENCE *sighs.*

BILL: Well, that puts quite a spin on things, doesn't it? Dolour ...

DOLOUR: Dolour.

BILL: ... if you get the next question right, you take home the three-pound jackpot.

HUGH: Three pounds? Gawn there, Dolour. Gawn.

The torch shines across him again.

BILL: Who is the patron saint of aviators?

The clock ticks.

HUGH: Oh, for—
MARGARET: Now, wait, Hughie.
HUGH: What kind of a fuckin' question is that?

The torch shines on him again.

ROIE: She knows saints. She does. Never stops!

DOLOUR *bites her lip* ...

DOLOUR: The patron saint of aviators. Is an aviator like an airman?
BILL: Or airwoman.

He winks at the AUDIENCE. *They laugh.*

DOLOUR: Patron saint of airmen and airwomen …
Is it …?
It's …

She looks confused.

Is it Saint Joseph of Cupertino?

BILL *looks stunned.*

BILL: Uh …

He checks his card.

Uh … yes. Correct.

A bewildered LYNDALL *holds up the applause sign.*

The AUDIENCE *obeys.*

HUGH *is on his feet, screaming.*

HUGH: Yes! *Yes!* That's my little girl! That's my Dolour! Smartest kid in Sydney!
DOLOUR: I thought it must be Saint Joseph of Cupertino! He wasn't very clever, as far as saints go, but he could levitate as high as a tree!
BILL: Is that right? Well, congratul—
DOLOUR: And I know when women were allowed to vote here too!

ACT THREE: THE HARP IN THE SOUTH

Nineteen oh-two! My Grandma Eny told me that. She died a few weeks ago.

BILL: Hahahaha! Did she? Now, Dolour, here's your three pounds. Don't spend it all at once. Unless it's on Ivory Soap, that is.

DOLOUR: I'd never waste it on soap, Bill Briggs.

BILL: Hahaha. Well, thanks for listening in, at home. Stay tuned for the evening news, brought to you by the smooth, rich taste of Camel cigarettes—the brand recommended by ninety per cent of doctors.

> LYNDALL *holds up the applause sign. The* AUDIENCE *obeys.*
>
> *The* TRIO *sings as the* AUDIENCE *is hurried out.*

TRIO: [*singing*] 'Junior … Junior … Junior Information, Please'! On 2MB …

> *As* HUGH *and* MARGARET *hurry off to find* DOLOUR, ROIE *lags behind.*

HUGH: Dolour! Show us the cash!

DOLOUR: Look, Da! Mamma, look!

> *The studio is almost empty.*
>
> ROIE *clutches her head as she follows.*
>
> *She falls, unseen by her family.*
>
> *A young man who is departing with the* AUDIENCE *turns back to see her. He is* CHARLIE. *He rushes to her. 'He had the sort of heart that great men have. Straightforward, undeviating and tranquil.'*

CHARLIE: Are you alright?

ROIE: I'm awfully sorry. It's … it's the heat. And the crowd. I've been poorly. Sorry.

CHARLIE: It's not your fault. Are you by yourself?

ROIE: No … my family are here. My sister just won three pounds.

CHARLIE: Oh, yeah! She was fun!

ROIE: She was.

CHARLIE: I'm Charlie.

ROIE: Oh. Rowena. Roie. Thank you.

> *He helps her to walk.*

MARGARET: Roie! We lost you in all the excitement!

DOLOUR: Look, Roie! Three pounds! Did you see?

ROIE: I did.
HUGH: Who's this, then?
ROIE: I … I felt a bit dizzy and this man helped me.
MARGARET: That's very kind of you, son. It's her first night out in a while.
CHARLIE: It's nothing. I hope you're feeling better soon, Roie. Good evening.

He goes to leave.

HUGH: Oy! You can't be goin' like that! Rescued our daughter, you did! Let's have a drink.
ROIE: Da, please … he's got somewhere else to go.
CHARLIE: I'm not one for drinking, sorry, sir.
HUGH: What's wrong with yer?
ROIE: Da!
HUGH: Where do you live, son?
CHARLIE: Got a lodging near Devonshire.
HUGH: We're practically neighbours!
Well, if you're ever near Plymouth Street, perhaps you'd like to drop by sometime for supper and wireless.

CHARLIE *breaks into a smile.*

CHARLIE: I'd like that. Thank you.
DOLOUR: We live at twelve-and-a-half.
CHARLIE: Alright. Goodbye.

And he wanders away.

HUGH: What a nice feller.
DOLOUR: Three whole pounds. I'm gonna buy you some new shoes, Mamma.
MARGARET: Think he was a native, that one.
HUGH: No. You think? Thought he'd just gotten some sun.
MARGARET: You just invited him to tea!
HUGH: You've got a Prod-hopper and a witch livin' upstairs, woman. What's an Aborigine for tea gonna matter?
DOLOUR: Three whole pounds!
MARGARET: Well, I suppose … What's his name?

ACT THREE: THE HARP IN THE SOUTH

ROIE *is still gazing in the direction* CHARLIE *left.*
ROIE: Charlie. His name is Charlie.

SCENE ELEVEN

The radio TRIO *sing a version of 'Toolie Oolie Doolie' as we shift to Plymouth Street.*

TRIO: When a fella meets a girl in Switzerland
    There's a certain thing he's gotta do
    He can never, never take her by the hand

    MR GUNNARSON's *voice takes over as he sings along with his barrel organ.*

MR GUNNARSON and TRIO: Till he learns to toolie oolie doo

    At Plymouth Street, MR GUNNARSON *waits on the street, singing the tune and beaming up at the Darcy house.*

    MISS SHEILY *peers out of her window down at him.*

MR GUNNARSON: When a Swiss boy goes calling
    On a Swiss miss in June
    Toolie oolie doolie doo
    He sings this pretty tune
    And he charms her like magic
    When he yodels this tune
    Toolie oolie doolie doo
    Beneath the Alpine moon

MISS SHEILY: Caesar's ghost!

    MISS SHEILY *appears at the door, looks around the street, and lets* MR GUNNARSON *in.*

    He kisses her on the cheek as he enters.

TRIO: The echo
    Goes higher
    And higher
    And soon their hearts are both on fire

    DOLOUR *runs inside, wearing a new dress. She spins in it*

happily. MARGARET *and* HUGH *follow behind.* HUGH *takes* MARGARET*'s hand and kisses it softly as they head inside.*

TRIO: When you get lonely
Now you know what to do
Toolie oolie doolie doo
And make your dreams come true …

ROIE *sits on the front porch and looks at the stars. She looks much better now.* MR DIAMOND *passes her, gives her head a ruffle as he cradles a bottle of brandy and totters inside.*

ROIE: When you get lonely
Now you know what to do
Toolie oolie doolie doo
And make your dreams come true …

As ROIE *sits on the porch,* CHARLIE *comes walking along the street.*

CHARLIE: Hello, Roie.
ROIE: Charlie. Hello.
CHARLIE: You waiting for someone?
ROIE: No. Just … getting some air.
CHARLIE: You're looking much better.
ROIE: Thank you. I've been feeling good lately.

He smiles at her.

CHARLIE: I just finished work so I thought I'd drop by again. Hope that's alright.
ROIE: How's the printery going?
CHARLIE: S'alright. Keeps me in a job. No chance of newspapers ever goin' outta style.
ROIE: I used to work at a factory.
CHARLIE: Did you?
ROIE: Yeah. On Marlborough Street. A long time ago. Never got fired either. Not like Dad.
CHARLIE: What'd you do?
ROIE: Poured lipstick. Once you know what's in 'em you'd never wanna wear 'em.

ACT THREE: THE HARP IN THE SOUTH

CHARLIE: [*smiling*] You don't need lipstick, Roie. You've got Irish hair. It's pretty.

ROIE: Do I? Thanks.

CHARLIE: I've got a bit of Irish in me. Apparently.

ROIE: Really?

CHARLIE: Not sure which side it's from. Never was told exactly.

ROIE: Couldn't your parents tell you?

CHARLIE: Don't know my parents. Not my real ones.

ROIE: Oh. I'm sorry.

He smiles at her. They fall into silence.

CHARLIE: Hey. If you could have anything in this world … anything at all … what would it be?

ROIE: Gosh, Charlie. No-one's ever asked me anything like that before. I guess … I'd like to see Paradise.

CHARLIE: You mean Heaven?

ROIE: No. More like the Garden of Eden.

CHARLIE: Where Adam and Eve lived?

ROIE: Yeah. Just a visit, mind you. Wouldn't want to stay there too long. Not fond of snakes.

CHARLIE: What would you do there?

ROIE: Climb a tree. Drink from a river. Ride a unicorn.

CHARLIE: That sounds nice.

She smiles.

ROIE: You know the one thing Mamma wants more than anything in the whole world? Besides getting Thady back.

CHARLIE: Who's Thady?

ROIE: My big brother. He got lost when he was little. But besides him, you know what Mamma wants?

CHARLIE: What's that?

ROIE: A permanent wave.

CHARLIE: What's that?

ROIE: Her hair curled. I've heard her praying for it when she thinks there's no-one home.

She smiles.

What would you have? If you could have anything in this world.

CHARLIE: I'd take you to the Trocadero. In the city. It's got red carpet. And a dance floor. And a bandstand. And men dressed in gowns and women dressed in suits!

ROIE: What? No!

CHARLIE: True! I'd take you to the Troc, Roie. With your Irish hair and no lipstick. And I'd dance you round that dance floor like you were the Queen of Sydney. Heck, you *are* the Queen of Sydney.

ROIE: Pffft. Get out, Charlie. No queens in Surry Hills.

CHARLIE: Hear that?

ROIE: What?

CHARLIE: The Troc. Callin' from George Street. Listen. Come on, let's dance.

ROIE: All I hear is Plymouth Street. Drunks and angry cats and rotting garbage.

CHARLIE: Beautiful. Come on.

A symphony of sound builds around them. He stands and holds out his hand.

She takes it.

They dance to the symphony of Surry Hills.

CHARLIE: When you get lonely
    Now you know what to do…

DOLOUR *appears above them. She watches them dance on …*

CHARLIE/ROIE: Toolie oolie doolie doo
    And make your dreams come true …

CHARLIE: Can I kiss you Roie?

ROIE: Yes please.

He does.

So … you've got no family, Charlie?

CHARLIE: Not that I know of.

ROIE: Well … you're welcome to visit mine as often as you like.

CHARLIE: Thanks. I will.

They smile at one another on the Surry Hills dancefloor, watched by DOLOUR. *She sings sadly…*

ACT THREE: THE HARP IN THE SOUTH

DOLOUR: When you get lonely
Now you know what to do
Toolie oolie doolie doo
And make your dreams come -

DOLOUR *watches forlornly as* ROIE *and* CHARLIE *dance on.*

SCENE TWELVE

DOLOUR *hurries down the stairs and into the kitchen where* MARGARET *is battling with Puffing Billy.* HUGH *is there too.*

MARGARET: Hang in there, Puffing Billy. Please. Just cook the damn sausages, you bastard piece of—
DOLOUR: What's that Charlie Rothe doin' at our house again? This is the fourth time this month! It's like he's bloody moved in!
MARGARET: Dolour! Language! Jesus, Mary and Joseph, what if God hears you?
DOLOUR: Sorry, God.
MARGARET: Now go and ask Mr Diamond if he's joining us for dinner, please.
DOLOUR: I thought he had twisted guts?
MARGARET: Go and ask him anyway.

 DOLOUR *sulks off.*

Hughie. About Charlie. And our Roie. She's in love with him. I think she's thinking about marrying.
HUGH: And why not? She's a pretty girl. She should be married.

He peers at MARGARET*'s face.*

And if you're thinkin' about her little slip-up with that Mendel bastard, then you can forget it, for there's many a girl who have made the same mistake and been no worse for it.

He looks at her pointedly. She's suddenly serious.

MARGARET: He's black, Hughie.
HUGH: And you're pink after a bath. What of it?
MARGARET: I'm scared of it.
HUGH: Scared of it? What are you scared of?

MARGARET: Of losing our past.

HUGH: Can't get more of a past than the likes of him, Missus. He's real Australian.

MARGARET: So are we!

HUGH: We're Irish!

MARGARET: I never even set foot in Ireland. I'm from Trafalgar. I'm from these Hills. I'm Australian.

Beat.

HUGH: You know ... sometimes ... when I look at him ... he reminds me of Jer.

MARGARET: Everything reminds you of Jer. A stool with a broken leg reminds you of Jer. A bent banana reminds you of Jer.

ROIE *enters with* CHARLIE.

HUGH: [*whispering*] I'll talk to him.

MARGARET: That's all I ask.

CHARLIE: Thank you for having me to dinner again, Mr and Mrs Darcy.

HUGH: Not at all. Not at all.

DOLOUR *enters.*

DOLOUR: Mr Diamond's guts are still twisted. And Miss Sheily and Mr Gunnarson are eatin' lobster.

HUGH: Jesus. That kraut would give her the eyes out of his head if she wanted to play marbles.

MARGARET *places a pot of stew on the table.*

MARGARET: Mutton sausages and baked potatoes. Say your own grace.

They serve.

DOLOUR *glares at* CHARLIE. ROIE *smiles at* CHARLIE.

MARGARET *glares at* HUGH *pointedly.* HUGH *smiles nervously at* CHARLIE.

HUGH: So ... Charlie. Don't get rumbustious now, mate, because there's no offence meant, and heaven knows I'm not the one to skite meself, having a hangman in the family, and me own brother Jer had a touch of *something* to him ... but could you be telling me where the dark blood in you comes out?

ACT THREE: THE HARP IN THE SOUTH

A moment of stunned silence.

CHARLIE: It comes out all over me, I guess.

HUGH: Righto.

HUGH shrugs at MARGARET *and eats on.* MARGARET *puts down her cutlery.*

MARGARET: It's just ... well ... what about the children?

ROIE *practically chokes.*

CHARLIE: What? My children?

MARGARET: Yes. I mean. What would they be?

CHARLIE: Oh, right. You mean if I were to, say ... marry Roie?

ROIE*'s jaw drops.* MARGARET *nods tersely.*

Yeah, right. I get you. Well ... I guess they'd be ... they'd probably be ... kids.

He grins winningly at ROIE.

HUGH: So ... so are you sayin' you want to marry my Roie, Charlie?

CHARLIE: More than anything. But it all depends on how Roie feels. Roie?

ROIE *is caught like a deer in headlights at the dinner table.*

CHARLIE *smiles at her.*

Beat.

Then ...

ROIE: How do I feel? I feel like ... Even here in twelve-and-a-half Plymouth South Street ... In the middle of Surry Hills ... I feel like I'm separate from everyone else. Like I'm ... an island.

She looks at CHARLIE.

But then, despite all the noise and people and voices, I met someone sort of ... quietly floating the same way, and I realised I don't need to be an island anymore.

Silence.

DOLOUR: What does *that* mean?

ROIE: It means yes.

She smiles at CHARLIE.

HUGH: [*beaming*] Not till I say so. I'm father. I'm the one that gets to say yes or no.

He thinks.

Yes.

MARGARET: [*same time as* HUGH] No.

CHARLIE: Pardon?

ROIE: Mamma!

MARGARET: How will we ever afford it? We can hardly afford a mutton sausage, let alone a wedding feast!

ROIE: It doesn't have to be big, Mamma. I just want to be married to Charlie. I'd be happy if there was no-one there at all except me and him.

DOLOUR: What?! Roie! Surely I'm a bridesmaid? You'll need someone to carry your train!

MARGARET: Goddlemighty, a train. Goddlemighty, a dress. Shoes. Goddlemighty. A church. Flowers. Goddlemighty. Goddlemighty!

HUGH: I'll work a few extra shifts. We'll have the money in no time.

MARGARET: You'll have to do more than that, Hughie. The grog will have to go too.

HUGH: Maybe you should wait a little longer, Roie.

The family squabble over one another. CHARLIE *finally gets a word in.*

CHARLIE: *Oy!*

They fall silent.

I wouldn't dream of taking your money, Mr Darcy. I've got enough saved up to make it a nice wedding. Simple, but nice. Dolour, I'll make sure Roie has a beautiful train you can carry. And, Mr Darcy, I'll get you some shoes that are so shiny you'll be able to watch yourself walk her down the aisle. I'll make sure everyone at the wedding has a good feed and a nice time. I only want the best for Roie. And that's what I'm gonna give her.

Beat.

So … do you give us your blessing?

HUGH: I do.

ACT THREE: THE HARP IN THE SOUTH

ROIE *squeals. She hugs her father close.*

I'll see if Diamond's got something to pop. Or whiskey.

ROIE: Come on, Dolour! I've got a scrapbook of dresses! Let's go practise walking up the aisle!

They run upstairs, DOLOUR *less enthused than her sister.*

HUGH *heads up to Mr Diamond's room.* MARGARET *and* CHARLIE *are left behind.*

CHARLIE: I'll always do right by her, Mrs Darcy. You don't need to worry about that.

MARGARET *busies herself with clearing the table.*

I know that Roie always had a circle of warmth around her. And I will never break that. I'm just asking for your blessing to love her as much as you do.

MARGARET: I don't want this for her.

CHARLIE: What, this?

He gestures to himself.

MARGARET: No. This.

She gestures to herself.

CHARLIE: I promise I will shield her from every grief the world might bring.

MARGARET *nods.*

Do I have your blessing, Mrs Darcy?

MARGARET: Just Missus.

Silence.

CHARLIE: If Dolour is getting a train … and Roie is getting a dress … and Mr Darcy a pair of shiny shoes … is there something I can get you for the wedding, Missus?

MARGARET: Can you bring back my little boy?

CHARLIE: I can't.

MARGARET *shrugs.*

MARGARET: [*shaking her head*] Then no.

She cleans.

CHARLIE: But I do know a lovely hairdresser down near Devonshire Street. Does a good permanent wave. Ladies come all the way from Point Piper to have their dos done there.

    MARGARET *stops.*

MARGARET: A permanent wave …?

    She touches her hair delicately.

Me?

    CHARLIE *nods.*

[*Beaming*] Praise the Lord.

SCENE THIRTEEN

The Church.

SISTERS THEOPHILUS *and* BEATRIX *lay flowers around the pews. They sing 'My Happiness' as they decorate the church.*

SISTERS: Evening shadows make me blue
    When each weary day is through
    How I long to be with you
    My happiness

    They smile at one another.

    Every day I reminisce
    Dreaming of your tender kiss
    Always thinking how I miss
    My happiness

    *The church begins to fill with singing guests—*MR DIAMOND, LICK JIMMY, DELIE, HUGH *and a few others …*

ALL: A million years it seems
    Have gone by since we shared our dreams
    But I'll hold you again
    There'll be no blue memories then
    Whether skies are grey or blue
    Any place on earth will do
    Just as long as I'm with you
    My happiness …

ACT THREE: THE HARP IN THE SOUTH

MARGARET *hurries into the church. Her hair is a frizzed helmet—stiff and high on her head.*

HUGH: Sweet jumping Moses, whatjer done to yerself, woman?

MARGARET: I been permed!

HUGH: You look like an electrified goat!

MARGARET: It's my permanent wave. Charlie got it for me. Now shut your mouth.

She takes her place amongst the CONGREGATION.

CHARLIE *takes his place at the altar as* FATHER COOLEY *waits before him, along with the* SISTERS.

Everyone stands and sings …

ALL: A million years it seems
Have gone by since we shared our dreams
But I'll hold you again
There'll be no blue memories then
Whether skies are grey or blue
Any place on earth will do
Just as long as I'm with you
My happiness …

HUGH *walks* ROIE *down the aisle as* DOLOUR *walks sulkily behind, carrying flowers.*

HUGH *takes great pleasure in watching his reflection in his shiny shoes.*

CHARLIE *places a ring on* ROIE*'s finger and they kiss deeply.*

The CONGREGATION *throw confetti as the wedding ends.*

SCENE FOURTEEN

At Plymouth Street, the GUESTS *celebrate in the street outside 12½. Dancing, music, boozing.*

ROIE *dances with* CHARLIE. HUGH *drinks with* MR DIAMOND. LICK JIMMY *dances with* DELIE.

MRS SICILIANO *dances with a baby on her hip.* MARGARET *sits resting her feet.*

MISS SHEILY approaches as MR GUNNARSON waits nearby with a suitcase.

MISS SHEILY: I've come to wish you goodbye, Mrs Darcy.

MARGARET: What's that, Miss Sheily?

MISS SHEILY: Mr Gunnarson has asked me to marry him. I said yes. So that's that, then.

MARGARET: Oh. Well. Congratulations, Miss Sheily.

MISS SHEILY: We'll be going to the registry tomorrow so I'll only be spending one night of sin with him. I figured you'll need the spare room for the newlyweds, so I'm sure God will forgive me my transgression. The bed is made and the room is clean for tonight. You needn't give up your own room for them.

MARGARET: Much appreciated, Miss Sheily.

MISS SHEILY: You were very kind to poor Johnny. Thank you.

MARGARET: I loved him, Miss Sheily. We all did. It was a pleasure to have him in the house.

MISS SHEILY nods, tearful. MR GUNNARSON hurries over.

MR GUNNARSON: Ready, my darling?

He kisses her cheek.

MISS SHEILY: Stop licking me, you old octopus.

She hits him.

MR GUNNARSON: [*beaming*] Ain't I a lucky one!

They start to walk away.

MARGARET: Miss Sheily …

MISS SHEILY turns back.

Before you go. Would you mind telling me … what's your first name?

Beat. MISS SHEILY's face softens unexpectedly.

MISS SHEILY: Isabel.

MARGARET: Isabel. Of course.

Beat.

The two women share a smile. MISS SHEILY leaves with MR GUNNARSON. HUGH drinks with MR DIAMOND.

ACT THREE: THE HARP IN THE SOUTH

HUGH: I'm not an old man yet, Diamond. I remember what old looks like. Me da with his angry fists and me ma with her stripped throat. Thass old. I'm not old yet. We're not old, are we, Missus? Missus?!

He calls out to MARGARET, *who is rubbing her feet, her hair in a perm.*

Jesus. We're old. My wife's turned into a damn nanny goat.

MR DIAMOND: You should have remained a bachelor like me, Darcy. There's nothin' like it for peace and contentment.

HUGH *weeps into* MR DIAMOND'*s shoulder.*

MR DIAMOND *pats him on the back gently and then winces in pain, groaning.*

HUGH: Indigestion, Diamond?

MR DIAMOND *nods and rubs his tummy.*

MR DIAMOND: Me old pal.

HUGH: Look at us in me shoes, Diamond.

HUGH *holds up his feet.*

MR DIAMOND: We look very handsome, Darcy. Very handsome indeed.

They stare at their reflection ... and drink the pain away. ROIE *and* CHARLIE *start to head inside.*

ROIE: Bye! Time for us to go!
CHARLIE: Bye!
ROIE: Bye, Da! Bye, Mamma! Bye, Dolour! See you in the morning!
MARGARET: Go well, my darling! I'll be up the hall if you need anything!

MARGARET *is a sobbing mess.*

ROIE: Oh, Mamma!
HUGH: Go! Go on, you two, before the street floods.

They hurry away.

DOLOUR *is with* HARRY DRUMMY *as she glares at* CHARLIE *leaving with her sister.*

DOLOUR: My sister, she is. And he just waltzes in like some kind of tomcat and takes her away.
HARRY: Aren't they goin' on a honeymoon?

DOLOUR: They wanna save up for a place to live. So they're honeymooning at home.
HARRY: So they could be sinkin' the sausage? Up there? Right now?
DOLOUR: Don't be so hideous, Harry.
HARRY: That's what newlyweds do, isn't it? Soon as they leave, they're at it. Knickers down and knocked up. Everyone knows that.

> DOLOUR *whacks him.*

DOLOUR: I'm warning you, Drummy. That's my sister you're talking about.
HARRY: Not anymore. She's his wife now.

> *Beat.*

DOLOUR: She'll never love him the way she loves me. Me and Roie are tight as trousers. He can't take that away, that Charlie Rothe.
HARRY: You look different.
DOLOUR: How'd you mean?
HARRY: Dunno.
DOLOUR: It's probably my diamante belt buckle. I bought it with my winnings from 'Junior Information' Quiz.

> HARRY *looks at the buckle then back at* DOLOUR.

HARRY: You definitely look different.

> *Beat.*
>
> *He pulls her hair.*

DOLOUR: *Ow!* What'd you do that for, Drummy?
HARRY: Felt like it.

> LICK JIMMY *passes with a piece of fruit.*

DOLOUR: Lick! Lick! Is that a poor man's orange? Can we have a bit?

> LICK JIMMY *eats a piece of orange.*

LICK JIMMY: Not ready.

> DOLOUR *groans impatiently.*
>
> *As ...*
>
> HUGH *stops weeping.*

HUGH: I need to dance. I need to *dance*, Diamond!

ACT THREE: THE HARP IN THE SOUTH 141

HUGH *leaps to his feet and dances around wildly, pulling* MARGARET *to her feet and twirling her as the night fades ...*

SCENE FIFTEEN

CHARLIE *and* ROIE *are upstairs. The room has been decorated with flowers and candles.*

ROIE: Charlie. It's paradise!

CHARLIE: Only the best for you, Roie. I asked Miss Sheily if I could do it up nice.

    ROIE *runs to the window.*

Look at them all down there. What a party.

    CHARLIE *watches her.*

CHARLIE: They'll keep going till morning. Come here.

    She turns, nervous.

Don't worry. I'll look after you.

    He starts to take off his clothes. She stares, stunned.

This is me, Roie.

ROIE: I know. I've just never …

CHARLIE: Come here.

    She goes to him. He runs her hands over his skin. Meanwhile ...

    MARGARET *leads a drunken* HUGH *and* MR DIAMOND *upstairs.*

MR DIAMOND: I love you, Hughie. I love you.

MARGARET: Quiet, Patrick. They'll be consummating.

    She puts him in his room where he passes out on the floor.

    MARGARET *gets* HUGH *to their bedroom.*

    DOLOUR *lays on her bed. All hers for the first time ever.*

    ROIE *takes off her wedding dress. She stands in her slip.*

    MARGARET *takes off* HUGH*'s shoes and socks.*

    DOLOUR *takes off her diamante belt.*

    CHARLIE *sits on the bed.* ROIE *doesn't move.*

MARGARET *takes off her dress, revealing old, tattered undergarments.*

HUGH: You want me to loosen your stays, Missus?

She smiles sadly at her husband as he stares up at her with bleary eyes.

MARGARET: That's what got me into this mess, Hughie.

In the newlyweds' room ...

CHARLIE: You're beautiful, Roie.

ROIE: I'm scared, Charlie.

CHARLIE: Of me?

ROIE: No. Of me.

CHARLIE: You don't ever have to be scared again, Roie. Not with me here. We'll make this Paradise.

He holds out his arms to her.

She walks to the bed and sits beside him. They kiss gently.

DOLOUR *lays back on her bed and reaches out for her sister. She's not there.* DOLOUR *starts to cry, alone in her room.*

MARGARET *prays by the edge of her own bed.*

MARGARET: Twenty years, seven months and …

She turns to see THADY *watching her. She smiles.*

What I wouldn't give to see him again.

HUGH *sits up groggily.*

HUGH: Who, Missus? Jer?

MARGARET: What I wouldn't give to smell his skin. His breath. Hold his little hand in mine.

HUGH *strokes his wife's hair.*

HUGH: Let's wait and see, Missus. Wait and see.

ROIE *pulls away from* CHARLIE *slightly. He looks her deep in the eyes.*

CHARLIE: I've never been with anyone before, Roie. I'm as new to this as you are.

ROIE: You're mine and I'm yours. You're mine and I'm yours.

ACT THREE: THE HARP IN THE SOUTH

ROIE *then lays* CHARLIE *down on the bed, sitting astride him.*

DOLOUR *puts her ear to the wall and listens in.*

DOLOUR: You're mine and I'm yours. You're mine and I'm yours.

MARGARET *sits on the bed as* HUGH *holds her.*

HUGH: Whatjer thinking of, my old hen? My Missus.

MARGARET *smiles sadly at* HUGH. *She kisses him deeply.*

MARGARET: I was thinking of … I was thinking of how lucky we are.

HUGH *grins.*

HUGH: You're mine and I'm yours.

He rolls over to sleep.

MARGARET: You're mine and I'm yours.

'You're mine and I'm yours' is picked up by the RESIDENTS *of Plymouth Street like a distant thrum.*

THADY *exits the house through the front door.*

A MAN *appears and pins up notices on houses.*

THADY *watches the* MAN.

The chanting of 'You're mine and I'm yours' resonates from every house on Plymouth Street.

The MAN *departs.*

THADY *takes a notice from the door of 121/2 Plymouth Street.*

He holds up the notice as the thrumming chorus builds. It reads: 'SLUM CLEARANCE—SURRY HILLS'.

'You're mine and I'm yours' starts to climax as THADY *holds up the notice. Behind him, a house crashes to the ground.*

The thrum is silenced.

Blackout.

END OF ACT THREE

Dinner break: baked potatoes for all.

ACT FOUR: POOR MAN'S ORANGE

SCENE ONE

The harp echoes ...

The Plymouth Street Church.

MARGARET, DOLOUR, *a pregnant* ROIE, SISTERS THEOPHILUS *and* BEATRIX *and a few others kneel in the pews, to the strains of 'Last Rose of Summer'.*

FATHER COOLEY *steps up to the pulpit, a little slower than the last time we saw him.*

FATHER COOLEY: There is great sadness in these Hills.
　Open the doors, there. Up the back there—open the doors. Let some air in.

The doors are opened.

Look at that Sydney sky. Not a cloud. Not a grain of dust between the earth and the planets, it seems. It seems … vastly empty. And we feel we are alone, here in these Hills of Surry, Sydney. But I can tell you that sky is in fact crowded with stardust. Celestial mayflies accompanying us to sleep every night. These are a sign of God's continuing creation above us all. And it is a reminder that although we don't always see Him, He is there.
　He is there.
　Wave to Him. Let Him know you're here.

　　　THE CONGREGATION *waves to God.*

　And Dear Lord, right now in Plymouth Street, Surry Hills, we need You more than ever. Because I have here a newspaper. I know there's many of you out there have trouble with the printed word, so I'll read it aloud for you.
　[*Reading*] 'It has been decided by the powers that be that the slum area of Surry Hills will be acquired and redeveloped. The reduction of the stinking labyrinth of unnecessary streets and houses will give

ACT FOUR: POOR MAN'S ORANGE

additional land for industrial purposes, and, consequently, additional revenue to the City Council. The acquisition of housing in the area has begun and will be completed within the year.'

The CONGREGATION *gasps.*

They are closing us down, my friends. They are moving us on. We are a pestilence. An embarrassment. We are a festering boil on the pristine buttocks of this Harbour City, just waiting to be lanced with a red-hot needle.

But I can't help but feel this church has been closing down for years now. Where are your husbands? Your children? Where are your neighbours? Where is the music?

This little church used to ring with the voices of the Hills.

Now we are falling into silence. We are being *forced* into silence. And so I'm declaring a mission.

I want each and every one of you to get these Hills back in God's heart. I expect these pews to be filled with backsides by next Sunday.

Before they raze us to hell, I want there to be a queue of sinners out the door, clamouring for forgiveness. If this neighbourhood is atoned for, then God will be on our side.

Now let us raise our voices so that those bastards can hear us at Town Hall.

SCENE TWO

MARGARET *makes her way from the church to the pub.* ROIE *and* DOLOUR *hurry after her.*

MARGARET: *Hughie!*
DOLOUR: Dad!
MARGARET: *Hughie!*
DOLOUR: *Dad!*

She leans through the window.

MARGARET: Oy! Get Hugh Darcy for me. *Now!*

She paces outside the pub.

Ninety years, my house has been on Plymouth Street! When Surry

Hills was still green and Lick Jimmy's was still loquat trees. Our house stood all by itself then.

Hugh Darcy!

And now they want to knock it down! They want to knock us all down!

A couple of BARFLIES *appear at the bar windows.*

BARFLY 1: What do yer mean, knock us down?

DOLOUR: They wanna make our houses into factories and flats.

BARFLY 2: Flats? What's flats?

MARGARET: It's them parliamenticians! I'd like to see them tossed out of house and home, the very places where their mothers and fathers were brought up, getting turned into shoebox towers and communist laundries and the dear knows what!

Hugh Darcy, get out here now!

Well, I won't go! They'll have to haul me out with ropes first! We got a grandchild on the way! And how will Thady know how to get home if they knock the damn thing down?

HUGH *appears at the pub door.*

HUGH: What is it, Missus?

MARGARET: Hugh Darcy, sinner that you are, I'm going to be forcing you to confession for Father Cooley's mission.

HUGH: What?

MARGARET: They're gonna rip the floor out from under us like they did right through Frog Hollow! They've already smashed the Sicilianos. The Maloneys. And the Chans. God's punishing us for the sins on our streets. He's hurling his vengeance down upon us. *So, you lot—get your arses outta that pub and into the bloody pews!*

HUGH: Ah, Missus. Can't God wait till after the swill?

Suddenly, a flurry of activity hurries up the street. A small mob of CAMERAMEN *and* REPORTERS *follow* DELIE STOCK *as she swaggers and poses in front of her brothel.*

KIDGER *lurks behind her.*

'*Delie's hair had been set and lacquered about three weeks before, and now it was like a doll's wig, growing in thick clumps, some in waves and some in a fuzz, all stiff and greyish with cracked lacquer.*'

ACT FOUR: POOR MAN'S ORANGE

DELIE: I ain't changed me slippers, but you won't want me feet when you can get me pan. Get out of me frame, Kidger.

The REPORTERS *chuckle as they snap her face.*

REPORTER 1: Now, Mrs Stock, you're a well-known citizen of Surry Hills …

DELIE: I'll say. Been up before the beak more times than you could count.

REPORTER 2: Would you care to give a statement about the proposed resumption of Surry Hills?

DELIE: Stinkin' mongrels. Howzat for a statement?

REPORTER 3: What about the electric stoves they're promising for every kitchen?

DELIE: Can't put yer head in an electric oven when you've had enough of livin', can yer?

The REPORTERS *chuckle.*

No-one asked us if we want to be chucked out of our houses. We've got along alright for years here. I spent a lot of money on my place too. Only last week I got the kitchen kalsomined a lovely blue, real pretty it is, and only a bit streaky round the sink. Now the bloody council comes and wants to widen the streets and put up factories and build flats with private fishponds. Who wants a bloody fishpond? A fish wouldn't last five minutes with the stray cats in these Hills. And where are they gonna put us while they put up these bloody beehives? How far out are they gonna send us? At this rate they'll have us livin' in bloody cardboard boxes in Kal-bloody-goorlie! Nah. This is where us lot belong.

Beat. She casts a gaze at the onlookers in the street.

'Course, they'd all be happy if I just fucked off. But they'd miss me. They would.

And me gettin' me mug in the paper will do more than any bloody church 'mission' will do. Half them town councillors are my clients.

So. Save Surry Hills. Girls?

DELIE'S GIRLS: *Save Surry Hills!*

DELIE: One more pic? Make sure yer get me do. Just had me pompadour lacquered.

She lifts her dress to bare her leg a little.

Get outta me fuckin' *frame*, Kidger!

> *The cameras click exuberantly.* DELIE *swaggers into her house and slams the door, as she and her girls chant 'SAVE SURRY HILLS!'* KIDGER *stands guard at the door.*

SCENE THREE

As the OTHERS *head into their abodes and the* REPORTERS *depart, a teenage girl,* SUSE, *is left leaning against a wall. 'She didn't care that there were holes in her black stockings, or that her greenish gym tunic was ripped at one side.'*

DOLOUR: Hi, Suse!
SUSE: What's buzzin', cousin?
DOLOUR: Nothin' much. Watcher waiting for?
SUSE: Fellas. Seems I'll have to go searchin'. Wanna come?

> DOLOUR *hesitates. She looks back at the house.*

Come on. Yer sixteen, aren't yer?
DOLOUR: Yeah. It's just … Mamma likes to know when I'm takin' off.
SUSE: Ugh. Yer such a pain in the tit, Dolour.

> CHARLIE *and* ROIE *appear.*

ROIE: Hello, Suse. How's your mother?
SUSE: Patchin' up the old pram for a bit more work. She's up to number six.

> SUSE *stares at* ROIE*'s belly.*

ROIE: Oh, send her my congratulations.
SUSE: Soon as she's sober.
ROIE: Pardon?
SUSE: Sure will!
ROIE: I'll tell Mamma you've gone for a stroll, Dolour.
CHARLIE: Here. Buy yourselves an ice-cream.

> *He hands* DOLOUR *some coins. She scowls.* SUSE *takes it and gives him a coquettish smile.*

SUSE: Killer-diller. Thanks, Charlie.

> *As they walk …*

ACT FOUR: POOR MAN'S ORANGE

He's nice, ain't he?
DOLOUR: Who? Charlie? No.
SUSE: How long they bin hitched?
DOLOUR: About a year.
SUSE: How many kids they got?
DOLOUR: None. Roie has tummy problems. But this one looks like it might get through.
SUSE: Ever caught 'em fucking?
DOLOUR: Get out …
SUSE: I'll bet he's a right stinger. I wouldn't mind a go.
DOLOUR: Shut your mouth! Don't you ever think of anything else?
SUSE: 'Course not. Do you?
DOLOUR: I just been to Benediction!
SUSE: Hey! He gave us two bob! Let's get some grog!
DOLOUR: I've … already had the blood of Christ today.

But SUSE *has hurried away.* DOLOUR *follows reluctantly … to the pub.*

It is raucous. SUSE *stands outside the window as* DOLOUR *stands beside her, trying to look invisible.*

SUSE: Bobby! Oy, Bobby! Get us a schooner! A sherry! Anything!

She waves the money at him.

Two bob! Oy, Bobby! Benny! Two bob!

A hand takes the money.

LEERING BARFLY: What else you got, Suse?
SUSE: I'll only show yer if yer get one fer me mate here.

The LEERING BARFLY *sizes up* DOLOUR.

LEERING BARFLY: Orright.

SUSE *looks around. Lifts her dress.* DOLOUR *is horrified. The* LEERING BARFLY *grins and heads back inside.*

HUGH *stumbles out of the pub.*

DOLOUR *sees him and hides, terrified, as he weaves down the street.*

DOLOUR: Cripes. Cripes. Cripes. Cripes …

The LEERING BARFLY *gives* SUSE *two glasses of beer. She hands one to* DOLOUR *and starts to chug down her own.* DOLOUR *does the same but spits it aside when* SUSE *isn't watching.* SUSE *downs the rest of the booze and tosses the glass aside.*

SUSE: Carn. Let's go to the pitchers. We can pretend our elbows are Rock Hudson.

DOLOUR: Huh?

SUSE *demonstrates. It's graphic.*

SCENE FOUR

Plymouth Street.

HUGH *is outside Mr Diamond's room.*

HUGH: Diamond! Oy, you ol' Prod-hopper! Why weren't you at the swill?

MR DIAMOND *lays on his bed in his underwear, clutching his gut.*

MR DIAMOND: I … I couldn't make it today, Darcy. Did you bring anything home for me?

HUGH: No. I was hopin' you might have a little somethin' in there. Let me in.

Beat. MR DIAMOND *groans in agony.*

Diamond?

Another groan.

Pat?

HUGH *tries the door. It opens.*

He sees MR DIAMOND *lying on the bed.*

Jesus, man.

MR DIAMOND: Hughie. Come here.

HUGH *walks to him, wincing at the smell in the room.*

HUGH: Christ almighty, Pat. Watcher been cookin' in here?

MR DIAMOND: You know me indigestion, Darcy?

HUGH: Like an old pal.

MR DIAMOND: Well, it ain't.

He takes HUGH*'s hand and places it on his bare belly.* HUGH *is horrified.*

ACT FOUR: POOR MAN'S ORANGE

HUGH: The fuck is that, Patrick?
MR DIAMOND: I think it's a fish, Hughie.
HUGH: What's it doin' inside yer?
MR DIAMOND: Swimmin'. Just swimmin' round and round the one spot over and over again. Burnin' and churnin' me up inside. Damn fish.
HUGH: Goddlemighty.

He goes to remove his hand.

MR DIAMOND: Leave it there, Hughie. Feels nice.

HUGH *leaves his hand on* MR DIAMOND*'s belly.*

HUGH: You're not well, Pat.
MR DIAMOND: I know.

Beat.

I'm enterin', Hughie.
HUGH: Enterin' what?
MR DIAMOND: The Church.

Dumbfounded silence.

HUGH: You mean the Catholic Church, Patrick Diamond?

MR DIAMOND *nods.*

MR DIAMOND: I've not got long, Darcy. So just in case.

Silence. HUGH *removes his hand.*

HUGH: You dirty, stinkin' scoundrel of a scab, Diamond. To think I been nursin' you in me bosom all these years and this is how you repay me.
MR DIAMOND: I thought you'd be pleased. I thought you'd want me to turn.
HUGH: Orangemen never turn Catholic! How dare you, man!
MR DIAMOND: But the fish, Hughie. The fish is makin' me turn. Put yer hand back on me belly, Hughie.
HUGH: Drinkin' me booze and eatin' me sausages all these years and then sayin' a thing like that. You're not fit for decent society, Diamond. You can't be trusted to stick to yer own principles.
MR DIAMOND: I'll do what I like without the interference of any boneheaded tike! *Put yer hand back on me belly!*
HUGH: Listen to yer! Blaspheming against the sacred name of the

Church while yer talkin' about enterin' it! Yer just a stinkin' old heathen who wants to seek grace when yer on yer last pins.

> MR DIAMOND *rears up furiously and the two men struggle with one another, dopily and drunkenly.*

MR DIAMOND: Put yer hand on me, Hughie! Please put yer hand on me!

> *They end up on the floor, entwined.*

> MR DIAMOND *weeps, holding* HUGH's *hand to his belly.*

Please, Hughie. I need yer to tell Father Cooley that I've joined his mission. I need yer to do it tomorrow, Hughie. Please. Tell him. Please. I can't do it by meself. And you're all I got.

> MR DIAMOND *weeps in* HUGH's *arms as we shift ...*

SCENE FIVE

ROIE *is at the doctors' rooms. She wears a long calico gown and lays on a cubicle table nervously. In the space, partitioned by a curtain, lays an old woman,* MRS WILEY.

HUGH *is also partitioned. He is reluctantly inside the confession box in the church, separated by a tatty curtain from* FATHER COOLEY.

DOCTOR EVANS *enters Roie's cubicle, along with three other young men,* TRAINEES *in white coats.*

DOCTOR EVANS: Hello. Rowena Rothe?
ROIE: Oh. Yes. Doctor Evans?
DOCTOR EVANS: Yes.
ROIE: Who … who are they?
DOCTOR EVANS: Oh, don't mind them. They're all going to be doctors one day. They have to learn somehow. Now lay back and don't worry about a thing.

> ROIE *looks worriedly at the men.* MRS WILEY *peers through the curtain.*

We're professionals, Mrs Rothe. You're just another woman having a baby to us.

ROIE: Yes … but … I'm not just another woman to me.

> *They stare at her blankly. She lays back reluctantly. The* DOCTOR *examines her as the others move in close to observe.*

ACT FOUR: POOR MAN'S ORANGE

In the confession booth ...

HUGH: Bless me, Father, for I have sinned. It has been ... thirty-one years since my last confession.

FATHER COOLEY: Thirty-one years? This may take some time then.

HUGH: Ah, Father. I heard about your mission. And it's a good thing you're doin', while they're tryin' to rip our streets out from under us. And I do have many things to confess. Many, many things. But I'm here today for a friend, you see.

FATHER COOLEY: I cannot give absolution to someone who is not here.

HUGH: He's unable to make it, Father. He's got a fish inside him. I don't think he's long for this world. And I'm not asking for atonement for him. Just to ask you to ask God to open the gates to him when he gets there soon.

FATHER COOLEY: It is not for me to say who God lets into the Kingdom, child.

HUGH: But He's less likely to let an Orangeman in than one of us, isn't that right, Father?

FATHER COOLEY: He's Orange, this fella who wants atoning?

HUGH: Was. He wants to enter our flock. Before he goes.

FATHER COOLEY: Is he Catholic in the heart, do you think?

HUGH: He is a few things in his heart, Father. What he holds in his heart may seem strange to the likes of you. He loves differently to most men I know. He is a bachelor of the most unique kind. He is a gentle man. A diamond, even. And I know that in his heart, he has true honour, Father. I know that. I've spent many an hour with the fella. He's the closest thing I've had to a brother since ...

FATHER COOLEY: I see ...

Beat.

I tell you what. I'll have a word to God about your friend if you confess to me what's in your heart after thirty-one years of sinning without penance.

HUGH: Ah, Father ... I'm really just here for me mate Pat.

FATHER COOLEY: Remember your soul, my child.

HUGH: I believe my choices over these past thirty-one years have delivered me plenty of penance, Father. Now, I don't want to take up your time. Just tell me that God will welcome my friend. Tell him his name is Mr Patrick Diamond.

FATHER COOLEY: But I must hear *your* sins, my child.

HUGH: Father, please. Tell him his name is Patrick Diamond.

FATHER COOLEY: Hugh Darcy, you confess your sins here and now or, by God, the wrath you'll be faced with when you meet the Maker will make my penance look like a smack on the knuckles.

In the hospital cubicle ...

DOCTOR EVANS: I thought this was your first baby, Mrs Rothe?

ROIE: It is ... I ... lost one a little while back.

DOCTOR EVANS: Yes, I can see that. [*To the* TRAINEES] As you can see, signs of severe trauma.

ROIE *winces as he pokes between her legs.*

Still, this one looks well enough. Note down this area here ... and here ...

He pokes around beneath the smock as the TRAINEES *take notes. One takes a picture.* MRS WILEY *hurls back the curtain and gapes at the doctors.*

MRS WILEY: 'Ere! What's she got, a picture house up her dress?

DOCTOR EVANS: These are future doctors, Mrs Wiley. It's important for them to see case studies like Mrs Rothe here. It's for the good of all women, you know.

MRS WILEY: Yeah? Then why not use *all* women as guinea pigs, eh? Why only public hospitals?

DOCTOR EVANS: We are here to help, Mrs Wiley. Regardless of locale.

MRS WILEY: Yeah? Do you ever go into a posh private hospital out Vaucluse or Point Piper with your tribe of louts with their eyes stickin' out like boiled onions and let them have a squint at those women's pampered poodles? Nice stink if you did, eh? No-one would dream of subjecting a rich man's wife to clinical rape, but the poor man's wife is different, eh?

DOCTOR EVANS *steps back, appalled.*

DOCTOR EVANS: Thank you, Mrs Rothe. That will be all we need today.

ROIE *gets off the bed quickly and smoothes down the smock.*

ROIE: Is ... is everything alright with my baby?

DOCTOR EVANS: Seems to be.

ACT FOUR: POOR MAN'S ORANGE 155

ROIE: And everything's alright with me?
DOCTOR EVANS: As right as can be.

> *And they are gone.* ROIE *gathers her things. She smiles shyly at* MRS WILEY.

ROIE: Thank you.

> MRS WILEY *stares intently at her belly.*

MRS WILEY: It's a boy.

> MRS WILEY *shuts the curtain.*
>
> *Scene Six can form here.*
>
> *In the confession box ...*
>
> HUGH *pulls back the curtain. Furious.*

HUGH: Fuck your mission, Cooley. You heartless bastard. All you had to do was tell God to welcome Patrick Diamond into His Kingdom. Why does that bearded bastard have to shut the door on us if we don't live up to His standard of man?

Why do we have to wallow in guilt every day of our fuckin' lives? I didn't ask Jesus to die for me! I'm perfectly capable of doing that myself! I die for my sins a little every fuckin' day of my life and He dares threaten my eventual salvation because I don't share them with *you*? A man in a fuckin' dress? A man who has never laid in the arms of someone he loves? Who has never held his own living, breathing child in his shaking arms? Who has never worked in a factory? Never fought in a brawl? Never drowned himself in liquor? What fear do you have?

What shame? What sins? Fuck you and your mission, Father. Fuck God and His fucking locked gates. Fuck you all.

> HUGH *storms out of the church and sits in a gutter, his head in his hands.*

SCENE SIX

A woman, FLORRIE, *sings on a street corner and sings in Italian—'Ti Parlero di'Amore'.*

FLORRIE: Ti parlerò d'amor
　　　　　e sfoglierò una rosa
　　　　　sulla tua bocca ansiosa
　　　　　che non conosco ancor
　　　　　　HUGH *lifts his head. Watches.*
　　　　　Ti parlerò d'amor
　　　　　con voce sospirosa
　　　　　non c'è più dolce cosa
　　　　　per far felice il cuor
　　　　　Dammi i tuoi folli baci
　　　　　stringiti forte a me
　　　　　chiudi i tuoi occhi amore taci
　　　　　voglio sognare con te
　　　　　　FLORRIE *smiles at* HUGH *as she sings. He is transfixed.*
Hello.
　　HUGH *looks around. Is she talking to him?*
HUGH: Hell … hello.
FLORRIE: Are you alright?
HUGH: Yes.
　　He stands.
Pretty song.
FLORRIE: 'Ti Parlero di'Amore'.
HUGH: Oh.
FLORRIE: 'Let Me Tell You About Love'.
　　HUGH *nods at her, transfixed.*
HUGH: Orright.
　　She laughs.
FLORRIE: That's what the song means. In Italian.
HUGH: Oh.

ACT FOUR: POOR MAN'S ORANGE

He laughs with her.

You headin' to church? For the mission?
FLORRIE: No. Just singing in the street. I don't care much for church.
HUGH: Me neither.

Beat.

Jupiter, Mars, Venutio and Mercutio, you look like you belong in a painting. If you don't mind me saying.
FLORRIE: No.
HUGH: You live around here?
FLORRIE: I have just moved into the neighbourhood.
HUGH: Oh, yeah ... Where?
FLORRIE: I live at Delie Stock's house. Do you know this place?

She smiles at him sweetly.

HUGH: I know it. But in all my years, I've never been inside it, unlike most fellas round here.

She smiles and nods.

Well ... I best be off. Hughie, by the way.
FLORRIE: Florentina.
HUGH: Itie, are yer?
FLORRIE: Yes.
HUGH: Florentina.
FLORRIE: Florrie.
HUGH: Florrie. Like a painting, you are.

Beat.

Welcome to Surry Hills, Florrie.

He smiles and walks away as FLORRIE *starts singing again ...*

SCENE SEVEN

At 121/2 Plymouth Street.

CHARLIE *sits at the table with* ROIE *and a newspaper.*

ROIE: Four pounds?! For Pyrmont?!
CHARLIE: Now Surry Hills is getting torn down, the rental prices are

through the roof. [*Pointing to the paper*] Look—this bastard's charging three bob for a bed on a landing.

ROIE: No children allowed ... No children allowed ... Six pound, four pound, no children allowed ... No ...

She stops herself. CHARLIE *takes the paper.*

CHARLIE: Blacks.

ROIE: [*furious*] How dare they? Wasn't long ago that Pyrmont was a slum too. Bloody suburb smells of fish scales and backyard booze and now they think they're the new Bellevue bloody Hill? Well, they can keep their backwards opinions to themselves. We wouldn't lower ourselves to their standards anyway. I'm not having my baby wading through fish guts with its first steps.

ROIE *throws the paper across the room.*

CHARLIE: So where will we go?

ROIE: We don't need to go anywhere. We've got a room right here.

CHARLIE: Ro, they're knockin' down houses along Albion Street. Frog Hollow doesn't even exist anymore. Plymouth Street is next. We'll be flattened by Christmas.

ROIE: The mission will help. God won't let us fall. We've got a church, a pub and a brothel all on the one street. We'll be the last to go.

CHARLIE: Ro ...

Beat.

I want to go.

ROIE: What?

CHARLIE: This house isn't the place to bring up a little one. It's dirty. There's people coming and going all the time. It smells of piss and shit and rising damp and rot.

ROIE: If Plymouth Street smells, at least we know where the smells come from. If it's rowdy, at least it's from people we love and who love us back.

CHARLIE: Sometimes I think you don't want to leave.

ROIE: This is the only place I've ever known. It's my home.

CHARLIE: But it's not *ours*.

Beat.

We deserve more than this, you and me. Our baby deserves more.

ACT FOUR: POOR MAN'S ORANGE

Please, Ro. We gotta get out of here before it falls down round our ears.

ROIE: But what about Mamma? And Da? And Dolour. Don't they deserve to get out too?

CHARLIE: 'Course they do.

ROIE: Well, where they go, I go. That's the way it's always been.

CHARLIE: Well, where you go, I go. So where does that leave the lot of us?

ROIE: I guess we're all bloody stuck with each other.

She gasps suddenly. Puts CHARLIE*'s hand on her belly.*

It's kicking!

CHARLIE *smiles sadly.*

CHARLIE: Probably more room in there than out here.

He rests his head on ROIE*'s belly as* ROIE *hums 'Last Rose of Summer' ...*

Outside, LICK JIMMY *sprays, humming along too.*

DOLOUR *passes. She is dressed like Suse. But not quite pulling the look off. She has lipstick all over her elbow.*

LICK JIMMY: G'day, Dolour!

DOLOUR: Ni hao, Lick! Letter come for you yet?

LICK JIMMY: Not yet. Where you off to?

DOLOUR: Goin' to find my friend Suse.

LICK JIMMY: Oh, yes?

DOLOUR: She lives on *Chapper Lane*. Next to an *opium den*!

LICK JIMMY: Opium, you say? Scandalous.

DOLOUR: She's in my class. Sometimes.

LICK JIMMY: Ah.

DOLOUR: The nuns reckon she's rambunctious.

LICK JIMMY: Ah.

DOLOUR: She reckons she's just confident.

LICK JIMMY: Ah. Why your elbow all red?

DOLOUR: No reason.

Beat.

Suse knows words I've never heard before. And I've got a pretty good vocabulary. She's killer-diller.

LICK JIMMY: Ah.
DOLOUR: That means amazing, Lick. She's amazing.
> LICK JIMMY *keeps spraying his stall.*

Hey, are they poor man's oranges?
LICK JIMMY: They are.
DOLOUR: Can I have one?
> *He shakes his head.*

LICK JIMMY: Not ready.
> DOLOUR *groans impatiently.*

But when they are, they'll be killer-diller. That means amazing.
> DOLOUR *saunters away.*

Bye, Dolour. Don't get too fresh with your arm! I hear they can be all hands!

SCENE EIGHT

Dusk.

DOLOUR *sits with* SUSE *on a street corner near a dilapidated house.* SUSE *drinks orange booze and smokes.*

SUSE: Who needs school anyway when I got other things to buzz?
DOLOUR: What do you mean, you left?
SUSE: I told 'em. Old cows. Give me the jips. I'd scrag 'em in a jiff if it didn't waste time.
> *She sticks out her breasts.* DOLOUR *attempts to do the same— unsuccessfully.*

You know they're into each other. Those brown joeys.
DOLOUR: What? Sister Theophilus?
SUSE: And that Beatrix one. I caught 'em once, whisperin' and gigglin' like they were a coupla corn-grinders.
DOLOUR: What's a corn-grinder?
SUSE: They're friends of Dorothy. Except they're *both* Dorothy. If you catch my drift.
DOLOUR: They're just close, I s'pose …
SUSE: Stuck me tits out proud and told 'em I'm never goin' back to that

ACT FOUR: POOR MAN'S ORANGE   161

damned school again, nor the Church neither. I couldn't give a fuck about no mission. I'm gettin' out of Surry Hills anyway. Gonna get meself a job usin' me moxie. Already started. Had two customers last week. Gave it to 'em for free but made 'em promise they'll pay next time.

DOLOUR: Suse, wouldn't your mum go crook if she knew about you and … fellers?

SUSE swigs.

SUSE: If she even tried to say anythin', I'll tell her a few things back. She tried everything she knew to get rid of me before I was born. Coathanger. Punch to the gut. Cupful of Persil. And what's she ever done for me but land me with one stinkin' baby after another to wash nappies for, give bottles to, put to sleep. Gawd, if I ever have to put another kid to sleep, it'll be for good.

She drinks.

DOLOUR: Suse, don't say things like that. Maybe you should go easy on that cocktail.

SUSE: Wanna know how I spent my tenth birthday? Dad was in the nick. Same day, Mum was droppin' another baby. Early. She couldn't hold 'em in long by then. I ran up the cop shop to get them to send us an ambulance, but they wouldn't. So Mum had the baby right there in the kitchen, biting holes in her cardigan and screaming. It was dead, that baby. All shrivelled up and blue. Know what Mum did? She made me put it in a pot, blood and everything, and carry it up the cop shop.

DOLOUR: Whaffor?

SUSE: So they could see what they'd done. Not just the coppers. Dad too. Happy birthday, Susan.

SUSE burps.

Right. I'm goin' in.

She stands, wobbling.

DOLOUR: Suse, you can't go in there, you dill. You'll get a hidin'. Come home with me, won't yer? Stay in my room till you feel okay. Yer dad's gonna belt you if he sees yer.

SUSE: **Killer-diller.**

A woman comes out. MRS KILROY.

> *'She was a little, shapeless woman with all the width in her body across the hips and buttocks, with snaggled yellow teeth and a baby slung across her hip.'*

MRS KILROY: Whass goin' on out here?

DOLOUR: Suse doesn't feel very well, Mrs Kilroy!

SUSE: Thass cos I'm drunk, Mum!

> *She calls inside.*

Oy, Dad! I'm drunk!

> *A huge man appears in the doorway.* MR KILROY. *'He was a gigantic man, with a bald head too small for the rest of him, so that he seemed a malformed creature, pin-headed, with bushy brows and a face carved in deep vertical grooves.'*

MR KILROY: I bin waiting fer you, girl. Tom Phelan told me he seen you going into the park with that dago from the shirt factory.

SUSE: Watcher gonna do about it, Dad?

> MR KILROY *unbuckles his belt.*

DOLOUR: I was there too! They didn't do anything, sir!

> *But he ignores* DOLOUR *and grabs* SUSE *by her hair roughly.*

MR KILROY: You're a whore! *You're a whore!* How many men 'a had yer?

> SUSE *purses her lips together in defiance.*

Oy! Answer me, you little bitch!

MRS KILROY: *Ralph!* Let's take it inside, ey?

SUSE: Whatta yer got, Dad? Ey? Whatta ya got?

> *He pins her to the ground under his foot and whips her with his belt. Over and over and over.*

DOLOUR: [*screaming*] Stop it! You beast! You beast. Suse! Help! Someone!

> PASSERSBY *duck their heads and walk away.*

> MRS KILROY *watches on, passively, the baby in her arms.*

> *Finally,* MR KILROY *stops his beating, leaving* SUSE *gasping on the ground, barely conscious, as* DOLOUR *stands horrified nearby.*

ACT FOUR: POOR MAN'S ORANGE

Scene Nine can form here.

MR KILROY: Yer right, Suse?

SUSE *nods, still gasping.*

Get up then, and come and have dinner, darlin'.

SUSE *nods.*

He helps her to her feet.

'Atta girl. 'At's my darlin'. 'At's my beautiful, beautiful girl.

He puts his arms around her and walks her inside, leaving DOLOUR *with* MRS KILROY.

MRS KILROY: Reckon you might wanna steer clear, little miss. Yer a bad influence.

She follows her husband and daughter inside and closes the door on DOLOUR.

SCENE NINE

Around the dinner table sit HUGH, CHARLIE, ROIE *and* MARGARET.

The sounds of construction in the distance. Buildings falling. Getting closer and closer.

MARGARET *serves sausages.*

DOLOUR *hurries in, still ashen and shaken. She sits.*

DOLOUR: Sorry I'm late.

The destruction of Surry Hills continues, audible to all.

DOLOUR *stands and impulsively hugs* MARGARET, *then sits down again.*

CHARLIE: You right, Dol?
DOLOUR: It's Dolour. And what would you care?
ROIE: Dolour.
HUGH: Any luck with the house hunting, Roie?
ROIE: Nothing. We've decided to stay on here for the time being. If that's alright with you, Da.
CHARLIE: I'm sorry, Hughie. I know I promised the best for your daughter. I'll keep trying. Promise I will. We'll earn our keep.

HUGH: As long as we've got a house, you've got a home.
MARGARET: As long as we've got a house. And why should God keep ours standing when we're doing nothing for His?
HUGH: Fuck God.
MARGARET: Hughie!

> *She hits him with a spoon.*

Dolour. Say grace. Quickly.

> *They all lower their eyes and clasps hands. Except* DOLOUR. *She just glares at* CHARLIE.

DOLOUR: How many babies are you gonna make her have?

> CHARLIE *looks stunned. The others look up at* DOLOUR, *confused.*

How many? It's cruel, bringin' more people into these Hills.
ROIE: Dolour, what are you talking about?
DOLOUR: All this place ever does is lose people. Da lost his brother because he wanted to move here. Mamma lost Thady because he walked out of here and never came back. Johnny Sheily's brains got splattered like a melon all over the road outside. And now you want to bring a *baby* into this place? When it's finally getting torn down? Good riddance, I say. Tear it down. Tear it all down.

Surry Hills is filled with nothing but no-hopers, whores and vermin. Us included. God's got every right to get rid of the lot of us.

> *They stare at her, stunned.*
>
> MR DIAMOND *appears. He looks desperately unwell.*

MARGARET: Oh, will you be joining us for tea, Mr Diamond?
MR DIAMOND: No, no. I just came down to pay my rent … and see how you went today, Hughie?

> *Silence.* HUGH *hesitates. Then nods.*

HUGH: It's done, Pat. You'll be right.

> MR DIAMOND *looks relieved.*

MR DIAMOND: Thank you, Hugh Darcy.

> HUGH *nods.*

If you'll excuse me, I'm going to retire.
ROIE: Are you sure you won't join us, Mr Diamond?

ACT FOUR: POOR MAN'S ORANGE

MR DIAMOND: I'm sure.

He shuffles away. Turns.

Thank you. All of you. For yer kindness.

As he walks away, MARGARET *sits.*

MARGARET: Sausages.

HUGH *groans.*

I'll say grace tonight then, since it's such a difficult task for anyone else at this table.

Dearest God in Heaven. We thank you for these sausages. We thank you for the home over our heads, when so many others are getting boarded up and knocked down all through the Hills. We pray that you find more people to join Father Cooley's mission. Those souls that haven't been to see You in awhile. Decades, even.

HUGH *opens his eyes and glares at his wife.*

We pray the safe return of our Thady. We pray that Dolour stops picking at her pimples and picks up her bottom lip a little instead.

DOLOUR *opens her eyes and glares at* MARGARET.

And we pray that the newborn on its way has lovely Irish skin.

CHARLIE *and* ROIE *open their eyes and glare at* MARGARET.

Upstairs, MR DIAMOND *has a shaving razor in his hand. He brings it to his throat.*

We thank You for keeping us all together in this house. For the souls of Surry Hills. Even if they be no-hopers, whores or vermin in the eyes of those who should know better. And we pray for the new life that will soon be joining us.

Beat.

Because any life is still a life. Isn't that right, Lord?

MR DIAMOND *looks skyward.*

Any life is still a life.

MR DIAMOND *slices his throat.*

Blackout.

The harp echoes.

Amen.

ALL: Amen.

SCENE TEN

A tortured cry from HUGH.

He stumbles from the house, weeping, as MARGARET *struggles to hold onto him. He shoves her away and departs, calling to the skies …*

HUGH: Pat Diamond! His name is Mr Patrick Diamond!

> DOLOUR *sits forlornly in her room alone. She rubs her eyes in pain, then puts her ear to the wall to listen into the next room …*
>
> *… as* CHARLIE *and* ROIE *hold one another in their bedroom.* ROIE *lays* CHARLIE *back and kisses him deeply …*
>
> *… as* MARGARET *trudges up the stairs to her own room. She takes off her dress and lays alone on her bed, her arm reaching out for an invisible* HUGH.
>
> HUGH *is outside Delie's house.*

Oy, Stock!

> DELIE *comes out onto the balcony.*

DELIE: What do yer want, Darcy?
HUGH: Is that Itie in there? Florrie?
DELIE: Yeah. Why?
HUGH: I need to ask her somethin'. Please.
DELIE: Learnin' Italian, are yer?
HUGH: Yer could say that.
DELIE: Well, make sure it's only *your* Italian yer brushin' up on, and not *my* Italian, capiche?

> DELIE *casts him a disapproving glance and goes inside. A* MAN *wanders past.*

MAN: Evening, Darcy.
HUGH: Evening, Malachy.

> FLORRIE *appears on the balcony.*

ACT FOUR: POOR MAN'S ORANGE

[*Whispering*] Florrie ... Florrie!

FLORRIE *peers down at him.*

FLORRIE: Hubert?

HUGH: Hughie. My God, you're beautiful.

FLORRIE: What do you want?

She gazes down at him.

He sways in the shadows.

HUGH: My brother Jer. We went together like finger and thumb. I've been waiting for him but he never comes. And I've never had another brother till Pat Diamond. And I tried to save him. But he died.

She stares down at him.

I had a son, too, Florrie. My Thady. Beautiful golden-haired boy. He went missin' on this very street. I tried to find him. But he's been lost all these years.

He stares up at her longingly.

And you know who else I lost, Florrie? I lost me.

All I see now is an old man. My old man. A mean bastard.

I think he might be dead, Florrie. Hugh Darcy. I think he might be a ghost, wandering around Surry Hills. Unseen and insignificant.

And you there, a painting that never ages ...

I reckon I might be dead. Or at least, I reckon I've forgot how to live.

Beat.

FLORRIE: I can remind you, Hughie. Would you like to come up?

HUGH *looks up at her, swaying in the moonlight.*

SCENE ELEVEN

The school.

SISTER BEATRIX *stands before the* CLASS.

SISTER BEATRIX: [*reading*] '... am I yourself
But, as it were, in sort or limitation,
To keep with you at meals, comfort your bed,
And talk to you sometimes?

Dwell I but in the suburbs
Of your good pleasure?
If it be no more, Portia is Brutus' harlot …'

The CLASS *giggles and repeats 'Harlot Um-ahh!'*

'… not his wife …'

She looks up from her book.

Who'd like to read Brutus? Harry Drummy?

HARRY: Not allowed to read about harlots, Sister. Goes against all my principles. I'd rather play King Julius Caesar when he comes on next. He's bonzer.

SISTER BEATRIX: What an excellent idea, Harry. We might even get up on our feet and let everyone have a stab at it.

HARRY: Whacko.

SISTER BEATRIX: Dolour Darcy. You've been rather quiet today. Could you please take the part of Brutus?

DOLOUR *blinks painfully.*

DOLOUR: But I'm a girl, Sister.

SISTER BEATRIX: Then you're just the right person to hear Portia's plea.

DOLOUR *sighs and blinks at the pages of her book.*

DOLOUR: [*reading*] 'You … are … my … true …'

She looks questioningly at SISTER BEATRIX *who stares back at her, confused.*

SISTER BEATRIX: Are you alright, Dolour?

DOLOUR *throws the book across the room.*

DOLOUR: I can't read! I can't read it!

SISTER BEATRIX: Dolour, you know how to read.

HARRY: Sister, she's got pus coming out of her eyes.

SISTER BEATRIX: Pardon?

DOLOUR: What?

SISTER BEATRIX: Good heavens! Sister Theophilus!

SISTER THEOPHILUS *hurries in and the nuns run to* DOLOUR.

HARRY: Been lookin' through keyholes at things, have you, Dolour?

DOLOUR: No! I haven't! Sister Theophilus, I haven't looked through any keyholes!

ACT FOUR: POOR MAN'S ORANGE 169

SISTER THEOPHILUS: Oh, Dolour ... oh, you poor thing.
DOLOUR: Am I going blind? My eyes are sticky.
SISTER THEOPHILUS: I'll have to send you home, Dolour. You're contagious.

The CLASS *respond.*

CLASS: Ewwwwwww ...
DOLOUR: What about my exams? I've been working so hard!
SISTER THEOPHILUS: You need to rest at home, Dolour. That's all. I'll walk with you.
DOLOUR: I'll be alright, won't I? Sister? What about my examinations?

DOLOUR *is hustled out ...*

SCENE TWELVE

... and into a doctor's chair ...

HUGH, MARGARET, CHARLIE *and* ROIE *stand nearby as an* EYE DOCTOR *places his hands on her face.*

EYE DOCTOR: Open them wider.
DOLOUR: I can't! They just won't!

He grabs her face and opens her eyes forcibly. DOLOUR *screams.*

He flicks at her eye with a pencil. She screams again.

HUGH *grabs the* DOCTOR.

HUGH: I got a good mind to give you a shirtful of broken ribs! What kind of doctor are you? She's a child!
EYE DOCTOR: Get your hands off me. Any nonsense from you and I'll have you up for assault, quick and lively. She's got ulceration of the retina. Probably from some parasite. No doubt from the kinds of conditions she lives in. Poor child.
　　Captain Phillip brought the bugs in the rotten timbers of his First Fleet, and they've remained ever since. Ferocious and ineradicable. The haunters of the tormented sleep of the poor.
HUGH: [*seething*] I'll give you tormented sleep ...
MARGARET: Hughie. Back. Please fix her, Doctor. She's got her exams.
EYE DOCTOR: Oh, there won't be any exams. She's condemned from any scholarly activity until at least the end of term.

DOLOUR *weeps.*

CHARLIE *goes to* DOLOUR *and holds her hand.*

DOLOUR: Roie?

CHARLIE: It's me, Dolour. It's Charlie. Roie can't hold your hand cos of the baby. But I will.

ROIE: I'm sorry, Dol.

DOLOUR *scowls a little but lets* CHARLIE *hold her. A* NURSE *enters.*

EYE DOCTOR: Nurse Watkins. Hold her down.

The NURSE *holds* DOLOUR*'s head back. The* EYE DOCTOR *pours fluid into them.*

DOLOUR *screams and screams as the others watch on, helplessly.*

MARGARET: [*repeating over and over*] Glory be to God … Glory be to God …

CHARLIE *does not let go of* DOLOUR*'s hand as the treatment continues.*

HUGH: It's those bed bugs. They've had enough of skin and now they're goin' fer the eyes. I'm gonna burn 'em out. Every last one of 'em.

HUGH *hurries out.*

Finally, the treatment ends.

EYE DOCTOR: You have to do this three times a week. No reading. No sewing. No cinema. And no school.

DOLOUR: *What?!!*

He places a pair of thick black glasses on DOLOUR.

EYE DOCTOR: No school. And no sunshine. Not till those eyes are clear.

DOLOUR: Gawdalmighty. Shall I cut my throat here or outside?

CHARLIE: Come on, Dolour. Let's get you home.

The family are hustled onto the street.

CHARLIE *sings 'Old Rugged Hills' softly as they head to the street.*

CHARLIE: Blue-grey majestic, eternal they stand
    Riding the shores of my native land
    Sheltering the valleys where blue waters run
    In adoration, kissed by the sun

ACT FOUR: POOR MAN'S ORANGE 171

The family help DOLOUR *walk through the streets of the Hills.*

Meanwhile, at Plymouth Street, HUGH *hurries into Dolour's room ...*

HUGHIE: You think I'm gonna be beaten by a bug?! I'm Hugh Darcy!

On the street ...

ROIE: Maybe I could read to you, Dol? Your schoolbooks. History, and things. Then when you go back to school –

DOLOUR: I won't ever go back, Ro. The school's probably not even gonna exist by the time my eyes are cleared up. What's the use of bothering about it?

MARGARET: Nearly home, Dol. This way to the Hills.

HUGH *sets the mattress alight.* DOLOUR's *bed starts to crackle and spit with flames.* HUGH *watches.*

HUGHIE: Take that you bastards! I'm Hugh Darcy!

He speaks to himself as he marches around the burning mattress ...

Think you can beat me? I'm Hugh Darcy!

This is my house ... *Burn! Burn, you bastards! Burn!*

CHARLIE: Old rugged hills of Australia
    Like sentinels stand wild and free
    Clad in their springtime regalia
    Guiding my loved ones for me

Meanwhile, the rest of the family walk together as a group, DOLOUR *in the middle, walking blindly.*

CHARLIE *keeps singing 'Old Rugged Hills' as they go.*

    And though I've travelled strange highways
    No matter where I roam
    I'll always ramble back
    Along a winding track
    To the old rugged hills of home

As the smoke billows around HUGH, *he walks around* DOLOUR's *room like he has a chest full of music. A heart like a drum.*

HUGH: [*yelling till the flames die*] Burn! Burn, you bastards!

The flames eventually die away.

SCENE THIRTEEN

DOLOUR *sits miserably in the kitchen with* MARGARET. *She has a cold flannel over her eyes.*

MARGARET: Tell you what, Dol. I'll make you a nice fried egg. How about that?

DOLOUR: I don't want an egg, Mamma. An egg looks just like a goopy eye.

MARGARET: Fair enough.

DOLOUR: What if I never get better, Mamma? What if I have egg eyes for the rest of my life? Who'll want me? I'll die alone like Mrs Rutson who no-one knew existed till her smell hit the street.

MARGARET: Oh, Dolour. This is just God's way of testing you.

DOLOUR: A fine thing to do when I've been so good lately. Been saying a rosary a night for the mission, I have. And what does God do? Strikes me blind.

MARGARET: Who's the patron saint of eyes, Dolour? Maybe they'll help.

DOLOUR: Saint Lucy. She got kidnapped and gouged out her own eyes to give to her captor on a plate.

MARGARET: Why would she do that?

DOLOUR: I don't know. Teach him a lesson, I suppose.

She begins to cry.

Ow. Owwww! Oh, Mamma …

MARGARET: Ah, Dolour … Dol …

DOLOUR: Can't even go to bed. Dad burnt me mattress like a madman.

MARGARET *bathes* DOLOUR's *eyes gently as she holds her.*

MARGARET: Let me tell you a story.

Once upon a time … in nineteen-twenty, not long after the big War ended, a young girl—around your age—named Margaret, met a young madman named Hughie Darcy.

They met at Carnival Day, in a little town west of here called Trafalgar.

DOLOUR: What did Margaret wear, Mamma?

MARGARET: A black silk skirt. And striped blouse. And stays.

DOLOUR: What's stays?

ACT FOUR: POOR MAN'S ORANGE

MARGARET: A torture device. And I had a hat!

DOLOUR: Really? What sort of hat did you have, Mamma?

MARGARET: Straw it was, and it had three big yellow roses along the front. And me red hair down me back with a big black ribbon bow just here. That's what I was wearing when I caught yer da's eye.

HUGH *enters.*

HUGH: I've not seen a bug in here for days. Look. No fresh bites either. I frightened 'em all away.

MARGARET: You burnt the house from the inside out, is what you did. Almost did the bloody council a favour.

HUGH: No bites on you, Dol, that I can see.

DOLOUR: None that I can see either.

HUGH: Told yer.

He's puffed up with masculine pride.

I could murder a cuppa. And a fried egg.

DOLOUR *groans.*

MARGARET: P'raps you'd like a few prawns too, Lord Muck.

She kicks Puffing Billy into life.

HUGH: Did she tell yer about Herbie?

DOLOUR: Who was Herbie?

HUGH: Your ma's beau.

DOLOUR: Ma had a beau before you, Da?

MARGARET: *I wasn't walkin' round with him!*

HERB LENNON *enters with a euphonium.*

HUGH: He took her to the carnival. Little oily yob with teeth that stuck out so far they arrived a full five minutes before he did.

MARGARET: Hugh Darcy … He was a lovely gent, was Herb Lennon. Played in the band. Euphonium.

HUGH: Worst sound I ever did hear.

HERB *parps and departs.*

MARGARET: At least he didn't career around drunk, with his trousers so saggy he showed six inches of red underpants, like you!

HUGH: You're not one to talk about underpants, Missus! You were walkin' around that day with your stays unstayed like everyone's business.

MARGARET: Yob or not, he was after me, Hugh Darcy, and if it hadn't have been for him you might never have come up to scratch! God rest him. Died in the big flu, he did, Dolour, and only twenty-five, poor Herbie.

HUGH: Yer can still find him in the Trafalgar graveyard. No headstone. Just teeth stickin' out of the ground.

MARGARET: *Hugh!*

> MARGARET *slides the egg in front of* HUGH.

HUGH: Ah, come here, me Missus.

> *He pulls her to him.*

What came over me, do yer reckon, eatin' that sod of a puddin' to get you a damn ring?

DOLOUR: What ring? What pudding?

MARGARET: Herbie had eight helpings.

HUGH: I had nine!

MARGARET: I wonder who ended up with it. The ring.

HUGH: Didn't stop me gettin' what I wanted.

> *He pulls her close.*

MARGARET: What has gotten into you?

HUGH: I'd have eaten Herb Lennon himself fer you, Missus.

DOLOUR: I'm still here, you know.

HUGH: Wanna walk through the House of Horrors with me, Missus?

MARGARET: I'd be delighted, Hughie.

> *He takes her hand and they dance around the kitchen as he sings a carnival tune.*
>
> DOLOUR *carefully makes her way out of the kitchen and upstairs to her burned-out bedroom. She listens through the wall as* ROIE *and* CHARLIE *lay together, then puts all of the bedding against it furiously, to block the sound.*
>
> *She cries wretchedly, in pain, as night falls.*

SCENE FOURTEEN

DOLOUR *lays in bed, in darkness.* ROIE *enters.*

ROIE: Dolour?

DOLOUR: You shouldn't come near me, Roie. You don't wanna catch what I got.

ROIE: You're not contagious anymore, Dolour.

She climbs into bed with DOLOUR.

Remember how many years we slept together? All curled up tight in a bundle like this?

She cuddles DOLOUR.

DOLOUR: Doesn't feel the same with that belly of yours poking me in the back, Roie.

Beat.

You gonna leave me, Roie? When the baby comes?

ROIE: I'll never leave yer, Dol. I'll always be around somewhere.

DOLOUR: But somewhere isn't right here. Everything's shifting. Falling down. Gettin' moved on. Dunno what to make of anything anymore.

Beat.

Did Mamma tell you anything—you know—before you were married? About … stuff.

ROIE: Yes, she did. She told me that tying a red ribbon round a cot will stop the fairies from stealing your baby away. And Lysol is very good for sweaty feet.

They giggle.

If there's anything you want to ask … about boys … or anything …?

DOLOUR: Why would I wanna know about boys?

ROIE: Because you're sixteen. And you're growing. And you're feeling things. And you're not sure where you fit in with the world and its people.

DOLOUR: I know plenty about the world. Even without me eyes workin'. I can smell it.

ROIE: Dolour, I knew a girl like you once. A nice girl. With big ideas about everything. And she went around with a fellow. And one night he asked her to … you know.

DOLOUR: What?

ROIE: You know. Let him maul her.

DOLOUR: She should have thudded him in the earhole.

ROIE: Yes. But sometimes you don't feel like that. Sometimes you feel like you have to do things … to make a boy happy.

DOLOUR: Not me.

ROIE: Even you.

DOLOUR: Girls who do that … they're just embarrassing themselves. They're fools. Bringing more fools into the world.

ROIE: Not all of 'em.

DOLOUR: Well, I'm not like your friend.

Beat.

Was it Rosie Glavich? The girl you knew who got herself in trouble? She's always got love bites on her neck.

ROIE: No.

DOLOUR: Ethel Jacobs?

ROIE: No.

DOLOUR: I'll bet it was Katie Raven. She taught herself how to jitterbug. Was it her? Bet it was her.

ROIE: It wasn't her. It wasn't any of them.

DOLOUR: What did she call the baby?

ROIE: It died … before it was born.

DOLOUR: It died inside her? Bloody hell. How'd she get it out?

ROIE: It doesn't matter how she got it out. It only matters how it got in there. And it only got in there cos she was made to feel like she had to. She wasn't a fool.

Beat.

And just because a baby wasn't planned or didn't get born doesn't mean that it wasn't loved, even for a moment, even while it bleeds out of you …

Even when it's just a stain on the floor … you still love it a bit.

ROIE *cries.* DOLOUR *finally understands.*

DOLOUR: Oh, Ro …

ACT FOUR: POOR MAN'S ORANGE

It was that Tommy Mendel, wasn't it? Oh, Ro … I was too young to … That night …
That bastard.
Roie.
Here.

She reaches for the talcum powder.

Just like the olden days.
Let's keep everything soft and sweet and safe. There. That's better. Isn't that better?
We won't let the dust settle, will we Ro? Even if they knock down everything around us. We'll keep the street smellin' sweet and cheap.

ROIE *smiles.*

ROIE: When did you grow up so fast, Dolour Darcy?

DOLOUR *smiles as she powders her sister.*

DOLOUR: While no-one was lookin'.

SCENE FIFTEEN

The crazy sounds of Spike Jones's 'Dance of the Hours' fills the street.
A MAN *places a cardboard box in the street ...*
So does a WOMAN *nearby ...*
A FAMILY *...*
We shift back to outside 12½ Plymouth Street.

CHARLIE *stands in the kitchen, grinning broadly, as* MARGARET *blocks her ears.*

MARGARET: What in God's name is it?
CHARLIE: It's a Breville radio, Mamma!
MARGARET: What's that awful racket?
CHARLIE: It's Spike Jones and his City Slickers! They make music sound like you're at the movies! Thought it might be nice for Dolour.

DOLOUR *makes her way blindly outside, helped by* ROIE. LICK JIMMY *dances outside his shop.*

MARGARET: I won't have that blasting through the house all day! It's louder than Delie Stock's on a Friday night! People will turn up on the doorstep wantin' favours!

CHARLIE: I got that sorted too. Look.

He pulls out a pair of headphones.

Come here, Dolour.

DOLOUR: What are they?

CHARLIE: Earphones. You put 'em over your ears and you can listen to the set like you were the only one in the world it was talking to.

He puts the earphones on DOLOUR. *She listens, enamoured.*

'*She looked grotesquely like a refugee from* War of the Worlds *with the horned black muffs over her ears and the large round goggles ...*'

She yells at CHARLIE.

DOLOUR: *You got these for me, Charlie?!*

CHARLIE: *All yours, Dol! I'll set it up in your room so you can listen to it every night if you like! Thought it might pass the time before you start your new job!*

DOLOUR: *Thank you, Charlie! Thank you! Look, Lick!*

LICK JIMMY: *You look like a blowfly, Dolour! Stay away from my fruit! Hahaha!*

DOLOUR: *What'd you say, Lick? You got a poor man's orange for me?*

LICK JIMMY: *Haha! Not ready!*

DOLOUR *groans impatiently.*

CHARLIE *pulls out the earphone cable and Spike Jones blares around the street again.*

MARGARET: Goddlemighty! Give me Bing Crosby any day.

The raucous music continues. DOLOUR *is by herself, lost in the sounds.*

ROIE *and* CHARLIE *run inside and set up a nursery in their bedroom. A cot. Clean and sturdy. They kiss ...*

Meanwhile, nearby, Surry Hills' RESIDENTS *set up more cardboard boxes in which to sleep. Like a beehive forming ...*

We shift again ...

Outside Delie Stock's ...

SCENE SIXTEEN

HUGH *fucks* FLORRIE *against a fence in an alleyway.*

FLORRIE: Hurry, Hughie. I've got to get back to Delie's.
HUGH: Wait! Florrie … Florrie …
FLORRIE: You have drunk too much, Hughie. You can never finish when you are drunk …
HUGH: I don't wanna finish, Florrie.
FLORRIE: Shh. If Delie finds out she'll have my garters for guts, Hughie.

They keep fucking.

HUGH: I love you, Florrie. I do. You're like a painting. You don't change. You don't age. Like a bloody … painting …

They finish. She waits as HUGH *recovers. He sways drunkenly.*

FLORRIE: Hughie …

He gasps for breath as he looks at her.

I have to go back.

She puts out her hand.

HUGH: But, Florrie … I'm not one of them fellas.
FLORRIE: I know this. But if Delie asks where I've been, I have to make her think I've been doing my job, yes?

HUGH *nods.*

You said you loved me, Hughie. I'm your bloody painting.
HUGH: 'Course I do, Florrie. 'Course you are.
FLORRIE: I make you feel like a man, yes? With a drum in his heart? Twelve foot tall?

HUGH *nods.*

How am I supposed to keep myself pretty if you don't pay me, Hughie?

HUGH *gets some money from his pocket.*

HUGH: There you go, love.

She waits. He rolls his eyes and gives her more.

See you again soon?

FLORRIE: Yes, amore.

> *She hurries away.* HUGH *clutches at his chest and grimaces. He stumbles drunkenly and retches a little. A voice comes from the fence.*

BUMPER: Ey up!

> HUGH *leaps in fright.*

HUGH: Whoozat?
BUMPER: I'm here.

> *He pokes his finger through a hole in the fence.*

Like a cuppa?

> *The fence opens, revealing a small hovel of asbestos sheets, plywood and hammered iron. 'It was shaped like a fowl-house, with sloping roof patched with tacked-on pieces of cardboard boxes and petrol tins, and it was divided into many little cubicles seven foot square. The man was a baggy, miniature creature like a full-sized man whom someone had allowed to deflate.'*
>
> *Each makeshift cardboard stall has a human crouched in it.* HUGH *looks around, gaping.*

I'm Bumper Reilly. Here, Hughie.

> *He thrusts a tin mug at* HUGH.

HUGH: How do you know me name?
BUMPER: I've heard it moaned many times in this alleyway.
HUGH: This a flophouse?
BUMPER: It is. Not the tidiest of places, but better than a whorehouse, hey?

> *He winks at* HUGH *knowingly.*

HUGH: How long you bin watchin' us for?
BUMPER: Couple of weeks. Know every bit of you now. Don't worry, your secret's safe with me.
HUGH: You pay for this place?
BUMPER: Half a frog.
HUGH: Strewth!
BUMPER: Leaves yer just enough to starve on. Each of us here got kicked out of our abodes over the past year or two. Luckily those rich bastards

that chucked us out saw a good opportunity to charge us ten shillings a week to sit under a plank of asbestos. Isn't that right, fellas?

The TENANTS *grumble in agreement.*

HUGH: I'd tell him to go fuck himself.

BUMPER: After you've slep' out of doors for a few nights you change your mind about the sorta roof you like best. 'Specially when you got angela pectoris like me. Heart trouble.

HUGH: Have you got no family you could stay with?

BUMPER: I 'ad a brother once. But he was killed in the second big war, at Singapore. An' me wife, she died on me a while back. Can still remember some of her face. You mightn't know, but I was a jockey once. Bumper Reilly! Fust-rate jockey! Me name was in the papers more times than I could count! Look!

He pulls a scrap of paper from his pocket.

There! See? It says 'Bumper Reilly rode such a race as has not been seen on the Australian turf!'

HUGH: Did you ever ride in the Melbourne Cup?

BUMPER: I did not. But that race is on its last legs anyway.

HUGH: I 'ad a brother once too. Jer. He had twisted feet. We went together like finger and thumb. And I had a son. Thady. But we lost him to the streets.

He looks blearily at BUMPER.

And I had a da that was mean. He looked like me. Could brand a pig with that man's glare.

BUMPER: Das can be mean, Hughie. I'm sorry your da was mean. And your brother's feet was twisted. And your son is gone. I'm real sorry about that.

HUGH: Are you?

BUMPER *nods sadly.*

Thank you. No-one's ever said that before.

Silence.

The couple in the next pen screech at one another.

FELLA: Move yer bloody arse, bitch!

WIFE: Move yer own arse, yer useless bastard.

BUMPER: Don't worry about them. When one dies, the other will commit suicide.

> HUGH *peers into Bumper's abode. The hovel is chock-full of small parcels, all neatly tied with string, clothesline and red wool.*

HUGH: Look, this might be the wine talking, but we gotta spare room in our place.
BUMPER: You and that young lady?
HUGH: No ... No. But sure, the missus wouldn't be objecting if we rented it to you. Used to belong to me best mate. Diamond. But he ... left the premises. Seven and six would do for the rent. That's all.
BUMPER: Seven and six ... Ooh! And what's the address?
HUGH: Twelve-and-a-half Plymouth Street.
BUMPER: Ahhh ... Tch, tch, tch. Tch, tch, tch.
HUGH: What is it? What?
BUMPER: This box will last longer than your street, Hughie. Thank you for your offer. But I'll stay here. Wrapped up nice and safe. I'll keep a box spare for you, my friend. We all end up in one eventually.

> *And with that,* BUMPER'*s gone.*
>
> HUGH *stumbles away, passing row after row of cardboard cubicles.*

SCENE SEVENTEEN

As we shift, ROIE *and* CHARLIE *continue their nesting, turning their room into a nursery. A mobile dangles above the cot. And a teddy bear is placed inside it, ready to meet its owner.*

Meanwhile ...

HUGH *tears down eviction notices as he traipses through the Hills ...*

Meanwhile ...

DOLOUR *peers into a mirror, trying to apply lipstick. She squints at herself — still terribly blind — then picks up a broom to sweep the Drummy general store. She is dressed in a pink apron that is far too small for her growing figure.*

'*The Drummy store sold milk and bread, butter and groceries, and*

ACT FOUR: POOR MAN'S ORANGE 183

delicatessan goods of a strictly utilitarian kind ... It smelt of bacon and cheeses and long-vanished tobacco and DOLOUR *hated it from the moment she entered it as its slave.'*

DOLOUR *practices greetings while she sweeps.*

DOLOUR: 'Ahhh. My first customer. Welcome to the Drummy Delicatessan! How may I be of service?' 'A thrippence-worth of corned beef? Of course, Mrs Jenkins. Coming right up.'

> DOLOUR *keeps sweeping.*
>
> LICK JIMMY *pokes his head into the store. He is wheeling a cart of fruit and vegies.*

LICK: Ahh … We in competition now, Dolour?
DOLOUR: What? Ah, no, Lick! Never. If anyone needs any fresh fruit and vegies I'll send 'em your way. Promise.
LICK: How are your eyes?
DOLOUR: Better, Lick. Thanks. I missed too much school to go back, but I get to take the glasses off soon.
LICK: You look very pretty, Dolour. Even in glasses. No more blowfly.
DOLOUR: I do? Ta, Lick.
LICK: And lipstick on your face instead of your elbow.

> *She smiles, embarrassed.*

DOLOUR: Yeah. Any news from Shanghai?
LICK: No. Not yet. See you later, Dolour.
DOLOUR: Zai jian, Lick.

> LICK JIMMY *turns and bumps into* KIDGER *and* DELIE.

LICK: Oopsy-daisy! Look Dolour! Your first customers! Bonzer!

> KIDGER *and* DELIE *enter as* LICK *leaves.*

DOLOUR: Oh. How lovely. Welcome to the Drummy Delicatessan, Ms Stock. Kidger. How can I help you?
DELIE: We've come to put in our monthly order. Where's Mrs Drummy?
DOLOUR: She's gone part-time. I'm her shopgirl now.
DELIE: Well, la-di-dah, midarlin'. Congrats. Kidger.

> KIDGER *reads from a shopping list.* DOLOUR *takes notes.*

KIDGER: Fifty boxes of Kelloggs Cornflakes. Sixty boxes of Sunshine powdered milk. Thirty boxes of Jatz crackers.
DELIE: Chuck some Milk Arrowroots in there too, love. Love an Arrowroot.
KIDGER: Eighty boxes of Edward's tea leaves. Twelve packets of Aeroplane Jelly.
DOLOUR: Any particular flavour?
DELIE: Whatever the green one is.
KIDGER: Ten packets of Carnation Custard Powder. Fifteen packets of French onion soup. Twenty boxes of Modess napkins. Twenty-five cans of Gerber baby food.
DELIE: Get the strained peas. Little bugger seems to like them. Which reminds me, chuck in a few bottles of Persil too.
KIDGER: Two vats of butter. Eight bags of flour. One-hundred-and-four eggs. Five tubs of lard. Eighteen packs of lamb chops. And Vegemite.
DOLOUR: How many jars?
DELIE: One. And chuck in a box of Bex. Add it to me bill.
DOLOUR: Mrs Drummy isn't allowing credit anymore, Ms Stock. You'll have to pay now.
KIDGER: Delie's good for it.
DOLOUR: I'll need the money now or I can't put the order in. If you can't pay you'll have to leave the premises.
KIDGER: You think cos you gotta job in a shop you're better than anyone else? Thass bullshit. We know yer family. Where yer live. We see everything. You'll never be more than these streets, Darcy. 'Delicatessan' or not.
DELIE: Kidger. Enough.
KIDGER: She was tryin' to get above yer, Delie!
DELIE: Yeah. Good on her.

She peers at DOLOUR.

Whassa matter? Whass all this?

She indicates the glasses.

You got pig-sty?
DOLOUR: My eyes have been bad. Had to leave school. That's why I'm workin' here. But they're on the mend.

ACT FOUR: POOR MAN'S ORANGE

DELIE: That's crook, love. I ain't too well meself these days. Dunno why. I feel sorta ... tired ... all over. Sorta heavy in here.
DOLOUR: Maybe you're pregnant.
DELIE: Mary Mother of God, I don't reckon.
DOLOUR: Maybe you work too hard.
KIDGER: Course she does. She's a woman.

DELIE gets out a wad of cash.

DELIE: Here. That's for the order.

She reaches into her bra.

And here's a tenner. Buy yerself somethin' nice. And remember, darlin...the people you meet on the way up are the same people you meet on the way down.

She goes to leave.

DOLOUR: Ms Stock!

DELIE turns back.

The Bex is on the house. Hope you feel better soon.

She hands her a packet of Bex.

DELIE: Nice lippy. Suits ya. See ya. Kidger.

She leaves with KIDGER, as HARRY DRUMMY enters.

HARRY: Whoa, Dolour!
DOLOUR: Hullo, Harry.
HARRY: I'll have to report yer to me Mother. She won't stand for givin' away pharmaceuticals to whores.

Beat. He looks at her, in awe.

You got lipstick on.
DOLOUR: So. What of it?
HARRY: Wrong colour. Brunettes shouldn't wear coral.
DOLOUR: Fat lot you know about it.
HARRY: Sure I do. I'm a tiger with the tomatoes.
DOLOUR: Really? And how'd yer exams go, tiger?
HARRY: Don't need exams. I'll own this shop one day. Which means I'll probably own you.

Beat.

Wanna go to the pitchers tonight? If you got a couple of bob you can shout me.

DOLOUR: Why would I do that?

HARRY: It's my mum that pays yer. So in reality, that money's mine.

DOLOUR: I can't go to the pitchers anyway. It hurts my eyes.

HARRY: You don't go to the pitchers to watch. You go to cuddle.

DOLOUR: Get off the grass, Harry. I wouldn't cuddle you if you were given away with a pound of prawns!

HARRY: Orright. Guess Ma will just have to find out yer bin givin' free comestibles to Delie Stock. You'll lose yer job on yer first day. Shameful.

A stand-off. DOLOUR *hangs her head. Beaten.*

DOLOUR: Alright, Harry.

He grins. Starts to leave…

HARRY: Missed a spot.

SCENE EIGHTEEN

At 12 1/2 Plymouth Street.

The Breville plays softly. MARGARET *sings along quietly. She chops potatoes in the kitchen as* ROIE *sews.*

MARGARET: Make sure you double-darn that sock. Big toes are the first to wear through.

ROIE: Yes, Mamma.

MARGARET *watches critically. She can't help herself…*

MARGARET: Here. Let me do it.

She takes the sewing from ROIE.

You've made a mess of this, Roie. Poor child will be tripping over the threads.

ROIE: Mamma …

But MARGARET *is already resewing Roie's work.*

Leave a plate aside for Charlie, tonight. He's workin' late.

MARGARET: Again?

ROIE: He wants to save up enough for when the baby's here. So we're not a burden.
MARGARET: What kind of a man thinks his child is a burden?
ROIE: He didn't mean it like that, Mamma. He just wants to make sure we've got enough put away to keep things comfortable.
MARGARET: To move out?
ROIE: No. But if we do stay, we gotta make things ...
MARGARET: What?
ROIE: It doesn't matter.

Silence. Puffing Billy belches wearily.

Where's Da?
MARGARET: Still at the factory.

Silence.

Is he ... is he a good husband, Roie? Your Charlie.
ROIE: Kind of question's that?
MARGARET: He never comes to church.
ROIE: He works seven days, Mamma.
MARGARET: He's never shown any interest in the mission.
ROIE: And the mission's never shown any interest in him, I'm sure.
MARGARET: Do you not see his ... past ... when you look in his eyes?
ROIE: What?
MARGARET: You know. The tar.

Silence.

ROIE: I see Charlie, Mamma. Sometimes at night, while he sleeps, I just stare at him in the moonlight and marvel that he found me and I found him. And then I feel the kick inside me and I think of the generations that have gone into making this little soul we'll soon meet. The lines of blood and bone and nerve and rock that meet up ... right here. His blood. Your blood. My blood. Then and now and the future all at once. Growing and kicking to get out and live. Live.
MARGARET: Oh.
ROIE: It's about time you realised that Charlie's as good as a man can get, Mamma. But maybe that's what scares you. You don't recognise goodness cos you haven't seen it in such a long time. You've been praying for it. But you don't see it when it's right in front of you.
MARGARET: I've seen goodness.

ROIE: When? When Da comes home half-cut instead of full? When your bunions don't throb quite as much as yesterday? When night-time comes and Charlie doesn't look quite as black? Is that goodness for you, Mamma?
MARGARET: Roie. Don't speak to me that way.
ROIE: Don't speak to *me* that way. Not about my husband. And not about my baby.
MARGARET: I just want the baby to have a place to be. I want it to belong.
ROIE: It belongs where we are, Mamma. Me and Charlie.
MARGARET: And where are youse?
ROIE: We're here. For now.

> MARGARET *rears up suddenly and fans her face.*

You right, Mamma?
MARGARET: Flushes and pricklings.
ROIE: Again?
MARGARET: It's the change … It's come.
ROIE: Sit down, Mamma.
MARGARET: You see black specks floating round in front of you. And when you straighten up again, yellow flashes and whirligigs in front of your eyes as your skin prickles all over. I suppose a woman's lucky it only lasts five years.

> DOLOUR *enters.*

ROIE: How was work, Dol?
DOLOUR: Fine. I sold five cans of stewed apples.
MARGARET: Oooooh! That's exciting.

> HUGH *enters with arms full of torn eviction notices.*

Speaking of stewed fruit.
HUGH: Evening. What's for dinner?
MARGARET: I'll tell you what's for dinner. Your liver with all the trimmings. Old Mrs Sibson got moved on today.
HUGH: How's that my fault?
MARGARET: You haven't been helping with the mission. You've been wasting your time at the swill when you should be on yer knees, praying your pub will stay standing at all!
HUGH: I got better things to do than kneel in front of Cooley while he

lauds over Surry Hills like a smug fuckin' politician. I'm out there givin' back, woman! Look at you—complaining that our house might get pulled down, and there's people out there living in shoeboxes! You can go on Cooley's mission all you like, Missus, but I'm out there doin' things proper. Helpin' where help is needed. Pullin' down eviction notices, shoutin' people drinks who've lost their homes! This is *Hugh Darcy*'s mission. Thass what it is.

He pours himself a drink.

I'm the man of the house, see? And I make the decisions, dammit. Don't you be questioning my authority again, yer hear? Any of yer. Now what's for dinner?

MARGARET, DOLOUR and ROIE: [*together*] Sausages.

HUGH: *Fuck!*

HUGH *walks out and slams the door.*

SCENE NINETEEN

Night.

As HUGH *drinks in the darkened street ...* MARGARET *prays alone.*

DOLOUR *rubs her aching feet.*

ROIE *lays back down on her bed and strokes her belly.*

She sings softly, as she listens to the rustles.

ROIE: [*singing*] 'Tis the last rose of summer,
    Left blooming alone;
    All her lovely companions
    Are faded and gone;
    No flower of her kindred,
    No rosebud is nigh,
    To reflect back her blushes,
    Or give sigh for sigh.

Outside, FLORRIE *and* HUGH *meet in the shadows. They kiss passionately.*

At home, ROIE *sits up suddenly.*

[*Spoken*] I see you, rat.

She keeps singing quietly as she grabs a broom and chases a rat in the darkness.

Outside, HUGH *and* FLORRIE *fuck against the wall ...*

[*Singing*] I'll not leave thee, thou lone one!
To pine on the stem;
Since the lovely are sleeping,
Go, sleep thou with them.

She raises the broom ...

HUGH *and* FLORRIE *disappear into the shadows ...*

ROIE *goes to bring the broom down on the rat, which runs up her dress. She screams.*

Argh! Argh! Fucking filthy rat!

The rat runs into a corner ... ROIE, *shaking, closes in on it again. She slams the broom down on the rat over and over and over again.* MARGARET *and* DOLOUR *come hurrying into the room ...*

Where's Da?
DOLOUR: Still out on his mission.
ROIE: There's a rat.
MARGARET: Filthy.
ROIE: I killed it. It's dead.

She stares at them, gasping, still holding the broom.

DOLOUR: Roie … is that the rat's blood or yours?

Blood drips down ROIE*'s legs. The women stare at it.*

Darkness.

The harp echoes ...

SCENE TWENTY

The sounds of prayer, whispered softly. A hospital.

ROIE *lays in a bed beside a cot.*

She is surrounded by MARGARET, DOLOUR, SISTER BEATRIX, SISTER THEOPHILUS *and* FATHER COOLEY, *who all whisper prayers.*

CHARLIE *runs in.*

ACT FOUR: POOR MAN'S ORANGE

CHARLIE: Where is she?

He shoves them out of the way.

Roie? Roie ...

She opens her eyes.

ROIE: Charlie.
DOLOUR: Roie! You're awake!
MARGARET: You're alright, lovey. You're alright, aren't you?
ROIE: Charlie ... it's a boy. You've got a little boy.

CHARLIE *peers into the cot.*

CHARLIE: You did good, Ro. I'm sorry I wasn't here.
ROIE: Lookut our baby, Charlie. He's an island. He caught us as we floated past. We're his and he's ours now.

Her smile fades.

Mamma ...
MARGARET: Yes, darling.
ROIE: I can see them black spots.
MARGARET: What's that, Ro?
ROIE: Them flushes and pricklings. What a whirligig, hey? How lucky we are.

She dies.

The harp stops.

The DOCTOR *checks her pulse.*

CHARLIE: What ... what's happening? Roie?
MARGARET: Roie.
DOLOUR: Roie, what are you doing?

The DOCTOR *shakes his head at* FATHER COOLEY, *who makes the sign of the cross over* ROIE*'s body.*

MARGARET *shrieks.* DOLOUR *wails.* CHARLIE *stands in shock, gaping at his dead wife.*

CHARLIE: No!

He climbs into the bed and puts his arms around ROIE.

I'll warm you up, Ro! Wake up, darling! Stay warm!

He holds her desperately.

Ro. *Roie!* Stay. Please *stay!* Roie! Breathe with me! Breathe with me, Roie!

> HUGH *stumbles in, drunk.*

HUGH: Where's my girl? *Where's my Roie?!*

> MARGARET *sobs.*

MARGARET: She's gone, Hughie.

> CHARLIE *leaps out of the bed and grabs* HUGH *roughly. He shoves him toward* ROIE *by the scruff of the neck.*

CHARLIE: This is *your* fault, you drunken bastard. You filthy rat. You and your dirty fucking house. Spending all your money on booze when you should've been looking after your family. You stupid Irish halfwit. Where were you? You did this. *You did this!*

> CHARLIE *runs out of the hospital, leaving them all behind.* HUGH *wails, keening over* ROIE*'s corpse.*

HUGH: Roie … Roie … Thass my girl … Thass *my* beautiful girl! See her? Look at her! See her? *I made her!*

> THADY *enters and takes* ROIE*'s hand.*
>
> *He leads her away.*

SCENE TWENTY-ONE

La Perouse.

Dawn.

CHARLIE *looks down at Botany Bay as he prepares to jump from a cliff. He weeps.*

An Aboriginal man, GUS MCINTOSH, *appears beside him. 'He was bent at the knees and the elbows into a comfortable workaday shape.'*

GUS: You up early this morning, boy. Bin fishing?

> CHARLIE *turns, shocked. He shakes his head.*

You look a mess. Bin on the booze?

> CHARLIE *shakes his head.*

What you doin' on the cliffs in La Perouse?

ACT FOUR: POOR MAN'S ORANGE

CHARLIE: My ... my wife just died.

> GUS *sits down and pats the ground beside him.*
> CHARLIE *hesitates, then sits.*

GUS: Want some tea? Goat milk and sugar. Nicen sweet.

> *He hands him a flask.* CHARLIE *drinks.*

Wonder where she'll go, hey? Your wife. Somewhere out there, hey?

> *He gestures to the dawn.*

Not Heaven. None of that rubbish. If you look close, there's still some stars. Look close, boy. See? Waragal. Waragal...

> *He waves goodbye to the stars.*
> CHARLIE *squints.*

There she goes. There she goes. Drink some tea and say goodbye. She'll be back tonight. Uru.

> CHARLIE *sobs.*
> GUS *sits quietly beside him.*
> *Then ...*

Here you go. Comb your hair, boy.

> *He hands* CHARLIE *a comb.*

You got kids?

> CHARLIE *nods.*

CHARLIE: One.
GUS: Baby?
CHARLIE: A boy.
GUS: Best you get back to 'im, hey?

> CHARLIE *nods. Combs his hair.*

You come back again sometime. Me and you go fishing. You just ask at camp for Gus. Thass me! Orright?

> CHARLIE *nods and hands* GUS *back his comb.*

CHARLIE: Yes.

> *Dawn glows.*

GUS: There she goes ... there she goes ... there she goes ...

SCENE TWENTY-TWO

Day.

MARGARET *walks through Surry Hills, laden with groceries.* PASSERSBY *hurry past as she hobbles onward, her shoes falling apart at the seams. She stops for a moment, exhausted.*

Then … a man with a bouquet of flowers, BRETT, *stops nearby to tie his shoe. He and* MARGARET *are still amongst the crowd. She watches him. 'All at once her heart gave a painful thump.'*

MARGARET: Thady …?

> *He hurries on. He darts in and around the crowd.* MARGARET *drops her groceries and hobbles after him.*

Thady … Thady?
Goddlemighty.

> *She chases him through the throng, her voice drowned out by traffic and noise.*

Thady!

> *He turns and sees* MARGARET.

Thady!

BRETT: You talkin' to me?

> MARGARET *runs to him, exhausted.*

MARGARET: My Thady!

> *She throws herself at him, kisses him all over.*

BRETT: Get off me, you old hag!

> *He shoves her away.*

MARGARET: It's me, Thady! Your Mamma! Oh, me little boy! Me little Thady! Hold my hand. Give me your hand!

> *She goes for him again and he starts to run.* MARGARET *gives chase.*

I'm not losing you again! Thady! I got presents for you at home! Thady!

ACT FOUR: POOR MAN'S ORANGE

They arrive at a house. BRETT *hurries to a man and woman on the porch,* BRETT'S DAD *and his mum,* ELSE.

BRETT: Mum! Dad! Old bag follered me. She's a loon! Look at her!
MARGARET: Which one of yer stole my boy? Which one of yer?
BRETT: She's bats! [*To* MARGARET] Get home, will yer? Garn, get!
MARGARET: Thady, darling, don't you remember? Twenty-one years, eight months and sixteen days ago! You were eight! Nearly. And yer had yer little navy pants on, with the patch, and yer red braces, new ones. You were so proud of them. And yer had three marbles in a flour bag, a yeller connie, and a sort of stripy one, and a big clay one you'd made yerself and baked in Puffing Billy. We've still got Puffing Billy! Can you believe it?!

The three of them stare back at MARGARET, *baffled.*

Come on. Let's go home!
BRETT: Get lost, yer old haybag. This is my mum. Happy Mother's Day, Mum.

He gives her the flowers.

They got crushed by that bloody madwoman.
ELSE: Brett! Hush. Look at her. Poor thing. [*To* MARGARET] Come inside. Have a cup of tea.
MARGARET: Don't you poor thing me! You'll be poor thinging on the other side of yer face when I get the coppers onto yer for pinching my baby.
ELSE: Now, look here—
BRETT'S DAD: Hold yer gab, Else. She's talkin' the truth, as far as she knows it.
MARGARET: Of course I am! I'm a good Christian woman!
BRETT'S DAD: Else. Get the album.

ELSE *hurries inside.* MARGARET *stares in awe at* BRETT.

MARGARET: Thady. Glory be. Thady. Yer haven't changed a bit. I ain't forgotten yer, Thady. Not one inch of yer body. You're mine. I bore yer down there on Plymouth Street. I got presents for yer, waitin' there.

ELSE *hurries out with a photo album. Hands it to* MARGARET.

ELSE: Look. Now, missus … here's Brett at six weeks.

MARGARET: That could be any baby.
ELSE: And here. At three. At five, in his nice velvet suit. And six. No braces. No marbles.
MARGARET: But I thought … I thought …

She keeps turning pages, then drops the album and sinks to the ground.

I'm sorry. I just lost another one, see. Roie.

She looks blearily at BRETT.

Thady…?
ELSE: No mother should ever lose their child. Let alone two.
MARGARET: I gotta go. You been nice to me. I'm sorry I said some things I did. Happy Mothers' Day.
ELSE: Give the lady a hug, Brett.
BRETT: Get out.
BRETT'S DAD: *Brett!*

BRETT *reluctantly stands before* MARGARET. *She holds his hand softly, searching. Then lets it go and walks away.*

ELSE: Have a nice day, missus … I hope you find what you're looking for.

As MARGARET *hobbles away,* ROIE *and* THADY *and* ENY *pass her on the street. She does not see them.*

MARGARET: Twenty-one years, eight months and sixteen days … twenty-one years, eight months and sixteen days … twenty-one years, eight months …

SCENE TWENTY-THREE

The sound of a baby crying.

DOLOUR *opens the door of the house to find her father and* CHARLIE *collapsed on the doorstep.*

DOLOUR: Jesus, Mary, Joseph and the donkey! What are you doing, Charlie?

CHARLIE *retches.*

You're drunk again! Tch. There's a baby in here needs a drink too.

ACT FOUR: POOR MAN'S ORANGE

I see Lick's delivered the milk. More of a man than the both of yer.

MARGARET *arrives home without groceries.*

Mamma, where've you been?

MARGARET: I was gettin' groceries.

DOLOUR: Where are they?

MARGARET: I lost 'em.

She sits wearily between CHARLIE *and* HUGH.

DOLOUR: Charlie, you never used to get drunk. What's going on?

MARGARET: It's natural for men to get drunk when they're upset, Dolour. You may as well learn that lesson now.

She slugs from Hugh's bottle.

DOLOUR: Mamma!

MARGARET: Don't show me the whites of your eyes, Miss. It's Mother's Day. I deserve it.

DOLOUR: That's not you. That's not Charlie. You know that. You wanna see him end up like Da? Is that it?

She throws CHARLIE*'s booze away.*

How can you do it? Don't you see what Da is? Do you want to be the same as him when you're old? It ain't fair for little Mikey for you to go the same way. You'll take a bottle from Da but you ain't ever given one to your own son!

CHARLIE *stares at* DOLOUR *blearily.*

CHARLIE: Why do you say 'ain't' for, when yer've had a better education than any of us?

He squeezes past her roughly.

Scene Twenty-four can form here.

DOLOUR: [*calling after him*] Call yourselves adults?
[*To her parents*] Children. The lot of yer.

DOLOUR *slams the door.*

MARGARET: I thought I found him, Hughie …

HUGH: Jer?

MARGARET: Thady. And for a moment there, everything was right …

She takes another slug of booze.

SCENE TWENTY-FOUR

Inside Plymouth Street, DOLOUR *is in the bath, wearing her bloomers on her head. Steam rises from the water. She soaps her skin.*
She speaks softly to herself.

DOLOUR: I'm finally a woman.
  I've got mirrors all over the wall of my palatial bathroom …
  When I get out, I'll put on my lovely pink—no, lilac—satin gown. And my slippers with very high heels and lots of feathers on them …
  And I'll powder my nose and perfume my soft flawless skin …
  Then I'll meet Harry Drummy at Luna Park and we'll—

  HUGH *comes crashing in.*

  Da! I'm having a bath! Get out!
HUGH: I wanted a bath!
DOLOUR: Da, you have more baths than anyone I know! Why do you need so many ablutions? What do you do in here?
HUGH: Never you mind.
DOLOUR: Well, it's my birthday and this is my present to meself. So bugger off.

  HUGH *leans mischievously against the door.*

HUGH: What are yer doing to keep your crankcase off the hot bottom?
DOLOUR: I'm sitting on the soap!
HUGH: And what's that you got on yer head there, Lady Muck?
DOLOUR: They're me bloomers! They keep me hair from gettin' wet, you big calonkus!

  HUGH *laughs and laughs.* CHARLIE *appears with the baby and looks shocked.*

  Get out! I've got a date with Harry Drummy and you're all gapin' at me like I'm some sideshow freak!
CHARLIE: I was just gonna bathe Mikey.
DOLOUR: *Get out!*

  CHARLIE *does.* HUGH *keeps laughing.* MARGARET *appears.*

HUGH: Look at that steam! 'Ere, Missus, throw some onions and potatoes in there and we'll have a lovely stew tonight!

ACT FOUR: POOR MAN'S ORANGE

DOLOUR: *Da, get out!*

MARGARET shuts the bathroom door. DOLOUR hurriedly gets out of the bath and dresses.

MARGARET: Stop teasin' the girl, Hughie Darcy.

HUGH: Just takin' some of the starch out of her.

MARGARET: You've got to remember, she isn't a child now. She's eighteen.

HUGH: Ahh ... nothin' I ain't seen before. Remember, I used to change her nappies when she was Mikey's size.

MARGARET: I can count on one finger the number of nappies you changed, Hugh Darcy.

Mikey starts to cry.

CHARLIE: What do I do? I've fed him already. What do I do?

MARGARET: Give 'im here, Charlie.

CHARLIE: Nah, Mamma ... just tell me what to do and I'll—

MARGARET: He needs a finger to suck on with a dab of sugar on it.

CHARLIE: Well, I've got fingers.

MARGARET: Yes, but yours are covered in printer's ink. You'll poison the poor little soul. Give 'im here.

She takes the baby.

She rocks him in the crook of her arm as she prepares dinner, cooing down at him.

HUGH: Four clearances down Reservoir this week. Three families on the street and one fella found hangin' from the rafters.

MARGARET: Goddlemighty. Who?

HUGH: Henry Dickson. Reckon he did it weeks ago. He'd been there so long his feet were touching the ground.

MARGARET: I'll say a prayer for his soul.

HUGH: He was an atheist.

MARGARET: Goddlemighty. Then I'll say two.

CHARLIE: Missus, please let me take Mikey.

MARGARET: Leave him. He's just dropping off.

He tries to take the child again. MARGARET *evades him.*

CHARLIE sits sullenly. DOLOUR *enters, in a pretty dress and heels.*

HUGH: Did you leave the bath water for me?
DOLOUR: Yes. And I hope you drown.
CHARLIE: You look nice, Dol. Where you off to?
DOLOUR: Luna Park. For my birthday. Got a date. With Harry Drummy.
HUGH: Send our regards to Humphrey Bogart, Miss Bacall!
DOLOUR: Shurrup, Da!

> *She bumps into a wall then saunters out, watched by* CHARLIE.
>
> CHARLIE *tries to take Mikey back, but is thwarted at every turn by* MARGARET *as she moves around the kitchen.*

CHARLIE: What's for dinner?
MARGARET: [*cooing to Mikey*] Sausages.

> CHARLIE *pours himself a drink.*

SCENE TWENTY-FIVE

The sounds of a distant carnival.

DOLOUR *walks with* HARRY DRUMMY. *'Of all the nice boys going to Luna Park, she had to draw this droob. It wasn't his fault he was a drongo.'*

HARRY: You haven't said anything about my moustache.

> DOLOUR *stares at his face.*

I've been growing it for three weeks and four days now.
DOLOUR: It's very ... refined.

> *He seems happy with that.*

Do you notice anything new about me?

> HARRY *looks* DOLOUR *up and down.*

HARRY: Your stockings. They're new.
DOLOUR: Oh ... Well, yes—
HARRY: You shouldn't wear them. They're snooty.
DOLOUR: They're all the go!
HARRY: Not in Surry Hills. In Surry Hills they're snooty. We prefer no stockings at all.

> *We are at Luna Park.*

Why don't you take off them black windows?

ACT FOUR: POOR MAN'S ORANGE

DOLOUR: I'm not supposed to, but ... Okay.

She removes her glasses.

HARRY: You know, you ain't half as funny-looking as you used to be.

DOLOUR: Thanks. Wish I could say the same.

A HOTDOG SELLER *passes.*

HOTDOG SELLER: Carman getcher dargies! Carman getcher dargies! Mustid dor termarter! Carman getcher li'l red dargies!

HARRY: [*to the* SELLER] One with tomato. Hate mustard.

The SELLER *hands it over.*

HARRY *tears it in two and hands half to* DOLOUR.

You can buy me somethin' another time.

DOLOUR: It's been real nice workin' for your mum at the delicatessan, Harry. She's super nice for takin' me on after me eyes went bad.

HARRY: She's alright, I s'pose.

DOLOUR: She's lovely. Sister Theophilus and Sister Beatrix think so too. They want to thank her personally for givin' me a future.

HARRY: Nuns? Pffft. What do they know about the world?

DOLOUR: I love them. They're so ... womanly.

HARRY: Pffft. What's that even mean?

DOLOUR: I dunno. They've got this ... secret kind of strength, I guess. They've sacrificed everything in the world for self-discipline. Hour by hour. Minute by minute. They don't even flinch at all the dirt. They just glide. Assured. Beautiful. Serene. Womanly.

HARRY *blinks at her, sauce dripping from his mouth as he stands under the Luna Park mouth.*

You might wanna wipe yer mouth.

They head through the mouth.

Two more young men, FRANKY *and* TUG, *appear with their partners,* SHIRLEY *and* MINNIE.

SHIRLEY: Who's she?

HARRY: Name's Dolour Darcy.

MINNIE: Thought you were bringin' Nelly.

HARRY: Nah. Not tonight.

FRANKY: Goin' on the River Caves?

HARRY: Too right.
DOLOUR: I wanted to try the Big Dipper.
TUG: Dipper's for kids. Caves for adults.

He slips some cash to an ATTENDANT *who pockets it.*

The couples get in a boat, chattering and giggling. Except DOLOUR.

Light shifts around them as they glide. HARRY *chomps down on his hotdog, dribbling sauce.*

HARRY: How'd you get rid of yer pimples?
DOLOUR: They just … stopped.

As she says this, so do the boats.

Suddenly, FRANKY *and* SHIRLEY, MINNIE *and* TUG *are making out passionately.* HARRY *lurches at* DOLOUR. *He kisses her sloppily. She reluctantly lets him.*

He finally stops.

HARRY: God, I could go for you, Dolour.
DOLOUR: Could you …?

The other boys start to unbutton their pants and climb on top of the girls. HARRY *tries to do the same to* DOLOUR.

Wait.
 Wait, no … what are you doing?
SHIRLEY: Shut up, yer big gollion. Yer disturbin' the peace.
HARRY: Come on, Dolour. Take this off.

He paws at her dress in the dim light.

DOLOUR: Harry … please don't. Why have the boats stopped?
TUG: The boats aren't gonna start for another ten minutes, love. Unscheduled dinner break. We got the Caves all to ourselves.
HARRY: So take this off.

He tugs at her dress.

Bloody stockings. Told yer they're snooty.
DOLOUR: Harry … no …

He rips the stockings off.

ACT FOUR: POOR MAN'S ORANGE

HARRY: Come on. You Darcys are always up for it. I seen your da fucking one of Delie's girls.

DOLOUR: What? No! Harry. Get off me. You're maulin' me.

He continues crawling all over her.

Harry! Stop!

She thumps him into the water.

HARRY: You bitch!

DOLOUR: Help! *Help!*

She starts to wade out of the River Caves. The others hurry after her.

FRANKY: Oy … where do you think you're goin'?

SHIRLEY: Stop ruinin' everyone's fun!

FRANKY: Come on. You'll enjoy it. Yer from the Hills, aren't yer?

The drag her back.

DOLOUR: Please let me go.

MINNIE: Pin her down.

They do, as HARRY *watches on.*

TUG sticks his hand up her dress. She gasps.

TUG: She feels like a virgin to me!

MINNIE *draws with lipstick on* DOLOUR*'s chest as she struggles to get away. She is branded 'WHORE'.*

DOLOUR: [*hollering over and over*] Stop! Stop it! No!

But her cries are to no avail.

Suddenly, the carnival music starts again and the boats begin to glide. DOLOUR *runs away as the others get back in their boats, laughing raucously.* HARRY *sits in his boat alone, looking peeved.*

SCENE TWENTY-SIX

Plymouth Street. DOLOUR *shivers as she walks along the dark street. She sees a figure stumbling ahead. It's* CHARLIE.

DOLOUR: Charlie?

He turns.

Oh, Charlie ...

She runs to him, crying. He catches her in his arms.

CHARLIE: What's the matter, Dol?

She sobs.

What's happened?

He sees her ripped dress and 'WHORE' written on her chest.

Who did that to you? Harry Drummy? I'll kill him.

DOLOUR: No! No, it wasn't him. The halfwit can't spell anyway. Ah, Charlie. People are awful. Just awful. We breed 'em here. We do.

She speaks furiously.

I can't escape these Hills, Charlie. And I don't know how to fight them.

She stops suddenly.

Why are you out? Are you lookin' for booze?

He can't answer.

Jesus, Charlie, you're as bad as the rest of 'em!

She goes to leave. He stops her.

CHARLIE: Wait. Dolour, I haven't had a drop. Promise. Come here. Let me clean you up.

He takes out a hanky.

Here. Spit.

She spits on it. He starts to clean her chest, gently, then stops. Gives her the hanky. She cleans herself up.

Dol, I know this city can get mean. But there are good things here, even in the Hills.

DOLOUR: Like what?

CHARLIE: Like ... Lick Jimmy and his milk. The songs you can hear through the walls on a hot night. An old magic fella at La Perouse watchin' over all of us.

And it's not just the Hills where those things happen, Dol. It's

ACT FOUR: POOR MAN'S ORANGE

everywhere. No matter where you live. No matter where you come from. There's bad. There's awful. But there's good too. Promise.

The 'WHORE' has faded a little from DOLOUR'*s chest.*

They stand awkwardly. A strange silence.

Soap will sort out the rest of that.

DOLOUR *nods, embarrassed.*

Where's yer glasses?

DOLOUR: Lost 'em at Luna Park.

Silence.

CHARLIE: You look a bit like her sometimes.
DOLOUR: Who? Roie?

He nods.

I won't ever be as pretty as Ro.
CHARLIE: You already are, kid.
DOLOUR: I'm not a kid, Charlie.

Not anymore.

They stare at one another.

Suddenly ... HUGH *stumbles backwards out of the shadows, shoved by* KIDGER. FLORRIE *is with them. Both* FLORRIE *and* HUGH *are unbuttoned and dishevelled.*

HUGH: Jesus, Kidge—
FLORRIE: Kidger, it was nothing—
DOLOUR: Da?!
KIDGER: This is yer last warnin', Darcy. You play by the rules or Delie's gonna cut off all commerce. No booze and no Florrie. You either fuck her at Delie's or you can fuck off for good.
FLORRIE: Kidger, we were just talking—
KIDGER: Charge for a chat now, do yer, Florrie?
DOLOUR: Da?

HUGH *turns to see* DOLOUR *and* CHARLIE.

KIDGER: Carn, Florrie. You got clients waitin'. [*To* HUGH] I catch you one more time, I'll cut it off, nail it to Delie's door and use it as a fuckin' knocker!

He drags FLORRIE *away.*

DOLOUR *and* CHARLIE *stare at* HUGH *in the dim light.* HUGH *sways drunkenly as he tries to button his fly.*

HUGH: G'day darlin'. You got any booze, Charlie?

CHARLIE *nods and passes* HUGH *a flask.* DOLOUR *is furious.*

DOLOUR: You're a damn liar, Charlie Rothe.

She storms away from them.

There's nothin' good in these Hills! Nothin'!

SCENE TWENTY-SEVEN

The harp echoes ...

More of Plymouth Street is boarded up. TENANTS *leave with suitcases.*

Eviction notices are posted, closer and closer to 12½. HUGH *stands before a wall of them, bewildered.*

Inside ...

Mikey cries in his cot.

MARGARET *enters and takes the baby away, despite* CHARLIE *trying to keep him there.* CHARLIE *leans against the wall of his bedroom.*

He puts an ear to the wall and listens as DOLOUR *moves around next door.* MARGARET *totters around the kitchen as Puffing Billy wheezes and coughs. She sings softly to herself.*

DOLOUR *comes downstairs sullenly.*

MARGARET: Dolour, did you hear? Father Cooley is sending Sister Theophilus away.

DOLOUR: What? Why?

MARGARET: It's a mystery. Probably something to do with the takeover. The church may well be the next to get knocked down.

DOLOUR: When does she leave?

MARGARET: I saw her this morning. She'll be heading to Central soon.

DOLOUR: But she's it. She's the one good woman left on this street.

She looks dumbfounded.

She looks around the kitchen with distaste, then at her mother.

This place is a pigsty, Mother.

MARGARET: [*stunned*] Well, daughter, why don't you get down on your

ACT FOUR: POOR MAN'S ORANGE

knees and give it a scrub if you're so fussy. Gettin' too big fer yer boots, you are.

DOLOUR: You shouldn't be holding Mikey. He could catch anything off you.

MARGARET: I beg your pardon ...

DOLOUR: He only just got through winter with his croup. There's diphtheria right through the Hills. Here, give him to me. I'm clean.

MARGARET *keeps the baby away from* DOLOUR.

MARGARET: Just because you're working as a shopgirl doesn't mean you get to speak to me that way. Don't forget where you come from, girl. Yer poor father didn't slave away to have you judge us under our own roof.

DOLOUR: 'Poor father'? I'd like to push him in front of a tram.

MARGARET *is shocked. She whacks* DOLOUR *across the head.* DOLOUR *cries out.* CHARLIE *hurries from downstairs.*

MARGARET: How dare you talk about your father like that!

CHARLIE: What's going on?

MARGARET: It's a pity the nuns can't hear you.

DOLOUR: I wish they could! I hate him! I wish he was dead!

MARGARET: Dolour!

DOLOUR: You wanna know why he has less money than ever before, Mamma? Why he takes so many baths and he's started parting his hair? Why he comes home smellin' of wine instead of whiskey?

CHARLIE: Dolour, don't—

DOLOUR: Because he's got a girlfriend. Everyone knows about it! He's been seeing her for months! He's been fucking her on the streets!

CHARLIE: Dol / our—

MARGARET: How could you say such a thing about yer / own—?

DOLOUR: I've seen her, Mamma. So's Charlie. So's most of the Hills. She's one of Delie's girls. I saw him with his pants undone and her skirt hitched. Saw one of your old bangles on her arm.

MARGARET: But ... he's mine.

DOLOUR: I'm sorry, Mamma. I didn't want to tell you. But everyone knows.

MARGARET *looks bewildered.*

I'm going to say goodbye to Sister Theophilus.

DOLOUR *leaves.* CHARLIE *is left with* MARGARET.

CHARLIE: You alright, Missus?

She looks weak.

He goes to take Mikey from her. She holds him tight in her arms.

MARGARET: He's mine.

CHARLIE: No, he's not, Missus.

He takes Mikey.

He's mine.

CHARLIE *takes Mikey upstairs.*

MARGARET *stands helplessly in the kitchen. 'She stood so still it seemed she could hear the very ticking of her body, staring straight ahead of her and not seeing a thing.'*

Silence.

Puffing Billy exhales a long, last exhale. Dead.

MARGARET *goes to a drawer and gets out her wedding wreath. It is brown and dried. She places it on her head.* YOUNG MARGARET *appears.*

MARGARET: Where's it all gone? Where's me hair that was so curly and pretty, and the way me complexion never got a spot, and the bust that made a five-bob blouse look like the front of a ship? Where's the Margaret that people smiled at in the street? That people *saw*. Where'd she go? The Margaret that could not be contained?

YOUNG MARGARET *departs.*

MARGARET *runs to the bath water and pours it over herself. Tries to scrub herself clean.*

HUGH *appears.*

HUGH: Missus. What's for tea?

MARGARET *rears up and runs at* HUGH.

She hits him and hits him, hollering and hollering, dripping. Her wreath still on her head.

MARGARET: You're mine and I'm yours! You're mine and I'm yours!

ACT FOUR: POOR MAN'S ORANGE

You're mine and I'm yours!

HUGH: Missus! Settle down! Jesus Christ!

MARGARET: What have you done for me, Hugh Darcy? What have you given me? Nothin' but nothin', that's all. Dragged me from Trafalgar to these Hills to see me spend my life gettin' bitten by bugs, wrestlin' with a stove that spits at me every fuckin' day, waitin' for you to get home at all hours and bein' afraid—so afraid—if there's a stammer to yer step … Moved me to this godawful place where a child can just disappear off the street and a girl can have her insides ruined by a pack of wild men and a rat. You did that. You told me to take a walk with you through the House of Horrors all those years ago and I'm still in it! I never got out! It makes you wonder what a body's born for!

She crumbles.

What's a body born for …?

She weeps.

HUGH: Missus …

MARGARET: I know about her, Hughie. The one you've been with.

He looks shocked.

You told me once you'd kill anyone who hurt me. So go on. Cut yer damn throat.

HUGH: Missus—

MARGARET: *My name is Margaret Kilker! Margaret Kilker! Margaret Kilker! My name is Margaret Kilker!!*

Silence.

Thady's not comin' back. He never was, not from the moment he had the bright idea to leave this house.

HUGH: Now, wait a minute there, Missus. You never / know—

MARGARET: He's dead, Hughie. And so's Jer.

HUGH: You don't need to get all—

MARGARET: Jer drowned himself on our wedding day.

HUGH: What?

MARGARET: And his body floated to the top of the dam in Trafalgar just as we arrived on the doorstep of twelve-and-a-half Plymouth Street. Josie wrote me a letter to tell me. She always did like to gloat.

HUGH: Jer what?

MARGARET: I didn't tell yer. I didn't want it hanging over us. And I wanted yer to always have hope. I used to love it when you were hopeful.

Beat. HUGH *is stunned.*

But then I got to know hope. And I realised it was mean and fickle and cruel. So I'm tellin' yer now. Jer's dead. And whether you care or not, so's your son Thady. And no matter how young the flesh is that you fuck, Hugh Darcy, you're closer to the end now than the beginning.

He sits in stunned silence.

Where'd we go, Hugh? Me and you.

HUGH: Nowhere. We're still here.

MARGARET: Why?

HUGH: Cos I promised you something more.

Beat.

I just never expected you to get old like everyone else, Missus.

MARGARET: I'm not too old to walk out of here and never come back.

A moment. HUGH *nods.*

HUGH: Yes. Margaret.

They sit in silence.

He tries to take her hand. She doesn't let him.

She takes his hand instead.

HUGH *sinks to the floor and wraps himself around her legs. She remains stoic.*

A missus and her man.

SCENE TWENTY-EIGHT

Central Station.

DOLOUR *is amid a crowd of* COMMUTERS.

She sees SISTER THEOPHILUS *on a platform, waiting with her bag. She calls above the din.*

DOLOUR: Sister Theophilus! Sister Theophilus!

As she hurries toward the sister, SISTER BEATRIX *hurries to*

ACT FOUR: POOR MAN'S ORANGE   211

SISTER THEOPHILUS. *She's crying.*

The two nuns embrace tightly. DOLOUR *stops and watches, curious.*

SISTER THEOPHILUS *whispers to* SISTER BEATRIX *as she holds her face in her hands.* SISTER BEATRIX *nods.*

SISTER THEOPHILUS *looks around nervously, then softly kisses* SISTER BEATRIX *on the lips.*

On the busy train platform. Two women, alone.

DOLOUR *watches, wide-eyed.*

SISTER THEOPHILUS *smiles at* SISTER BEATRIX *and the two women depart in opposite directions, leaving* DOLOUR *among the* COMMUTERS.

As she walks home, a shift in light.

SCENE TWENTY-NINE

Each house member prepares for bed.

DOLOUR *lays in her bed and places her ear against the wall.*

CHARLIE *does the same on the other side of the wall.*

Mikey is in a cot by his bed.

HUGH *watches* MARGARET *undress.*

He pats the bed beside him and she lays down. He holds her close.

Stillness as each room breathes in and out.

CHARLIE *strokes the wall.*

CHARLIE: *Dolour ...!*

    DOLOUR *turns to the wall.*

DOLOUR: Charlie?! Is Mikey alright?!

    CHARLIE *covers his head with a pillow, horrified that she has heard.*

Charlie?!

    DOLOUR *hurries out of bed and into Charlie's room.*

Charlie?

CHARLIE *sits up in bed, embarrassed.*

CHARLIE: Yeah. What?

DOLOUR: Did you call for me?

CHARLIE: No.

DOLOUR: Oh.

She stands embarrassed in her nightgown.

CHARLIE: Dolour ...

He gets out of bed. It's awkward.

I ... I got you this.

He hands her an ornament from under his pillow.

For Christmas. It's carved out of bone. It's a Chinese water-seller. He reminds me of Lick. And I know how much you love Lick Jimmy.

DOLOUR: Thank you.

Beat.

Nobody's ever given me a gift like this before, Charlie. It's so ... grown-up.

CHARLIE: Well, so are you, Dolour.

They sit in awkward silence.

Dolour, I've been thinking ... about you ... And I was wonderin' ... Why don't you bugger off?

DOLOUR *is slightly taken aback.*

DOLOUR: What?

CHARLIE: I mean leave home. Get out of the Hills.

DOLOUR: I will one day. Anyway, it doesn't matter much. I'm too old to go back to school. I s'pose I'll always be a shopgirl now. So I might as well stay here.

CHARLIE: But you'll be gettin' married one day. Some day soon.

DOLOUR: 'Course I'm not. You've got a nerve.

CHARLIE: Sorry. It's none of my business. I've just been thinkin' about you ... you know ... going on dates with people. Young men showing interest in you. Thought it might be on your mind, that's all. You don't seem to wanna be a nun anymore.

DOLOUR: Stop talking about it, Charlie. It's embarrassing.

CHARLIE: I know you don't have your big sister to talk to about these

ACT FOUR: POOR MAN'S ORANGE

things, Dol. And you're becoming a beautiful young woman. So I thought I'd just—
DOLOUR: Just what? Just … take the place of my sister?

CHARLIE *looks ashamed.*

CHARLIE: Sorry, I—
DOLOUR: You're not Roie, Charlie. You'll never take the place of her.
CHARLIE: I'm not trying to—
DOLOUR: And who do you think you are, talking to me about being a woman? Why does *any* man think he gets to speak to me about being a woman?

I know what it is to be a woman. It gets beaten into us, that knowledge. Beaten for being young. Beaten for getting old. Beaten by our husbands. Our fathers. Our lovers. Beaten by complete strangers. Beaten by friends. Beaten by other beaten women. Beaten if we laugh. Beaten if we cry. Beaten if we fight back. Beaten if we lay down and take it. Beaten if we speak up. Beaten if we stay silent. Beaten by stories in the damn Bible. Beaten by dumb rules and stupid laws. Beaten by a world that tells us we're here to be beaten. That we somehow deserve it. Like the blood of women is something to be shed. Beaten for just being.

Beat.

CHARLIE: I'm sorry the world makes you feel that way.
DOLOUR: Men make me feel that way.
CHARLIE: Is that how you feel about me?
DOLOUR: What? No. Of course not. You're not a man.
CHARLIE: What am I then? Just your black brother-in-law?
DOLOUR: No! I didn't mean it like that—
CHARLIE: What do you reckon Mikey's gonna turn into? Will he ever be a good man in your eyes? Will he ever be anything with my blood in him?
DOLOUR: Of course he will. He's Mikey.
CHARLIE: Yes. He's Mikey. He's my beautiful little boy, and I'm his father. And I'm a good man, whether you can see it or not.
DOLOUR: I know. I see you.
CHARLIE: And I see you.

Silence.

> *He reaches out and touches* DOLOUR'S *hair.*
> DOLOUR *lets him.*
> *Then ... Mikey lets out a cry.*
> DOLOUR *pulls away.*

DOLOUR: I'm not Roie, Charlie.
CHARLIE: I know. And neither am I.
I won't ever let you be beaten, Dolour.
DOLOUR: I think I already am.

> *She leaves.*
> CHARLIE *curls up on his bed, mortified.*
> DOLOUR *enters her room.*
> *She stares at the ornament in her hands ... and goes to throw it. But can't.*
> *The harp echoes ...*
> *All that is standing is 12 1/2 Plymouth Street, Delie Stock's, the church and Lick Jimmy's.*
> *The symphony of Surry Hills plays across the desolate landscape.*
> CHARLIE *gets up and goes to Mikey. He picks him up. Smells his skin.*
> *Looks out over Surry Hills as a breeze comes through the window ...*

SCENE THIRTY

At 12 1/2 Plymouth St, Bing Crosby sings 'You're all I want for Christmas' from the crystal set as HUGH *stirs a pudding and* MARGARET *cleans the house frantically.*

HUGH: Maggots in the flour.

> MARGARET *enters.*

Missus. I got you a present.
MARGARET: Oh, Hughie...?

> *He gives her a gift. It's a cardigan. She puts it on.*

It's too small.

ACT FOUR: POOR MAN'S ORANGE

HUGH: Not to worry. Just goes to show you don't look as big as you are.

Silence. MARGARET *smiles. Strokes his face.*

MARGARET: Ah, Hughie. There's something we've gotta do. Help me get Thady's presents.

She repacks the gift, then opens Thady's cupboard of gifts.

Bing Crosby sings ...

Down on Plymouth Street, LICK *hands out fruit and vegies to a hungry* PASSERSBY.

A hoard of MEN *smash on the door of the pub. But it's boarded up. Shut down. The song continues ...*

HUGH *and* MARGARET *drop Thady's gifts off along the street.*

HUGH *drops one at Bumper's hovel. They walk on, dropping the gifts of* THADY *throughout the Hills, hand in hand ...*

CHARLIE *walks a pram through the streets of Surry Hills. He weaves through the debris and traffic. As he passes, more houses are boarded up.*

DOLOUR *approaches from the other direction, weaving her own way through the debris.*

CHARLIE: Where you headed, Dol?
DOLOUR: That way. Where you headed?
CHARLIE: That way.
DOLOUR: Pub's been shut down.
CHARLIE: I know. I'm just takin' Mikey for a walk.
DOLOUR: Yeah, right.
CHARLIE: You headin' to the church? For the final mission?
DOLOUR: Nah. Doesn't seem much point anymore.

LICK *appears, peeling a poor man's orange. He stands with them.*

DOLOUR: Ni hao, Lick.

LICK: G'day, Dolour.

All of the residents of Plymouth Street make their way up the road toward the church. They keep singing. LICK, DOLOUR *and* CHARLIE *watch as they pass.*

I have to go now.

DOLOUR: To church?

LICK: No. I get notice. No more Plymouth Street. No more Surry Hills. I've been cleared.

DOLOUR is devastated.

DOLOUR: What about your daughters? And Roger? And your Mum and your grandparents?

LICK: A letter came, Dolour.

Beat.

A letter came.

He smiles sadly. DOLOUR *is devastated.*

DOLOUR: Oh, Lick.

LICK: I still have them. My family. In here. And in here.

He gestures to his head and his heart.

DOLOUR: No, Lick … No … Come and stay at ours. They haven't got to us yet. We'll make the room. We always make the room.

LICK *smiles.*

LICK: Dolour. You're the best friend I ever had. Killer-diller. That means amazing.

DOLOUR *embraces him.*

He smiles as he watches the people file along the street.

They have rough skin on the outside, see? Dirty. Hard. And when they are young, the inside is bitter. Makes you pull a face. But … when the poor man's orange ripens, its fruit loses all bitterness and it becomes sweet and delicious.

Beat.

See you later, Dolour. See you later, Charlie.

ACT FOUR: POOR MAN'S ORANGE   217

DOLOUR/CHARLIE: Zai jian, Lick …

>LICK *follows the congregation.*

>DOLOUR *calls out to her friend.*

DOLOUR: Lick. You never gave me a piece of poor man's orange.

>LICK *smiles. Take off a piece. Holds it out to her. She reaches for it. He pops it in his mouth.*

LICK: Not ready.

>*As* LICK *goes, his house falls.*

SCENE THIRTY-ONE

Inside the church, FATHER COOLEY *is weary …*

FATHER COOLEY: Well, how lovely of you to turn up today.

>*Beat.*

I see faces in this flock that have grown old and haggard in the past year.
Faces falling like so many of the Hills houses. Souls crumbling like so many of our homes.
This church is next. The mission failed.
God works in mysterious ways. The bastard.
Let us pray.

>DELIE *bursts in, with* KIDGER.

>*The* CONGREGATION *stares at them in shock.*

DELIE: Alright, alright. It ain't a bloody peep show. What yer gawkin' at? Can't a woman step inside a bloody church without judgement?

>KIDGER *glares at them all.*

There's an ambulance waitin' outside for me. I won't be comin' back to Plymouth Street. Just wanted yerse all to know.

>*They stare at her in silence.*

I know yerse don't think much of me, unless yer need a girl or a bit of dosh. But yer my people and yer won't be seein' me again. I'm dyin'.

KIDGER *weeps.*

Shurrup, Kidger.

I won't ask yer to pray for me cos I reckon I'll get on just fine with the Devil. I don't reckon God's got a pair of wings on the hook for me.

But I do have ten cases of bombo in me backyard. First in, best dressed. Be nice to me girls.

Merry Christmas. See yas.

She leaves.

KIDGER *pauses. Leaves in a different direction. A moment of silence.*

The entire CONGREGATION *hurries into the street.*

SCENE THIRTY-TWO

As Bing Crosby starts to sing again, the RESIDENTS *of Plymouth Street pass around bottles of bombo, getting progressively drunker.* DOLOUR *and* CHARLIE *find themselves caught up amongst it.*

DOLOUR *watches* CHARLIE *get a bottle of bombo. She is devastated. She leaves.*

The street party gets more and more debauched. Fights break out. DELIE'S GIRLS *leave the brothel with suitcases and yell at* MEN *who try to get a piece of them.*

FLO: Fuck off. You want action, you'll have to come up the Cross to find it.

FLORRIE: Hughie, where you been? I miss you …

HUGH *ducks his head.*

MARGARET *shoves in front of him and scowls.* FLORRIE *laughs at the old woman cruelly as she hurries away.*

If you need me, I'll be up the Cross, Hughie! Just like Jesu Christo!

DELIE STOCK *falls. The revelry continues.* POLICE *arrive.*

The street is left desolate, leaving only CHARLIE *and a crying Mikey and an* INEBRIATED MAN, *passed out nearby.*

CHARLIE *pours the bombo out.*

It trickles away down Plymouth Street.

The INEBRIATED MAN *crawls to the river of bombo. He sucks it from the ground.* CHARLIE *wheels his son away from the river of booze.*

SCENE THIRTY-THREE

MARGARET *is packing up the church, shuffling around the altar, placing things in a box.*

CHARLIE *enters.*

CHARLIE: Need a hand?
MARGARET: Bit late for that, doncha think?

She looks at him suspiciously.

Yer can pack away the prayer candles.
CHARLIE: They're still lit.
MARGARET: Then blow 'em out. Someone's got to.

CHARLIE *hesitates. Blows one out.*

Silence.

CHARLIE: I … I wanna tell yer, Mamma. I'm leaving.
MARGARET: What?
CHARLIE: I thought if I cleared out, it might be easier. For everyone. I don't wanna be a burden.
MARGARET: What about Mikey?
CHARLIE: I'd take him with me.

She looks at CHARLIE, *stunned.*

MARGARET: You can't raise a child by yerself. You're a man! Unheard of.
CHARLIE: He's my boy. He'd always know about Roie. I'd tell him every day who she was. But I'm not havin' him taken away from me the way she was. And so I've got to get out of Surry Hills. Now.
MARGARET: Why? Coward. You should count yerself lucky. You've got a roof over yer head. A bed to sleep in. Food. Warmth.

She falters.

Love.

Silence. They stare at one another in the church.

You think I don't see it, Charlie? I'm a mother. I know when my girls have a flush to their cheeks, a twinkle to their eye. When their skin smells like new soap and their hair is brushed smooth. When their moods duck and weave like a fairground ride and their silences are filled with secrets. I know. Cos I was a young girl once too.

And I see it in you. You loved one of my daughters. And now you love the other one.

Silence.

CHARLIE: I catch her looking at me. Dolour. Across the table. When we pass in the hall. I see … something … At first I didn't know if it was love or hate.

MARGARET: Sometimes they're the same thing.

CHARLIE: She must get that from you. You've taught me that more than anyone.

MARGARET: What? I don't hate you. You've lived in my house for nearly four years.

CHARLIE: Doesn't matter. There's still that little part of you that can't love me.

MARGARET *busies herself at the altar.*

And I feel the same about you, Mamma.

MARGARET *stops. Hurt.*

I don't wanna leave. These Hills are my home. More than you'll ever know. But if I stay … I want Dolour.

MARGARET: But she's family.

CHARLIE: Not to me. I'm no relation. Mikey's more related to her than me.

MARGARET: But … what would everyone say?

CHARLIE: There is no everyone. Look around you. The pews are empty. The Hills have been cleared. The mission's failed.

MARGARET: But … God.

CHARLIE: God's buggered off, Margaret. He's left us to blow out the candles. We're all that's left. And now it's time for me to go.

CHARLIE *goes to leave.*

MARGARET: But, Charlie …

He turns.

You'll break her heart.
CHARLIE: I know.

    CHARLIE *leaves.*

MARGARET: You'll break all our hearts.

    MARGARET *is left alone in the pews as the church crashes down around her.*

    The harp echoes.

SCENE THIRTY-FOUR

At 12 1/2 Plymouth Street, MARGARET *finds* HUGH *in the kitchen, cooking over a small gas ring.*

MARGARET: What are you doing home?
HUGH: Cookin' you a meal. Sit down.
MARGARET: What are we havin'?
HUGH: A stew. Fit for a queen.
MARGARET: England's?
HUGH: Surry Hills'.

    DOLOUR *enters.*

DOLOUR: Where's Charlie? Where's Mikey?

    Beat.

MARGARET: They left, Dol.
DOLOUR: What?
MARGARET: Charlie said he'd write. Let us know when they're settled.
DOLOUR: Oh.

    Silence.

HUGH: You right, Dol?
DOLOUR: So it's … it's just us three now.
MARGARET: Seems so.

    An empty a silence as there ever was.

HUGH: These arrived for you, Dol. They were sitting on the doorstep.

    He lifts a crate of poor man's oranges. There's a note left on top.

DOLOUR: [*reading*] 'Dear Dolour. The poor man's oranges are ready now. Eat your first one on the roof. Love, Lick Jimmy.'

> DOLOUR *can hardly hold back her tears.*

HUGH: Want some stew, Dol?

> DOLOUR *shakes her head.*

DOLOUR: No thanks. I'm not hungry.

> DOLOUR *hurries up the stairs.*
>
> *In La Perouse,* CHARLIE *sits on a cliff, holding Mikey. The stars twinkle in the distance.*
>
> GUS *appears.*

GUS: There you are. Hallo, bub! Hallo! Hallo!

> *On Plymouth Street, the rest of the street is now razed, leaving a clear view of the stars. The bays. Twinkling lights in the distance.*
>
> DOLOUR *sits on the roof and finally peels a poor man's orange.* ROIE *sits on the roof beside her.*

DOLOUR: That you, Roie?

> *In La Perouse,* GUS *sits beside* CHARLIE.

GUS: You look rough, mate.

CHARLIE: I love a lot of people at once. One's here. One's not. The rest are in between. What are the rules, Gus?

GUS: No rules for that. No rules for love. No rules for hope. No rules for life.

> *On the Plymouth Street rooftop ...*

DOLOUR: I love Charlie, Ro. I'm so sorry. I tried hard not to. But I do.

> ROIE *smiles. She strokes* DOLOUR*'s hair.*

And now he's gone. What now, Roie? What do I do now?

> *On the clifftop ...*

CHARLIE: I keep trying to leave. But those Hills ... They keep calling me back.

> *On the rooftop ...*

DOLOUR: Ah, Roie. To have what you had would be worth dying for.

ACT FOUR: POOR MAN'S ORANGE

On the clifftop ...

GUS: We have to live. Thass what we have to do, Charlie. Live.

'He walked around Charlie, brushing at him with the flat of his hand, and clucking anxiously. He did not treat the young man as a stranger at all.'

On the rooftop ...

DOLOUR: Look at that sky. Crowded with stardust.

On the clifftop ...

GUS: Get up, Charlie. Gawn. Stand up. Stand up.

CHARLIE *stands.* GUS *neatens him up. He combs his hair, straightens his clothes.* CHARLIE *stares at the stars.*

CHARLIE: Waragal.

GUS *nods and smiles.*

GUS: Waragal.

Beat.

Go on. Get going. We gotta live. We gotta live.

He gently shoos CHARLIE *away.*

There he goes ... there he goes ... there he goes ...

CHARLIE *leaves.*

On the rooftop ...

DOLOUR: How do I survive it all, Ro, when you couldn't?

ROIE *kisses* DOLOUR *softly on the cheek ...*

... as CHARLIE *arrives on the roof, holding Mikey in his arms.*

He sits beside DOLOUR.

ROIE *strokes his head as she leaves.*

DOLOUR *looks out over Surry Hills.*

You came home.

CHARLIE: I did.

DOLOUR: Lick Jimmy left us some poor man's oranges. They're ready. Finally. Wanna share one?

She peels an orange as they look out over the razed Hills.

It looks like the end of the world from up here.

No Lick Jimmy's. No Delie Stock. No church. No pub. No shop. No voices. No songs. Even the cardboard boxes got flattened. We're all that's left.

They eat their oranges. Finally. They are surprised by its taste.

They're so ...

DOLOUR and CHARLIE: Sweet.

Silence. He stares at her.

CHARLIE. Dolour … I want us to keep going together. Me and you and Mikey.

DOLOUR: You only feel like that because you miss Roie.

Silence.

CHARLIE: No.

Beat.

I'll always love Roie. Just like you'll always love her. But I love you too. Because you're Dolour Darcy.

Beat. She smiles.

DOLOUR: And you're Charlie Rothe.

A long moment and then ... they kiss. Surrounded by the peel of a poor man's orange. When they finally part, they look out over the detritus of Surry Hills.

What now?

CHARLIE: There's something more. Something meant to be. Something coming that's worth the fight.

Silence.

I just want to survive, Dolour.

She nods.

DOLOUR: Then let's survive.

Beat.

You're mine and I'm yours?

ACT FOUR: POOR MAN'S ORANGE

CHARLIE *smiles.*

CHARLIE: You're mine and I'm yours.

DOLOUR and CHARLIE: You're mine and I'm yours.

They kiss ... and look out again over the ruined remains of Surry Hills, laden with detritus, the homeless, the poor, the lost ...

DOLOUR: We gotta remember, don't we?

Beat.

We must always remember how lucky we are.

The harp echoes ...

ROIE *sings.*

ROIE: 'Tis the last rose of summer,
Left blooming alone;
All her lovely companions
Are faded and gone;

DOLOUR and ROIE: [*together*]
No flower of her kindred,
No rosebud is nigh,

CHARLIE, DOLOUR and ROIE: [*together*]
To reflect back her blushes,
Or give sigh for sigh.

HUGH and MARGARET join them on the roof beneath the stars, overlooking the remains of Surry Hills.

The harp soars, finally, with their song ...

HUGH, MARGARET, CHARLIE, DOLOUR and ROIE:
I'll not leave thee, thou lone one,
To pine on the stem;
Since the lovely are sleeping,
Go, sleep thou with them.

The other RESIDENTS *of Surry Hills and Trafalgar and beyond join them.*

Familiar ghosts are among them.

ALL: Thus kindly I scatter,
Thy leaves o'er the bed,

>   Where thy mates of the garden
>   Lie scentless and dead;
>   So soon may I follow,
>   When friendships decay,
>   And from love's shining circle
>   The gems drop away.
>   When true hearts lie withered,
>   And fond ones are flown,

THADY *is there. As ever. He sings alone.*

THADY: Oh! who would inhabit
This bleak world alone?

The harp echoes resoundingly.

Blackout.

THE END

www.ingramcontent.com/pod-product-compliance
Lightning Source LLC
Chambersburg PA
CBHW040305170426
43194CB00022B/2907